Sharing Jesus Holistically

with the

Buddhist World

D0109120

Sharing Jesus Holistically
with the
Buddhist World

David Lim and Steve Spaulding, Editors

William Carey Library
Pasadena, California
www.WCLBooks.com

Cover design: Joseph Gil

Copyediting and text layout: Sharon Edwards

Published by William Carey Library Publishers
1605 E. Elizabeth Street
Pasadena, California 91104
www.WCLBooks.com

William Carey Library Publishers is a Ministry of the U.S. Center for World Mission, Pasadena, California.

ISBN 0-87808-508-4

Printed in the United States of America

CONTENTS

INTRODUCTION

This book contains the works of a group of Evangelical mission "reflective practitioners," who are committed to developing more biblical and more effective ways to evangelize the Buddhist peoples of the world. While various forms of Buddhism gain popularity in the world, this network tries to disclose some creative approaches to reach them with the gospel communicated in culturally sensitive ways and with transformational impact.

We thank God for the publication of this second volume of well-researched papers that seek to help the world church to reach Buddhists for Christ. These works were presented first at a Missiological Forum, which specifically focused on this theme. We thank God that we were able to hold this Forum at the start of the fifth assembly of SEANET in March 2003 in Chiang Mai, Thailand.

We invite readers to gain access to our first volume entitled *Sharing Jesus in the Buddhist World*, which was also edited by both of us. It consists of nine papers that provide the main framework and some concrete models of culture-sensitive "contextualized" witness to peoples of Buddhist faith. It will serve as a rich resource for those concerned with the issues raised in this book.

This second volume demonstrates the five major dimensions of a holistic witness among Buddhist peoples. These five aspects are: experiential dialogue, intellectual dialogue, biblical exposition, cultural sensitivity, and economic development.

The first chapter, "Counting the Buddhist World Fairly," provides an update on the status of Buddhism today. Alex Smith (D.Miss., Fuller Theological Seminary), an OMF missionary in Thailand for almost 30 years and presently a mission mobilizer based in the U.S., concludes his chapter with an estimate of almost one billion Buddhists in the world today!

Each of the subsequent chapters in this compendium focuses on one of the five major aspects of a holistic approach in evangelizing Buddhists. The second and third chapters emphasize the *experiential dialogue* dimension of witnessing to those of Buddhist faith. Chapter 2, "The Power of the Kingdom for Encountering Buddhist Worldviews," is written by Kang San Tan (D.Miss., Trinity International University), a Chinese missiologist based in Malaysia and a member of the World Evangelical Alliance Missions Commission. The chapter highlights some of the issues in a personalized "dialogue of life" approach. This is also indicated in another way in chapter 3, "Practical Applications of the Good News into Some Doctrinal Black Holes in Buddhism" by John R. Davis (Ph.D. Theology, Birmingham University), who heads an inter-denominational missionary retreat center.

The second dimension of *intellectual dialogue*, especially to those trained in Buddhist philosophy, is discussed in the next three chapters. Chapter 4, "The Value and Limits to Dialogue," has been written by Russell Bowers, Jr. (Ph.D. Systematic Theology, Dallas Theological Seminary), who is professor of theology at East Asia School of Theology in Singapore. The author argues for the importance of working on truth claims in the encounter between Christians and Buddhists. Chapter 5, "Transfer of Merit in Folk Buddhism," is Alex Smith's second article in this book, written in mainly in the context of Thailand. In chapter 6, Johannes Aagaard, head of the Dailog Center in Denmark, gives a theological critique of "Serpent Power and the New Adam: Religion and Sexuality in Tantric Traditions."

Next, we have a unique chapter on the third dimension of evangelical holism: *biblical exposition.* Chapter 7 is "An Exploration of the Book of Ecclesiastes in the Light of Buddha's Four Noble Truths," a work that serves as a model of doing biblical exegesis *in context.* It has been written by Michal Solomon Vasanthakumar (Th.M., British Open University), a biblical scholar who teaches at Lanka Bible College in Sri Lanka and who has authored about twenty Bible Study books in the Tamil language.

The fourth dimension on *cultural sensitivity* is demonstrated in chapters 8-10. Alan Johnson, an Assemblies of God missionary in Thailand who heads a Buddhist Studies program, shows "A Contextualized Presentation of the Gospel for Thai Buddhists" in chapter 8. Ubolwan Mejudhon (D.Miss., Asbury Theological Seminary), who co-pastors a culture-sensitive church in Thailand with her husband, presents an outstanding model of effective contextualization in chapter 9, "The Ritual of Reconciliation in Thai Culture." This work challenges readers to be more resourceful and creative in finding cultural forms that can build bridges to reach *entire families*, which is probably applicable not just in Buddhist contexts. In a different context, Mark Dominey (Th.M., Dallas Theological Seminary), an OMF missionary in Japan since 1988, depicts and analyzes a distinct Mahayana Buddhist phenomenon in chapter 10, "Abortion and *Mizuko* Rites in Japan."

The final chapter shows the fifth dimension on "economic development," which is the first, but hopefully not the last, work on this subject in our series. In chapter 11, James W. Gustafson gives a missiological reflection on "Holistic Mission: A Thai Church's Ministry to the Whole Person." We hope that more case studies of this approach will appear in our future publications.

With such excellent papers in our first two books, we look forward to editing a third book in the near future. Readers who wish to participate in the Forum or this publication series may contact the publishers. We thank God for a Foundation, which has humbly asked not to be recognized, that provided most of the funds needed for the event and the publication of these papers.

We hope to continue to facilitate this type of sharing of the "best theologies" and the "best practices" of Christians, particularly of Evangelicals worldwide in reaching Buddhist peoples for Christ in their various contexts. May this series help us to be more faithful and effective in fulfilling the Great Commission among Buddhist peoples in our generation!

DAVID LIM and STEVE SPAULDING, editors

Quezon City, Philippines

November 2004

CHAPTER 1

Counting the Buddhist World Fairly

Alex G. Smith

The valuable annual world statistics of Dr. David Barrett, printed in the *International Bulletin*, January 1999, showed the Buddhist population in mid-1999 at 358,527,000 (1999: 25). This figure was also reported the same month in *Pulse*. Global Mapping International, Christianity Today, and other groups usually utilize similar figures for the Buddhist world, relying on Barrett's figures. But this estimate of the Buddhist world population seems to be an understatement, especially if all Folk Buddhists are to be included.

Normally world religion statisticians state the Christian figures in very broad terms including all types of Christians. In 1999 Dr. Barrett showed North America as having above 224 million Christians, which was almost 75% of the people on that continent (1999: 25). On his radio program, "Live at Night," on February 3, 1999, Jim Macintosh said that America, according to a recent article, has only 7% practicing Christians. So why is there such a wide discrepancy—75% and 7%? Both are affected by definition and perspective. Both are correct from different viewpoints. Barrett is right to use his inclusive figures for Christians, according to his definitions. Similarly, Barrett's large Muslim statistics are inclusive, though actually there are considerable animistic accretions in many of the Islamic groups. Hindu figures are treated similarly. When it comes to the Buddhist group, however, though not necessarily by intention, the statistics are frequently understated or minimized.

"Well," it is often argued, "these numbers are for 'practicing Buddhists'." What about all the other nominal Folk Buddhists practicing in today's world, in both East and West? Should they be treated differently than nominal Christians, Muslims, or Hindus?

At the Lausanne Congress on Evangelism in 1974, Dr. Ralph Winter helped clarify the big picture of religious populations. However, he unwittingly did a slight disservice to viewing the world religiously by mixing oranges and apples in his major unreached blocs—Muslim, Hindu, Buddhist, and Animistic Tribes—plus *Chinese*, the largest! This problem has persisted in missiological circles ever since. At the time in the mid-1970s, before it was opened to outsiders, China was difficult to define religiously. Most people thought of its peoples as communist and consequently, atheistic or at least non-religious. We now know better. Most Chinese, especially the dominant Han, have an ingrained Buddhist bent mixed with superstition, traditional religions, and animism. But an overriding influence on the Chinese Han is their underpinning Buddhism, and a widespread resurgence of Folk Buddhism and associated cults in China has occurred over the last quarter of a century.

Maybe it is time for missiologists to rethink and correct faulty, or at least inadequate, formulae for calculating the number of Buddhists in the world. The current paradigm may well be out of date. If the majority of Han Chinese is added to the Buddhist figures a more correct Folk Buddhist population is calculated. Patrick Johnstone's 1993 edition of *Operation World* more accurately recognized a much larger Buddhist population. He noted that

Buddhist-Eastern Religion totaled 613 million in 1990, today's equivalent of about 700 million (1993: 23). This was double the total of Dr. Barrett's figures at the time. Even *Eerdmans' Handbook To The World's Religions,* published in 1982, suggested that, "the total world membership of the Buddhist religion may be as high as 600 million" (1982: 228). This probable total in 1982 took into account the number of expected Buddhists within China proper. With the world's population growth since then, that figure would translate into one billion or more in today's early 21st century.

Whenever I have asked Taiwanese what their religion is, the answer automatically is "Buddhist." They never answer, "Chinese Traditional Religionist," which is a somewhat artificial term concocted by Western missiologists. Johnstone correctly recognized that the Buddhist, Taoist, Confucian mixture of China, Korea, Japan, and other peoples are so intertwined and intermingled "that a clear differentiation is hard to make" (1993: 23). The same could be said of the Theravada Buddhist populations of Southeast Asia, where animism, ancestor worship, shamanism, and even Brahmanism are syncretized into one Buddhistic whole.

Some Western analysts question this interpretation of oneness, but eminent scholars like Dr. S. J. Tambiah, who studied this phenomenon in Thailand and elsewhere, concluded that all these elements are really galvanized into one whole system in the Buddhist's mind. The indigenous people do not define or isolate each religious system into separate parts, as do Western analysts. The majority of Asians see all the elements of their local Buddhist mixture fused together into one integrated whole, unified Buddhism, and their own particular brand of Buddhism.

Furthermore, as Johnstone pointed out, beside the usual broad statistics for Buddhists, another 40 million in Japan, Korea, and Vietnam adhered to "New Religions" in the 1990s, mostly founded on Buddhism such as Soka Gakkai in Japan, or Cao Dai and Hoa Hao in Vietnam (1993: 322, 336, 577). These cults are often excluded from compilations of Buddhist statistics, though these groups are offshoots of Buddhism. Furthermore, the multitude of Falun Gong Buddhists in China needs to be added also. The strength and perceived political threat of the Falun Gong Buddhists caused the communist government to censure and outlaw them. Some estimates of this group are as high as 160 million.

The First International Buddhist Propagation Conference held in 1998 in Kyoto, Japan, claimed the Japanese nation to be seventy percent Buddhist. By way of contrast, the early AD 2000 Gateway Cities projects identified Japan as Shinto but not Buddhist. This was corrected in later years. Actually, most Japanese are both. They usually have a Shinto god shelf in the upper corner of some room, a large and very expensive Buddhist *butsudan* (altar) in a central room, and their Confucian ancestral tablets dutifully placed in the center of the *butsudan*. Do they then follow three religions or one? It is all integrated into a single unity and not conflicting for the Japanese.

In the early 1990s, the State Statistical Bureau of the People's Republic of China released some conservative figures (according to outside Chinese experts) for religious followers in the world's most populous nation. Of about 200 million religious practitioners acknowledged, more than half were Buddhists. Yet Johnstone noted only 33.6 million Buddhists in China in his 1993 *Operation World* (1993: 164). He did note that another twenty-seven percent, or 306 million, followed Chinese Religions, "a blending of Buddhism, Taoism, Confucianism and folk religion" (1993: 164). Some scholars consider that at least a quarter to a half of the majority Han Chinese to be significantly influenced by Buddhism. Others believe it to be even higher than that.

The Lausanne II *Christian Witness to Buddhists* fairly declared,

> It is unlikely that, during the last three decades, centuries of Buddhistic philosophical thinking in China has been erased. Changes have occurred, but Buddhistic conceptualizations

mixed with various spiritistic beliefs still permeate the thinking of that great nation today (1980: 4).

That 1980 paper and report also noted, "Peoples influenced by Buddhistic thinking comprise one of the largest blocs of unreached peoples in 1980, claiming over a billion people."

In their stimulating article, "World Mission Survey," Ralph Winter and David Fraser, while not recognizing the strong Folk Buddhist influence among the Han Chinese, acknowledged that, "Beyond them (that is, Chinese, Hindus, and Muslims) are some 850 million other Asians—most of whom are influenced by Buddhism" (1999: 365). This was an encouraging direction in the *Perspectives on the World Christian Movement.* It revealed that Buddhist populations ranked with Hindus and Muslims in sheer numbers. Interestingly, a joint agency publication of Frontiers and TEAM included a personalized Strategy Map that identified the number of unreached in each people group. In that short list, Han Chinese had 418 million in 2,000 people groups and Buddhists 264 million in another 1,000 people groups. Together these mostly Folk Buddhists totaled 682 million relating to 3,000 unreached people groups.

So what is the more accurate assessment of world population influenced by Buddhism in all its forms including classical, syncretistic, and folk religion? The attached schedule of 1998 estimated populations by country shows a low figure of 680.4 million, (90% more than Barrett's 1999 figures), and a high figure of 953 million—close to one billion Buddhists! The full nominal and Folk Buddhist total today is likely to be higher yet.

Wherever the diasporan Chinese, Japanese, or Koreans are located in the world, there Buddhism will be found in one or more of its variegated brands. Today, like the proverbial Jews, Asians are found scattered in large numbers across the globe—many millions of them. At least 40 million Chinese, two and a half million Japanese, one million Koreans, and 13 million Vietnamese are among them. Primarily, these are also Buddhist peoples. Only a minority of them are Christians. Africa has few Buddhist Asians, though they are increasing in strength in South Africa. Four of the Central Asia States, though predominantly Muslim populations now, also have 430,000 mostly Buddhist Koreans in their midst. Europe has over half a million Chinese. In France alone are 385,000 Vietnamese and 70,000 Cambodians. Saudi Arabia strangely boasts 58,000 Chinese and 66,000 Koreans.

Oceania has a quarter of a million Chinese scattered widely, while North America has about 24 million Chinese, and almost one million each of Vietnamese, Japanese, and Koreans, plus one and a half million Filipinos! Significantly, the population of Kuala Lumpur, capital of the Islamic State of Malaysia, has 4.5% Christians and 48.6% Buddhists. Most of these two groups are Chinese. Surprisingly, Latin America has two million Chinese, Japanese, and Koreans—the largest group of which is 1.4 million Japanese, most of whom are in Brazil. About fifty percent of these Brazilian Japanese follow Catholicism often mixed with Buddhist beliefs and practices. No wonder it is hard to get a handle on accurate statistics for Buddhist populations worldwide.

The conundrum is complicated further when trying to estimate accurate numbers of Folk Buddhists in the West, where the popularity of all kinds of Buddhist personalities, practices, and beliefs are saturating Western culture, thinking, and even worldview. Besides the Asian immigrant and refugee practitioners of Buddhism, there are now more than ten million "nightstand Buddhists" in America. Scholars such as Thomas A. Tweed (1999) use this term, primarily for those Westerners who privately practice variegated varieties of individualized Buddhist meditation and devotion. Most are not directed by priests or gurus. Add to these the exploding "hyphenated Buddhists" and "Buddhist-Christians" strewn throughout the Western nations from Scandinavia to South Africa and from Russia to Australia. Even Buddhist statisticians struggle to estimate the number of followers of their religion since "it's still hard to get an accurate count because of the people we call 'nightstand Buddhists'."

Currently the world Buddhist population of all types, shapes, and sizes is approximately one billion. In 1999 Mahayana claims 810 million, Theravada 130 million, and Tantric (Tibetan) Buddhism 15 million. Together these three branches total 955 million. However, unlike Muslim extremists or fanatical Hindus, Buddhists seem, because of their eclectic nature, assimilative tolerance, and peaceful coexistence, to be largely unnoticed and often underestimated. In addition, Western Buddhists, including some "New Age" and other "crypto" and Folk Buddhists, already number in the tens of millions. Besides this, modern Buddhist propagation is aggressively reaching out to Asian tribal groups. This is also adding new adherents daily to worldwide Buddhism. Lewis M. Hopfe in his *Religions of the World* suggested that, "Buddhism is perhaps on the verge of another great missionary outreach" (1987: 170).

The First International Buddhist Propagation Conference was held in Kyoto, Japan, in April 1998. This was a Buddhist milestone at which vocal criticism of Christian propagation, especially among the poor Buddhist groups, was openly discussed and evangelists were reproved and censured (Dhammananda 1998: 207). In the 21st century, with its attitudes of relativity and universalism, there is an urgent need to reawaken the church to the enormity of this growing religious kaleidoscope of Buddhist people groups. As advocates for this immense and complex bloc of peoples, let us stimulate a fresh movement of gracious prayer, compassionate concern, sensitive outreach, and loving evangelization of Buddhists everywhere. Their numbers and locations are broader than we think. They are often in our own backyards. Their temples sprout all over the West. Today more than 3,600 of them are in the U.S. A billion Buddhists still wait for Christ's unique saving power through the eternal Gospel. Let us join hands and hearts together to bless Buddhists and reach out to them everywhere with genuine meekness and humility.

1998 WORLD BUDDHIST POPULATION

COUNTRY	Population (millions)	Percentage Buddhist	Buddhists (millions)
India	988.7	*0.71	7.02
Bangladesh	123.4	0.6	0.74
Sri Lanka	18.9	70.3 – *75	13.29 – 14.18
Nepal	23.7	7.2	1.71
Bhutan	0.8	70.1	0.56
Tibet (China SAR)	6.7	70	4.69
Myanmar	47.1	*94	41.35 – 44.27
Thailand	61.1	95	58.05
Laos	5.3	59.4	3.15
Cambodia	10.8	87	9.40
Vietnam	78.5	57.2 – 70	44.9 – 54.95
Brunei	0.3	11.7	0.04
Malaysia	22.2	25	5.55
Singapore	3.9	52.4	2.04
Indonesia	207.4	1	2.07
Philippines	75.3	1.4	1.05
Macao	0.5	44.3	0.22

COUNTRY	Population (millions)	Percentage Buddhist	Buddhists (millions)
Hong Kong (China SAR)	6.7	66	4.42
Taiwan	21.7	70.4	15.28
Japan	126.4	58 – *60	73.31 – 75.84
South Korea	46.4	28.9	13.41
North Korea	22.2	1.7 – 31.2	0.38 – 6.93
China (PRC)	1,242.5	30 – 50	372.75 – 621.25
Mongolia	2.5	26 – 78	0.65 – 1.95
Russia	146.9	0.6	0.88
Central Asian states (4)	50.5	0.84	0.42
Europe	728	0.08	0.58
Canada	30.6	0.36	0.11
USA	270.2	0.4 (East Asian)	1.08
		0.18 (American)	0.49
Central & South America	500	0.11	0.56
Oceania / Australia	30	0.7	0.21
Africa	763	0.01	0.08
WORLD TOTAL			680.44 – 953.18

1. Population figures from Population Reference Bureau, Washington D.C., *1998 World Population Data Sheet.*

2. Percentage estimates from Patrick Johnstone's *Operation World* 1993 (and include his traditional Chinese religions).

3. Those marked * are from First International Buddhist Propagation Conference, Kyoto, Japan, April 1998.

Collated by Dr. Alex Smith, OMF International, February 1999 for the first draft.

CHAPTER 2

The Power of the Kingdom for Encountering Buddhist Worldviews[1]

Tan Kang San

The Need for Christian-Buddhist Encounters

Christianity's relationship with non-Christian religions is a key missiological inquiry for Evangelicals concerned with the Great Commission. Traditionally, Evangelical missions have concentrated on proclamation of the gospel and avoided interfaith approaches (John Stott, 1975). Increasingly, most missionaries in Asia work within restrictive environments which prohibit direct evangelism. Do we have a theology of witness for genuine encounter with Buddhists? In the West, the privatization of religious faith has made direct evangelism socially unacceptable. Globally, rising ethnic-religious tensions threaten peace and racial harmony in many countries in Africa, India, Indonesia, and the Middle East, to name a few. Even in seemingly "peaceful" Buddhist countries, Christian proselytization efforts are problematic. Another concern is the partial conversion of people groups in Asia, where church growth is not accompanied by worldview transformation. From a variety of perspectives then, wherever the gospel is preached, there is a need for deeper encounter with traditional Buddhist worldviews. The purpose is not to compromise the gospel but to confront underlying belief systems at their deepest level.

Some key questions for this study are: What theological implications does the kingdom of God have for the Interfaith Encounter with Buddhists? In particular, can conservative Evangelical theology provide an adequate and creative foundation for a genuine Interfaith encounter with other truth claims such as Buddhism? How will a distinctive Evangelical encounter be different from pluralist models?

This article is an attempt to explore a theology for Interfaith encounters from the perspective of an Asian worker serving within a Malaysian environment characterized by religious plurality and multi-ethnicity, and from a desire to position the Interfaith encounter as a key Evangelical approach for missionaries working among East Asian Buddhist peoples.

The notion of the kingdom of God, as defined by Scripture and developed by Evangelical scholars (John Bright, 1953; Richard T. France, 1990; George Eldon Ladd, 1993), is used here to construct an Evangelical approach toward the Interfaith Encounter. Following Johannes Verkuyl's article, "The Biblical Notion of the Kingdom: Test of Validity for Theology of Religion" (1993: 71-81), it is envisaged that the kingdom of God theme, as defined by Scripture and developed by Evangelical scholars and missiologists, has the potential to provide a programmatic framework for Interfaith encounters. For the purpose of the present study, I shall follow Ladd's definition of the kingdom of God as:

> the redemptive reign of God dynamically active to establish
> his rule among men, and that this kingdom, which will appear

as an apocalyptic act at the end of the age, has already come in
human history in the person and mission of Jesus to overcome
evil, to deliver men from its power, and to bring them into the
blessings of God's reign (1993: 89-90).

I define the Interfaith encounter as an inter-religious
conversation whereby both the Christian and the Buddhists desire to
witness to their faiths as well as listen and learn from the neighbor's
faith. Worldview can be said to be "a set of shared framework of
ideas of a particular society concerning how they perceive the
world" (Burnett 1990: 13).

The article begins by outlining a brief survey of the Buddhist
scriptures that influenced East Asian cultures, followed by an outline
of foundational axioms for a theology of Interfaith Encounter that is
based on a distinctive Evangelical theology of the kingdom of God.
Based on those seven foundational axioms, theological implications
for Interfaith Encounters with Buddhists are drawn. Theology *per se*
is fine, but as reflective practitioners, we are also interested in how
theology should be applied in real life situations.

In the second part of the article, I seek to demonstrate how an
Evangelical Interfaith Encounter might work in real life. First, by
using Groome's model of shared praxis as a model for a kingdom-
oriented Interfaith Encounter. Second, I will illustrate from the life
and ministry of E. Stanley Jones as a model of a reflective
practitioner of Interfaith Encounter with Hindus and Buddhists. I
will end with some proposals and summarize with a kingdom-
oriented model for encountering Buddhists.

Scriptures in Buddhist Traditions

Although we do not have good historical evidence on the life
of Buddha, Christians must be willing to engage with the Buddhist
scriptures because these are the sources of their religious beliefs. It is
true that the extant versions of Buddha's life were created long after

his death by his followers, our purpose in religious encounters is to understand what Buddhist believe and how the Christian gospel addresses those belief systems.

The words of the Buddha, which became the Buddhist scriptures, were stories of how he seeks after truth and finally achieves *nirvana*. The words he spoke were intended to exhort others to enter into the same experience of release. These words were new and different from the handed down Hindu Vedas:

> That this was the noble truth concerning sorrow, was not, O Bhikkhus, among the doctrines handed down (i.e., the Vedas), but there arose within me the eye (to perceive it), there arose the knowledge (of its nature), there arose the understanding (of its cause), there arose wisdom (to guide in the path of tranquility), there arose the light (to dispel darkness from it) (Coward 2000: 140).

Buddhists hold that the authority of Buddhist scriptures arose out of Buddha's enlightenment experience. Unlike the Christian's position on the Bible as divinely revealed and inspired, Buddhists are open to subsequent scriptures from "other Buddhas." Tradition records that within the year that Buddha died (c. 483 BC), five hundred monks gathered and agreed to codify the Rule of the Monastic Order. Ananda, Buddha's closest follower and relative, were reported to recite all the "remembered words" which were then approved by the world community (*Sangha)*. Ananda is said to have recited the original five *Nikayas (*also called *Agama)* in the *Sutra Pitaka*, or *The Basket of Discourses*. Centuries later, these were compiled into *Sutras* (Buddha's teachings) as part of the Buddhist canon. In addition, the School of Elders (Theravada) expanded texts (*Abhidharma)* were judged necessary part of the *Dharma*. Consequently, we have the *tripitaka* or "three baskets of scripture": *sutra* (Buddha's teachings), *vinaya* (monastic rules) and *Abhidharma* (philosophic treatise). Many Theravada Buddhists felt that only these transmitted sayings of the Buddha could be part of the scriptures while others take a more open view of the Buddhist canon. These more open groups accepted the same general *sutras and vinayas* but developed their own *Abhidharma* or *sastra* (philosophic literatures). The Mahayanas also add many new *sutras* such as *Prajnaparamita Sutras* and the *Lotus Sutras.* Later, other devotional texts such as *Tantras* (inspired words of Buddhas) and *Jatakas* (popular stories or fables about Buddha) were developed. Although folk Buddhists may not be literate in Buddhist scriptures, it is arguable that the teachings of Buddha shape the worldviews of Asian societies.

There is certainly more to Buddhist religious life than their doctrines, but with the revival of Buddhist intellectualism and complexities of various streams of Buddhism, it will be difficult for the Christian missionary to gain an appreciation of what Buddhists really believe without a good grounding of Buddhist doctrines as found in these scriptures.

Foundational Axioms for a Kingdom-Oriented Theology of Christian-Buddhist Encounters

The following foundational axioms for a kingdom-oriented theology of Christian-Buddhist Encounter are highlighted: (1) The kingdom-oriented Encounter is based on the belief that God alone is king; (2) the kingdom-oriented Encounter is Christ-centred; (3) the kingdom-oriented Encounter is Trinitarian in nature; (4) the kingdom-oriented Encounter transcends narrow ecclesiology; (5) the kingdom-oriented Encounter is about God's reign, not merely abstract ideas; (6) the kingdom-oriented Encounter must be suffused by the eschatological hope in Christ; and (7) the kingdom-oriented Encounter is totally dependent upon God's sovereign activity.

God's Kingship as the Basis for the Christian-Buddhist Encounter

Buddhists do not hold on to the existence of a creator God or a supreme personal Being, although in some streams of Buddhism, they do believe in the existences of divine beings and deities (Williams 2002: 25). Christians cannot expect our Buddhist friends to engage from a theistic viewpoint. By the same token, neither can Christians engage without at some point bringing the ontological argument for God. Buddha was a human being who found the way that brings release from infinite series of sufferings and rebirths. The remedy to our sufferings lies in letting go of our attachments to things (including God). We cannot prove God exists beyond reasonable doubt but we can begin with humble confession that we believe in a creator God, as revealed in the Christian scriptures.

Three theological implications from God's sovereign kingship may be highlighted as providing foundations for a kingdom-oriented theology of religious Encounters. First, God's character and his sovereign dealings with humankind provide the basis for engagement with humans. As a righteous and holy God, Yahweh cannot tolerate sin. Because humanity has sinned and continually rebels against God's kingship, God intervenes in history as judge. Interfaith relations cannot ignore humanity's persistent rebellion against God's kingship.

In the midst of judgment, God provides salvation due to his mercy. Yahweh is not only a God of wrath, but also a God of mercy and boundless grace. This pattern of "sin-judgement-salvation" provides a paradigmatic approach to all religions. The emphasis is on salvation as the goal of the kingdom, although judgement is also clearly communicated as an inevitable consequence on those who continually reject God's kingship.

An Encounter that is firmly rooted in God's sovereign character must hold both aspects of God's righteous judgement and loving kindness in creative tension. Without such "biblical realism,"

Christianity's approach to other religions is bound to fall into reductionism. Christopher Wright comments:

> The fallen duplicity of man is that he simultaneously seeks after God his Maker and flees from God his Judge. Man's religions, therefore, simultaneously manifest both these human tendencies. This is what makes a simplistic verdict on other religions—whether blandly positive or negative—so unsatisfactory and indeed, unbiblical (1984: 5).

Thus Christians, who are the recipients of God's mercy and who are worshippers of the righteous and holy God, have an epistemic and ethical duty to engage in dialogue with Buddhists, even if they are atheistic or agnostic. In a stimulating and intensely personal book, *The Unexpected Way: On Converting from Buddhism to Catholicism*, Paul Williams, Professor of Indian and Tibetan Philosophy at University of Bristol, among other things, presented the arguments for the existence of a God. After over twenty years as a Buddhist, Williams was challenged by Thomas Aquinas' writings in seeking after the question: "Why is there something rather than nothing?" He struggled over two viable alternatives:

> Buddhist position: The fact that there is something rather than nothing, and the way things are, in terms of causal processes and so on, as discovered by the Buddha, just *is* how it is. End of the matter.

> Christian position: The reason why there is something rather than nothing, and things are the way they are, is because they are grounded on a necessary being who has in some sense brought it about (Williams 2002: 33).

Beyond Williams' philosophical arguments, a kingdom-oriented theology of religion moves on to the affirmation that God's kingship is universal. God's universal kingship in the Old Testament is reflected in the repeated accounts of God's ruling activities over Israel and the nations. In particular, God is often depicted as exercising his power over foreign nations, for example, in his concern for Nineveh in the book of Jonah, his use of the Assyrians and Babylonians as instruments of judgment on Israel, his sovereign rule over Nebuchadnezzar (Dan. 1-4), his use of Cyrus as agent of restoring his kingdom (Isa. 44:28; 45:1, 13), and his providential use of Xerxes as agent of preservation of Israel in the book of Esther. Believing that God is actively at work among unbelievers, Christians can approach non-Christians looking for evidences of his work.

God's kingship is not only universal, but also covenantal. God's redemptive action is expressed and exercised through successive covenants: Noahic, Abrahamic, Mosaic, Davidic, and culminating in the New Covenant (Dumbrell 1984). In the Old Testament, God's kingship is associated most closely with Israel, a particular people with whom God chose to establish a covenantal relationship. In the New Testament, God's covenant people is identified with the Church of Jesus Christ. Membership in the kingdom is predicated upon the "new birth" (John 3), possible today only through faith in Jesus Christ. The theological implication for interfaith relations is that, at some point in the dialogical process, kingdom-oriented dialogue will issue the call for a covenant relationship with God through faith in Jesus as Lord and Savior.

In summary, God's sovereignty as expressed in his kingship provides the basis for a missionary encounter with Buddhists. God, who is the Heavenly King, must become king in the hearts of people. Therefore, those already subjected to God are *obligated to persuade others to submit themselves to God.* This is the philosophical basis for interfaith relations. It is based on the fact that there are others who do not acknowledge God's kingship and that their search for truth has something to teach us about God and his kingdom.

Yet, why should the Interfaith Encounter be utilized instead of simply relying on proclamation as the means of propagating the gospel? The primary reason is that God's rulership must be brought to bear on the existing faith-commitments, presuppositions, and worldviews of our Buddhist friends. However, in order to be genuine, their submission to God cannot be coerced or manipulated. Therefore, Christians need to enter into dialogue in order to witness effectively and persuade others regarding the challenge of God's kingship.

The Kingdom-Oriented Encounter is Christ-Centered

Salvation is accomplished through the person and work of Christ. *Commitment to Christ is the precondition for the kingdom-oriented Encounter*, after which Christ becomes the model for approaching Buddhists. Although God's salvation plan begins with the call of Abraham and the nation Israel, it ultimately looks forward to Christ, the Seed of Abraham. Due to Israel's failure to be a faithful instrument of the kingdom, God invaded human history through the person and work of Jesus. In contrast to Israel's misguided ethnocentrism, Jesus makes it clear that all people are welcome into God's kingdom, with special attention being shown to the poor, the oppressed, and the marginalized. Not only is Jesus the embodiment of the kingdom, he alone ushers in the kingdom of God. No one enters into a relationship with the Father except through Jesus Christ.

What are the implications of a kingdom-oriented Encounter where Jesus is confessed as Lord? First, *Jesus is both the ultimate judge of all truth and the criterion against which conflicting truth-claims are evaluated.* "Jesus is for the believer the source from whom his understanding of the totality of experience is drawn and therefore the criterion by which other ways of understanding are judged" (Newbigin 1981: 4). More specifically, a distinctive Evangelical theology of religion (in contrast to an Ecumenical perspective) holds a high Christology that does not compromise the truth of the supremacy of Christ over all the world's religions. Christ is the only way to the Father and, without him as king, there is no kingdom of God. Evangelical encounters with other religions, therefore, reject any form of relativism that undermines the unique person and work of Christ in bringing salvation to the world.

High Christology need not mean rejection of the truth of other religions such as Buddha's teaching on morality, or that Christians cannot learn anything new from Buddhists, including truths that the philosophical riches of Mahayana Buddhism may bring to Christian views of life, purity, disciplines, and the meaning of suffering. Buddhist background Evangelicals have a tendency to degrade everything about Buddhism as idolatry and pagan. I think it is possible to retain a high level of sympathy and even admiration for Buddha's compassion and his teachings, if only one ventures with love for Christ and the Buddhists he so loved.[2]

In a Christ-centered encounter, *Jesus becomes the model for approaching unbelievers.* His preaching and teaching methods, his lifestyle, and his commitments are the way that Christians should approach unbelievers. In particular, Christ's incarnational model provides the key toward meaningful dialogue. Jesus radicalized the law of love, "that we love God by loving our neighbor as we love ourselves, with neighbor unlimited, as the only measure of membership in God's reign" (Groome 1991: 16). Such an approach to Buddhists *needs to be shaped by Jesus' total mission.* Jesus' total mission encompasses the challenge of discipleship, the confrontation with demonic powers and religious authorities, a compassion for the lost, and the creation of a new society. The implications for interfaith encounters are profound. In particular, Christians are not merely to be interested in sharing the gospel, but also to be seeking the total transformation of the person and society.

Finally, *Jesus is the message.* In interfaith encounters, the Christian makes accessible the gospel story about the Christ who brings salvation to the world. However, our message must be presented with humility and grace. "The cross is not merely the centre of the message of salvation; it is crucial for Christian living and ministry" (Covell 1993: 169). Therefore, commitment to Christ is both a prerequisite and a goal for Evangelical engagements with Buddhists. Without religious commitment to Christ, one cannot truly engage with people of other faiths because nothing is at risk. With a deep commitment to Christ, Christians will naturally and logically enter into missionary encounters for the purpose of persuading their dialogical partners about the truth of the gospel.

The Trinity and the Interfaith Encounter

Verkuyl proposes that a kingdom-centered theology of religion should be thoroughly trinitarian in nature: "It is a theology that has God the Creator, the Redeemer and the Comforter at its very heart" (1993: 72).

Within a trinitarian perspective of Interfaith Encounters, one must take into account the role of the Holy Spirit in the world and in the Church. George Peters insightfully distinguishes a pre-Pentecost ministry and an extra-Pentecost ministry of the Holy Spirit:

> The pre-Pentecost ministry is fully exposed in the Old Testament and in the gospels, while the extra-Pentecost ministry relates to world missions. We may speak of it as the general or universal ministry of the Holy Spirit, keeping in mind that the Holy Spirit is the presence of God and is omnipresence (1972: 76).

A more recent attempt was made by Amos Yong in his article, "Discerning the Spirit(s) in the World of Religions" (Stackhouse 2001). Yong sought to make a methodological claim that "a pneumatological theology of religions not only commits but also enables Christians to engage empirically the world's religions in a truly substantive manner with theological questions and concerns" (2001: 38). What implications can we draw from the universal work of the Holy Spirit for Christian Encounters with Buddhists? First, *Christian-Buddhist Encounters are possible because the Holy Spirit is the one who reveals the mystery of the kingdom.* He was active before Christ's earthly ministry and he continues to reveal God's truths to all people, Buddhists included. Evidences of the hidden work of the Spirit include revealing truths about Christ in dreams to unbelievers, planting in the minds of unbelievers an irresistible desire to worship the creator, and convicting unbelievers of their sins through their conscience that was created in the image of God.

Second, *the active work of the Holy Spirit assures Christians that despite the rebellion of humanity and the depravity of certain practices within other religions, humanity has not been totally left alone* (John 16:7-8). "There was total depravity but not total destitute and deprivation" (Peters 1972: 79). The element of mystery coupled with the ongoing role of the Holy Spirit points to the place of prayer and spiritual discernment in Christian engagements. Recognizing the hiddenness of God's working in people's minds and hearts, the role of the Christian in Interfaith Encounters is to explain truth in an intelligible fashion and to help unbelievers discern God's work in their lives. God's part is to make that truth effective. In the process of encounter, God can open the spiritual eyes of unbelievers. God can also open the spiritual perceptions of his children. Therefore, the Interfaith Encounter is a discovery process about God for Christians and Buddhists alike.

Third, *pneumatological engagement also reminds the Christian of the spiritual battle of the kingdom* (Eph. 6:10-18). The real enemy is Satan, who blinds the eyes of unbelievers, and not unbelievers themselves (2 Cor. 4:4). The Interfaith Encounter proceeds with a combined attitude of prayer and spiritual warfare against the powers of darkness as well as reconciliation and compassion toward unbelievers. Prayer that centers on the real enemy will generate within believers an attitude of dependence upon God and an attitude of humility and compassion in relation to people of other faiths.

The Trialogue between God, the Church, and the Buddhist Communities

The kingdom of God is not to be equated with the Church; neither should it be separated from the church because God's presence and redemptive activity are administered primarily, though not exclusively, through the church. The kingdom of God is not to be equated with the church because God's ruling activity extends beyond the church into the world (see Hiebert 1993: 151-161; Scherer 1993: 82-88). The kingdom of God, however, cannot be separated from the church because the church is the sign and subject of the kingdom. God's presence and redemptive activity are administered through the church. It is the church, not the world, who is the "subjects" of the kingdom. The church, however, is to exist for the sake of God and his kingdom and never for its own.

As "subjects" of the kingdom, the church must proclaim the message of the kingdom and rely on the power of the Holy Spirit to lead Buddhists to repentance and to bring them into the kingdom of God. To the degree that the church submits itself to God's rule and participates in Christ's mission, the kingdom of God is manifested through the church (Pannenberg 1969: 77). When the church becomes concerned only with its religious needs and loses its kingdom-orientation toward serving the world, then the church can no longer be identified with the kingdom of God. The failure of Israel and the disciples remind the church of this tendency toward self-centeredness and self-righteousness.

Four implications for Interfaith Encounters arise from the nature of the relationship among the kingdom, the church and the Buddhist communities.

First, *the Interfaith Encounter does not begin with the church but with "God who himself entered into dialogue with man"* (Stott 1975: 61). All humans, irrespective of their religions, are created in the image of God and remain the object of God's boundless mercy.

Whether the church engages with other religions or not, God continually encounters those who seek him. Christians must not assume that the Sovereign Lord is inactive outside the walls of the church. Instead, they should enter into encounters with Buddhists with the conviction that the Lord has taken the dialogical initiative and that the church has the privilege of being allowed to participate in God's work of encountering his creatures. In encountering Buddhists, the Christian is called to trust in God's dynamic power to communicate God's truth to and to illuminate God's truth in unbelievers. In such a relation, Christians are not merely story tellers (proclaimers) but also "story makers" (helping unbelievers to make sense of God's work in their lives).

Second, because God's rulership extends beyond ecclesiastical and religious boundaries (Hiebert 1993: 153-161), *Christians can approach Buddhists with a confidence that God is already at work in the lives of unbelievers and, in some respects, even in their religious systems.* Holding such a dynamic view of God's kingship means that Christians should be willing to acknowledge the signs of God's common grace in the lives of unbelievers and their religions and be eager to find bridges that will open avenues for gospel penetration.

Third, although the kingdom of God is broader than and must not be identified with the church, neither must the kingdom be separated from the church. Just as Israel is God's chosen instrument for establishing his kingdom in the Old Testament, so too the church is God's chosen instrument today. Therefore, a kingdom-oriented Interfaith Encounter requires the involvement of the whole church, not just of individuals. Although *individual Christians may participate in missionary encounters on informal basis, they should engage the religions within the perspective of the community of faith.* Christianity's encounter with Buddhism as a religious system, whether formally or informally, is a communal affair. Such a view asserts that Interfaith Encounters between religious communities can only be undertaken by individuals who are identified with *specific* communities of faith, rather than "global, semi-fictional entities" (Griffiths 1991: 6). In this strict sense, an Interfaith Encounter that is undertaken by pluralists who are not committed to any religious community is ruled out.

A fourth implication of a kingdom-oriented Interfaith Encounter arises from the notion that *the church is the sign of the kingdom of God where God's presence is manifest in the world.* In restrictive environments, where evangelism is prohibited, the church, according to Newbigin, can "bear in its own life the presence of the kingdom" (1978: 54). The church, through her dialogical engagements with every aspect of the nation, can bear positive witness to the power of the gospel and the person of Christ. In such situations, despite the lack of opportunity for direct proclamation, the church is still able to represent faithfully the vitality and presence of the kingdom of God.

Traditionally, due to the confusion that the church and kingdom are the same entity, Evangelicals have been reluctant to enter into any collaborative ventures that were not centered on the church. Based on the above explanation of the relationship between the church and the kingdom, it should be obvious that the concerns of the church cannot fully account for the comprehensive scope of the kingdom. In other words, the works of the kingdom cannot be confined to the service of the church. In any case, it is appropriate to stress that the concerns of the kingdom will never marginalize the church. The dynamic tension between church and kingdom is subsumed when the underlying motive for Interfaith Encounters is the glory of God rather than the service of the church.

The Kingdom-Oriented Encounter is about God's Reign, not merely Abstract Ideas

The nature of the kingdom provides further insights for a kingdom-oriented theology of Interfaith Encounter. The kingdom of

God: (1) is about God's reign, not realm; (2) extends into every arena of human life; (3) has past, present and future aspects; and (4) is God's gift to humankind.

As stated in axiom 5 above, God's reign is not an abstract notion but a situation in which he is acknowledged as king. Within a kingdom perspective an Interfaith Encounter is an encounter between *people* (rather than between religious ideas), where the focus is on "lived issues." By emphasizing God's kingship rather than abstract ideas, the Interfaith Encounter is prevented from becoming mere "religious chatter." In other words, the kingdom-oriented Interfaith Encounter is about encounters between people within the context of an actual community. According to Verkuyl,

> Kingdom-oriented theology of religion requires the type of dialogue in which a true exchange of information regarding deeply held convictions takes place, one in which each of the partners listen[s] attentively to each other's articulation of beliefs concerning the fundamental questions of life and death and tries, in turn, to convince the other of the worthiness and truth of the core message to which he or she has given assent (1993: 78).

Second, the kingdom of God is concerned with every aspect of human life. As God the king exercises his authority and people respond to his kingship, the kingdom of God is experienced in its many dimensions. In other words, *the kingdom of God is not merely concerned about other-worldly affairs but is also concerned about social and structural transformations on earth.* Therefore, the kingdom-oriented Interfaith Encounter seeks the total transformation of society through a holistic witness (proclamation, dialogue, and social concern). Given the complex situation of mission in a pluralistic world, the church's participation in God's kingdom must include holistic engagement with peoples. There must be dialogues between Christians and non-Christians regarding issues of common interest. In the Malaysian context, for example, evangelicals should be willing to engage with other religious groups on common concerns such as constitutional freedom of religion, human rights issues, the role of religion in society, racial polarization and the general decline in morality. Such engagements on structural evils are not to be considered as "second-class" involvements within the mission of the church.

Third, based on the above two implications that kingdom encounters are concerned with "living issues" and the total transformation of the whole society, the church needs to approach non-Christian religions as all inclusive systems. Such an approach was advocated by Kraemer, and referred to as a "totalitarian approach" (1947: 102). The totalitarian approach refuses to dichotomize religious issues from social and cultural issues.

In the Malaysian situation, for example, where religion and ethnicity coincide sharply, evangelizing Chinese Buddhists involves dealing with the cultural issues and the worldviews of the Chinese. More than merely contextualizing biblical themes to the local situation, the Church needs to address the racial and religious overtones of unbelievers. What are their perceptions of Christianity? In what ways have the forces of colonialism and nationalism shaped their ideas about Christianity, or formed barriers against the claims of Christ? Where are the meeting points between, for example, the Chinese worldview and the teachings of Jesus? In order to deal with these worldviews and cultural issues, sensitive and creative engagements are essential.

The Kingdom-Oriented Encounter must be Suffused by the Eschatological Hope in Christ

Another implication of the nature of the kingdom is based on the insight that the kingdom has past, present, and future aspects. The kingdom is past in that it has definitively come in the person of Jesus Christ. It is future in that its full consummation awaits the *parousia*, and it is present in that its signs are evident in our midst whenever God's will is done on earth.

God's kingship has been inaugurated in the person and ministry of Jesus (axiom 2), but its full consummation awaits the *parousia*, when God in Christ returns as Judge and is fully acknowledged as King. The future has an imperative claim upon the present; as God's kingship is proclaimed and accepted, God's rule is presently experienced and we can even now glimpse its future glory. *The eschatological dimension of the kingdom requires a provisionality in truth presentation, and Christians must be prepared to live within a framework of penultimate knowledge.*

The dynamic interrelationship among the various time-aspects of the kingdom suggests an important insight for Interfaith Relations. God's salvation history and the vision of the kingdom in the future become meaningful and "arresting" only when people "see" their significance to present and existential needs. Because existential issues vary from individual to individual at different stages of life, Interfaith Encounters are necessary to uncover those issues. Within this perspective, the agenda for discussion must be determined by the unbeliever, rather than by the Christian. Theologically speaking, *the purpose of the Interfaith Encounter is to generate a critical consciousness in the minds and emotions of Buddhists so that the significance of the gospel story and the vision become relevant and meaningful to their existential concerns.*

The future, however, has an imperative claim on the present. Therefore, the kingdom-oriented Interfaith Encounter must be suffused by eschatological expectations of the future hope. *We approach people on the basis not only of who they are but also of what they will be in Christ.* The vision for the future is rooted not in their religiosity, but in what God will do in the lives of those who submit to his kingship. Another important insight is that due to the nature of the *eschaton*, we must be willing to acknowledge that we do not have all the answers and that we are living within the framework of penultimate knowledge. In Interfaith Relations, we can anticipate surprises as the Spirit guides us into fuller understanding. Dialogue demonstrates in a real way that there is always room for growth in our understanding of God. Through the process of good dialogue, believers can learn to understand truths of the Scriptures and experience God's dynamic power in a new way.

The Kingdom-Oriented Encounter is Totally Dependent upon God's Sovereign Activity

The final implication from the nature of the kingdom relates to an understanding that the kingdom of God is a divine gift to humanity. We cannot build the kingdom through human efforts; it is totally dependent upon God's sovereign activity (France 1984: 41-42). People do not enter into God's kingdom through our clever arguments or persuasions, but through the supernatural and operative work of the Holy Spirit. Our primary calling in Interfaith Encounters is to join God in what he is already doing in the lives of unbelievers. God is drawing people out of the kingdom of darkness into his marvellous light. Without the presence and power of the King, the Interfaith Encounter degenerates into mere godless chatter.

The Model of Shared Praxis

A variety of engagement models have been proposed in educational circles.[3] For our purposes, we shall adopt Thomas Groome's model of shared praxis. Groome first introduced his shared praxis to the religious community through his book, *Christian Religious Education: Sharing Our Story and Vision*, in 1980, and in 1991 he expanded his concept of the shared-praxis approach in *Sharing Faith: A Comprehensive Approach to Religious Education and Pastoral Ministry.*

Groome's model is primarily intended for Christian religious education in the local church, but he asserts that the way of shared praxis is just as applicable in evangelistic situations (1991: 334-335). In adopting Groome's approach, we should note that there a number of criticisms have been levelled against his shared-praxis approach. The first has to do with Groome's understanding of faith, which is heavily influenced by his Roman Catholic background. In her critique of Groome's definition of faith, Jackie Smallbones notes:

> Groome defines it as a lifestyle and, therefore, emphasizes the necessity of works to attain it. Evangelicals describe it particularly as a gift from God, having an object, Jesus Christ, and, therefore, emphasize the necessity of belief in and commitment to the person and work of Jesus Christ, which would, in turn, evidence itself in the life of the believer by works (1986: 58).

A second criticism revolves around Groome's understanding of praxis as a way of knowing. Groome defines praxis as,

> The consciousness and agency that arise from and are expressed in any and every aspect of people's "being" as agents-subjects-in-relationship, whether realized in actions that are personal, interpersonal, sociopolitical, or cosmic (1991: 136).

For Groome, praxis is the basis and the total process for all knowing. For Evangelicals, knowledge of God has to do with God's self-revelation in scripture, rather than praxis (see Smallbones 1986: 61). In addition, D. A. Carson criticizes Groome for his selective use of scripture, which has contributed to a false conclusion about Christian belief and knowledge. Carson writes:

> Certainly Christian belief and Christian knowledge are not exclusively intellectual; but by being selective with the evidence, Groome has managed to conclude that Christian belief and knowledge are exclusively experiential and nonintellectual. The result is a theory of education that consistently depreciates content (1984: 55).

One should also distinguish between the use of praxis as a theological reflection that is informed by a biblical understanding of the kingdom, and that which is drawn from a Marxist or liberation theologian's use of praxis that is confined to existential reflections (see Schreiter 1985: 91-94).

The above-mentioned criticisms, however, do not mean that Evangelicals should not adopt Groome's model. On the contrary, the model has exercised much positive influence on Christian education. For the purpose of this project, there are at least five factors that can be forwarded regarding the suitability of the shared-praxis model. First, Groome's shared-praxis is based on his understanding that the kingdom of God provides the theological basis for Christian education and ministry (1980: 35-55). He suggests that "our meta-purpose as Christian religious educators is to lead people out to the kingdom of God in Jesus Christ" (1980: 35), by which he means that

> Christian religious educators are to lead people out by inviting them to accept Jesus Christ as their Lord and Saviour. . . as well as continually calling them to change with works that verify repentance (1980: 46).

Second, shared praxis has been acknowledged to be a particularly useful and powerful tool for the oppressed or members of minority communities (Schreiter 1985: 92). Schreiter believes that "as a form of reflection, it [praxis] is geared toward transformation and remains the most powerful approach to social transformation available to theology at this time" (1985: 92). Given the contextual realities in majority Buddhist communities, where Christians are the minority group, shared praxis offers a powerful tool that can "help disentangle true consciousness from false consciousness" (1985: 92).

Third, the approach is dialogical, in contrast to being a one-sided presentation of the gospel; the Christian and his dialogue partner interact as equals. Instead of the traditional image of the evangelist/missionary as the "teacher" who has all the answers and the non-Christian as the "student" who has nothing to contribute, the

Interfaith Encounter needs to take "the subject and person seriously" (Stott 1975: 61). It recognizes that both the Christian and the non-Christian have something to contribute to the interreligious relationship. Dominance and control are abandoned, and the Christian, in particular, does not determine the agenda of the religious conversations.

Fourth, the approach is person-centered. The Interfaith Encounter I am advocating is audience-sensitive in the sense that the unique qualities of individuals, not abstract theory, guide the process. In addition, it is flexible and acknowledges that there is no one right method or strategy for encountering people of other faiths. Groome explains:

> The movements of shared praxis are dynamic activities and intentions to be consistently honored over time rather than "steps" in a lockstep procedures. There can be great variety and flexibility in the sequence of the movements (1991: 279).

In Asian-Buddhist contexts, how a person encounters Theravada Buddhists must be highly differentiated from the way that the same individual interacts with Mahayana Buddhists. Similarly, different evangelistic approaches are needed for reaching rural Thais and urban Thais, for reaching the old as opposed to the young, and for reaching English-educated Chinese and their Chinese-educated counterparts. Instead of applying a reductionistic approach, shared praxis takes the individual person and his worldview seriously.

Fifth, Groome's model is an inculturation approach. Inculturation takes seriously both Christianity and the culture of the unbelievers in the interreligious encounter. He defines inculturation as follows:

> The process of historically realizing the intimate relationship between "culture" and "the Christian faith" so that (a) Christian faith is expressed in people's lives through symbols and modes native to their culture; (b) it is a source of transformation for its cultural context; (c) each cultural

expression of it renews and enriches the universal Christian community (1991: 154).

Overview of Shared Praxis

Groome's shared praxis is implemented by means of a focusing activity and five subsequent pedagogical movements. The focusing activity turns people to their own "being" in time and place, i.e., to their present praxis, and establishes a focus for religious discussion. The focusing activity may also turn participants to their present praxis through an engaging symbol so that as they look at it they begin to recognize a particular aspect of their own and/or their society's praxis. To engage people in their present praxis is to turn them to the consciousness that emerges in their whole being as agent-subjects-in-relationship, and to reflect critically on what is "being done" by them, and on what is "going on" around them, to them, and to others in their sociocultural context. Groome outlines the dialogical process in five movements.

Movement 1: Naming/Expressing "Present Praxis"

Movement 1 invites participants to "name" or express their own and/or their society's "present action," typically of a generative theme or around an engaging symbol, as they participate in and experience that praxis in their historical or religious context. Movement 1 begins with people "naming" their present reality as they perceive it, not as a missionary telling them what it is.

For example, participants might share on the following themes: reminders of God's presence, answered prayers, guidance, or attitudes toward other races. Participants might also read a scriptural text through which Buddhists could express either their sentiments, attitudes, beliefs or assessments, or how the theme is being lived and produced in their lives. Movement 1 provides the participants an opportunity to express their religious beliefs or doctrine and for others to listen and learn "first-hand" about the religious faith and belief of their dialogue partners.

Movement 2: Critical Reflection on Present Action

Movement 2 encourages "critical reflection" by participants on what was expressed as "present action" in movement 1. Critical reflection can engage people in any or all activities of critical or social reasoning. "The intent is to deepen the reflective moment and bring participants to a critical consciousness of the present praxis: its reasons, interests, assumptions, prejudices, and ideologies" (Groome 1991: 147).

The most essential activity of movement 2 is critical reflection on the "present action" that is shared in dialogue. Critical reflection is an activity of discerning what to affirm, what to refuse and what to transform in one's historical reality (1991: 147). As participants engage in interreligious reflections, each listens to and interprets the emerging conversation and consciousness of the group regarding present praxis. The process encourages participants to discern what is true in their interpretations of present praxis, what is false or inaccurate, and what needs to be changed or transformed.

Movement 3: Making Accessible the Christian Story and Vision

In the first two movements, through critical reflection on their own/or society's present praxis, participants can appropriate and share together their own stories and visions from an aspect of present praxis. The third movement makes accessible the Christian *story* (namely, the gospel) and the Christian *vision* (of the kingdom of God). The Christian story "reflects God's covenant encounter with humankind in the people of Israel, in Jesus the Christ, and in the community of Jesus' disciples since then" (1991: 216). Its vision reflects the demands and promises that arises from the story to mandate and empower people to live under God's reign. The style of making accessible the Christian story avoids imposition and seeks to present the Christian perspective on the generating theme or issue. Groome writes:

> Educators are to teach the Vision of the Christian faith as something *immediate* and *historical*, in that it calls people to do God's will on earth now as if God's reign is at hand, and as something *new* and *ultimate*, in that it always calls people beyond their present horizons of praxis in faith until they finally rest in God (1991: 217; emphasis added).

Movement 3 is where Evangelical Interfaith Relations depart from a pluralist or syncretistic model of religious engagement. A kingdom-oriented model seeks not only to have Christians listen to individual stories, but also to have them present the gospel story and then to allow the gospel to critique personal stories. Just as evangelicals have the opportunity to witness about their faith, so they must also accord the same courtesy to their dialogue partners by listening attentively to their witness.

Movement 4: Dialectical Hermeneutic to Appropriate Christian Story/Vision to Participant's Belief Statements

In movement 4, participants wrap their critical understanding of their present praxis around a generative theme or symbol (movements 1 and 2), using a dialectic hermeneutic to appropriate the Christian Story/Vision (movement 3). In the fullest expression of its dynamic, participants ask: "How does this Christian Story/Vision affirm, question and call us beyond the present praxis?" Conversely, they query: "How does present praxis affirm and critically make use of the version of the Story/Vision made accessible in movement 3, and how are we to live more faithfully to the Vision of God's reign?"

The essential purpose of movement 4 is to enable participants to align the Christian Story/Vision with their historical reality and perceptions. Groome explains:

> Beyond establishing accuracy of understanding, movement 4 is to bring participants into dialogue about what they are thinking, and doing in response to what was made accessible in movement 3, to encourage them to judge and personally appropriate it to their own lives and contexts (1991: 290).

The Christian is to respect the freedom and discernment of participants in movements 4 and 5. If some participants appear to reject the gospel during the process of movement 4, the Christian is responsible first, to listen and understand their reasons; and second, if feasible, to engage in both positive and negative apologetics (Griffiths 1991: 14-16). Throughout the process, the Christian is to maintain an environment of openness to the discernment and decisions of the participants. For himself, the Christian is to reflect critically on whatever new insights he gains from the dialogue within the hermeneutical community of faith and the Bible.

Movement 5: Decision/Response for Lived Religious Faith

Movement 5 offers participants an explicit opportunity for making decisions about how to live Christian/religious faith in the world. Responses chosen by participants, depending on the generative theme, context, and so on, can be primarily or variously cognitive, affective, or behavioural, and may pertain to the personal, interpersonal, or socio-political levels of their lives. Whatever the form or level of response invited, the practical intent of the dialogue in movement 5 is to enable participants—by God's grace working through their own discernment and volition—to make historical choices about the praxis of Christian/religious faith in the world.

E. Stanley Jones: Christ at the Round Table

The life and ministry of E. Stanley Jones, the Methodist missionary to India, were controlled by his understanding of the kingdom of God as the central theme in scripture and the controlling motif for life. For Jones, there are essentially only two absolutes: "'the Unshakable Kingdom, the absolute order; and the Unchanging Person, the absolute Person" (1972: 34). These two belong together, for they both find expressions in the life and ministry of Jesus. Although Jones' ministry was primarily with Hindus, he had numerous opportunities to work with Buddhists as well.

Jones initially went to India with a closed mind, "with everything to teach and nothing to learn" (1928: 48). As he engaged in dialogue with Hindus, he discovered many parallel truths between Christianity and Hinduism. Years later, Jones was to conclude that Indians are "supreme seekers after God and the greatest spiritual race" (1925: 35).

Behind Jones' approach is his perspective on Christ's relation with people of other religions. He writes:

> Christ was related to all other faiths as fulfillment. I saw Christ gathering up all these scattered truths within Himself and completing and perfecting them. I could therefore be a friend of truth. I could look with appreciation on the religion and cultures of the people; I could be eager to see the best, for that best found fulfillment in Him (Christ). . . . In Him all things hold together (cited in Thomas 1955: 161).

In other writings, Jones is clearly an exclusivist when it comes to the finality of Christ for world religions. His writings are full of teaching about Christ, exalting him and placing him above all (see 1925: 59-72). Jones has a high regard for the Indian people, declaring that "if any people on earth should have found God apart from Jesus Christ the Indian people have earned that right" (1925: 50), but he concludes that the one thing that India lacks is Christ:

Fine things in their culture and thought—we admit it and thank God in real sincerity for them—but the real lack, the lack for which nothing else can atone, is just—Christ. They have no Christ. And lacking him, life lacks its supreme necessity (1925: 52).

A Hindu once remarked to Jones that he was a broad-minded Christian. In reply, Jones said:

My brother, I am the narrowest man you have come across. I am broad on almost anything else, but on the one supreme necessity for human nature I am absolutely narrowed by the facts to one--Jesus. It is precisely because we believe in the absoluteness of Jesus that we can afford to take a more generous view of the non-Christian systems and situations (1925: 54).

To illustrate Jones' model of Interfaith Encounters, we shall highlight three specific ministries in which he participates: ashrams, mass meetings, and the Round Table Conference.

Ashram

In order to understand the spirit of India, Jones spent two months in 1923 at Tagore's Santinikethan, an Ashram founded by Maharishi Devandranath Tagore. This episode is significant for our discussion. It reflects Jones' openness to learn from Hinduism. Later, as Jones was looking for a concrete expression of the kingdom of God, Jones adopted the Ashram as a model for community living. He writes: "It was this quest for a Kingdom-of-God order that drove some of us to adopt the Ashram as a possible mold in which this order might be expressed" (1939: 184). Jones' ashrams were essentially for Christians, with Christ in the center. However, Jones welcomes Hindu and Muslim participation in dialogue with Christians as a community.

Mass Meetings

Jones was dissatisfied with traditional evangelistic methods of his day. Christians usually began by attacking the weakness of other religions and then attempted to establish Christianity on those weaknesses. Instead, Jones followed these principles: (1) being frank that the purpose of the meeting is to introduce Christ: "I try to make Him (Christ) the last word on everything" (1939: 8); (2) making an announcement beforehand that there would be no attack upon any one's religion and that there would be only positive witness about Christ; and (3) concluding every meeting with a question and answer time or a dialogue session moderated by a leading non-Christian as chairperson. All types of questions were directed at Jones, some sincere and some critical. At the end of each meeting, Jones would close with prayer and with an invitation to receive Christ. A decision card was given to all who attended the meetings. Years later, Jones reflected on his approach:

> I have, therefore, taken my faith and have put it out before the non-Christian world for these seventeen years and have said, "There it is, my brothers, break it if you can." The more they have smitten on it, the more it has shone (1925: 98).

Round Table Conference

Jones' most well-known Interfaith Encounter example is an informal gathering called the "Round Table Conference," where members of each religious tradition have the opportunity to witness positively about their own faiths. Jones defines the objective of the Round Table Conference as follows: "The reproduction of Christ-like character, through faith in and fellowship with Christ the living Savior and through the corporate sharing of life in a divine society" (1928: 185). According to Jones, the Round Table Conference method consists of three fundamental elements: "Experimentation, Verification, and the Sharing of Results" (1928: 21).

The Round Table Conference usually consisted of fifteen members of other faiths and five or six Christians. The non-Christians invited were the most respected religious leaders of their faith that could be found. While in the public meetings Jones presented the Christian faith, at the Round Table, the best speakers of various faiths shared their religious experiences. It usually opened with a prayer for reality, for God and for an answer to the meaning of life (1928: 27). Within that positive climate, Jones developed a sensitivity to and appreciation for others' faith. In addition, religious beliefs formerly taken for granted and left unexamined were put to the test and examined experientially by the participants. After many years of such encounters, Jones concluded that Christ had never come out second best. He writes:

> Nevertheless—and I do not overstate when I say it, for no one could escape the impression—at the close of the meeting, everything else had been put to the edges as irrelevant and Christ controlled the situation. As men listened to what those who were in touched with him were quietly saying, they instinctively felt that here was something redemptively at work at the heart of life, redeeming men from themselves and from sin, putting worth and meaning into life, giving an unquenchable hope to men, lighting up the inward depths of life, bringing them into fellowship with God in beautiful intimacy and furnishing a dynamic for human service (1928: 51).

Some Proposals for Approaching Buddhists

In contrast to many Christian writers who interpret Buddhism mostly from a polemical standpoint, Evangelicals must be concerned with understanding Buddhism within its own traditions and faith perspective. It was through such a positive appreciation of Buddhism that one is able to respond authentically to the "real" rather than "prejudiced" Buddhism. The type of engagements that I am advocating is that which includes the sharing of faith-experiences rather than of mere faith-statements.

We must question the authenticity of theology that limits its reflection within Christendom and does not critically engage itself with other religions. Our theological vision is to deal not only with the presentation of the gospel, but also with the "prepossession" of other religions' perception of Christ. We need to know the attitudes and worldviews that were already present within our Buddhist friends and attempt to "prepossess" them for Christ of the New Testament (to borrow Kenneth Cragg's word for mission among Muslims). To put it in practical terms, no serious witness can occur without reading and understanding Buddhist literatures.

In addition to religious literature, we are to understand the place of Buddha, the Sutras, and the Buddhist traditions in the minds of today's Buddhists. Contemporary literature, poetry, and novels are sources for understanding Buddhist mindsets. More important than study of literatures is the quality of person-to-person relationship with Buddhist friends. This is one reason that I have reservations when the primary strategy to reach Buddhists is *dominated* by "Strategy Coordinators" who live far from the Buddhist peoples geographically, culturally, and economically. In such scenarios, how can we enter into genuine friendships and impact of worldview transformations? Within a context of personal friendship, there is a need to stimulate a Buddhist study of the New Testament that will face responsibly all it contains. I am aware of the challenge and difficulty facing Christian-Buddhist relations. The so-called "closed mindset" of Buddhist itself is the rationale for retrieval.

Buddhism is far more complex than most Christians are willing to acknowledge, and work among Buddhist people will continue to be far more difficult and "resistant" than we now experienced. We must not come as teachers but learners and must be prepared come alongside our Buddhist friends and take their questions seriously so that we can better share the story of Jesus. In that process of learning, we should not be surprised to meet God in a new way, in ways that we can never know if we come with a closed gospel.

Toward an Evangelical Model for Interfaith Encounter?

To summarize, a kingdom-oriented model for Christian-Buddhist Encounter is proposed in the figure below:

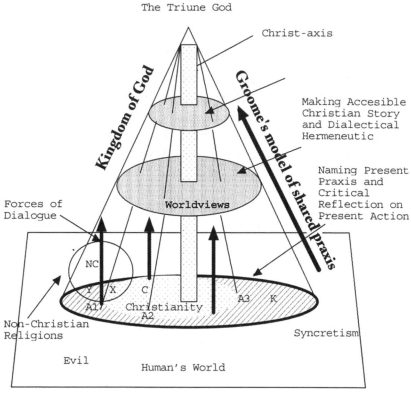

A kingdom-oriented model for Christian-Buddhist Encounter

In the kingdom-oriented model on the facing page, Christianity's encounter with other religions takes into account the *tripolar* dynamics between God, humankind, and Satan (Beyerhaus 1996: 16). Every evangelical's encounter with non-Christian religions is an encounter between systems, principalities, and people. The dialogical process takes place when the Christian and non-Christian come together as equals, admit their differences in worldviews and agree to a mutual search for understandings that best explain the totality of human experience (Clark 1993: 117).

Christianity (C) is totally within the domain of the kingdom (K). Although God is already king of the whole world, he needs to be acknowledged as king in human lives. God's kingship extends beyond Christianity into some parts of non-Christian religions (NC). Although Christians acknowledge that there are common elements of truths (X) shared between Christianity and other religions, Christianity's evaluation on religions are negative because major areas of non-Christian religions are still under the influence of Satan (S), as well as positive because they represent genuine seeking after God. Evangelicals confess that we believe the non-Christian religions do not possess the salvation that comes by faith through the Christ (shown by the separation from Christ-axis).

Guided by foundational axioms of the kingdom of God (e.g., A1, A2, A3), the five pedagogical movements of Groome's "shared praxis," are used to move the dialogical encounter along the Christ-axis to a worldview-level of mutual witness and ultimately, to a critical appraisal of nature and reality. In the process of the Interfaith Encounter, Christians will discover: (1) truths that are compatible with Christian faiths (X); (2) falsehoods that are the result of Satanic influences (S); and (3) mysteries of the kingdom that were the results of the Holy Spirit's general work among the religions (Y). From the Christian perspective, genuine and effective dialogue ultimately leads participants to the Triune God and the restoration of the kingdom of God upon the whole creation.

Notes

[1] This paper was first presented at World Evangelical Fellowship General Assembly, May 6, 2001, and has been revised specifically as a programmatic proposal for Christian mission among Buddhists.

[2] While I may not fully agree with the views of individual writers, I commend Rita Gross and Terry Muck's *Buddhists Talk about Jesus, Christians Talk about Buddha* (New York: Continuum, 2000) as one attempt toward deeper exploration of Christian-Buddhist dialogues.

[3] I find Stephen Bevans' *Models of Contextual Theology* most helpful. He presented Avery Dulles' definition of model as "a relatively simple, artificially constructed case which is found to be useful and illuminating for explaining realities that are more complex and differentiated."

CHAPTER 3

Practical Applications of the Good News into Doctrinal Black Holes[1] in Buddhism

John R. Davis

The subject of why people in the Buddhist world (BW) are so reticent to respond to the "Good News" of the Gospel is probably *the* most important issue facing us today. As ambassadors of the Good News, it is disheartening to see so few turning to Christ. To say that we have penetrated the Buddhist heartland to the extent that these folks eagerly respond would be a gross misrepresentation of the facts. We must be realistic and begin to ask some serious questions. Maybe just one serious question: Why? Before we come to the "Black Holes" later in the paper, the following are some precursors necessary to laying a basic foundation.

It is generally understood that there are numerous factors that impinge on the subject of *effective communication of the Gospel within the BW*. It should be recognized by the Communicator that each one of these factors are necessary "givens" before the Recipient can clearly understand the message within his own cultural context. Some of these factors would be:

The Theological Factor

In the final analysis we recognize that it is God who opens the minds of unbelievers through the light of the Gospel of Christ shining into their hearts by the power of the Holy Spirit. This cataclysmic divine event in the hearts of human beings is as miraculous the Creation itself! We become a "new creation" in Christ Jesus when we are saved. But since it is clearly God's will that "none should perish, and that all should have eternal life" (2 Pet. 3:9, ESV), there must be other factors involved in the plan of salvation.

That there is the human factor involved in the *proclamation* of the Gospel is self-evident. Otherwise, there would have been no need for Christ to give the Great Commission to his disciples. God in his sovereign prerogative has chosen those whom he redeems *to take the message* to those who are not redeemed with the purpose that they be redeemed; otherwise, there is no sense or need for us to be ambassadors for Christ, and nor would Paul have stated: "To the Jew I become and Jew…. I have become all things to all men so that by all possible means I might save some" (1 Cor. 9:20-22, ESV). Our task is to "beseech" others on Christ's behalf to be reconciled to him (2 Cor. 5:20-21, ESV).

The Sociological Factor

Some contemporary missiologists would say that this subject is so old hat as to not warrant further discussion. But this cannot be the case since we are still not learning lessons today, even in countries that are just opening to the Gospel. We are still perpetuating the same old mistakes of earlier mission enterprise. Donald McGavran stated that "the principal reason why people in other cultures do not turn to Christ is not 'theological', but 'sociological'."[2] In other words, the closely knit cultural networks in some societies can work both ways, so that if a group wanted to believe, there would be a "multi-individual" decision. Households, families, and clans would turn to Christ. Such turnings lessen or help resolve the problems of what to do with transitional rites, birth, marriage, deaths, etc. The new community can together embrace the Christian (not Western!) way, using functional substitutes for the old ways. On the other hand, if *individuals* are persuaded to accept Christ they are often pressured to not only become Christian, but at the same time, to reject their own culture and social structures. Our Western emphasis of inviting *individuals* to turn to Christ creates an immense sociological barrier, for in most other cultures it is virtually impossible for individuals in any other area of their lives to make decisions unilaterally on their own. The stigma and pressure of others within the group would not permit such "anti-social" behavior to such an extent that any perceived break-away would be regarded as a betrayal of one's culture and identity, and would therefore be dealt with in the way that particular culture felt appropriate—from social ostracism, to eviction of the person from their social web so they could no longer function within that group. (Note the problems of births, weddings, and funerals within a social matrix, even when two or three individuals turn to Christ.) It is well known that many societies have resorted to killing those who would turn to Christ. When individuals do break away and decide for Christ, they are stigmatized or persecuted not only because of the Cross, but because the majority in the culture understand that they have rejected their own culture and all its values as well, and this to them is the ultimate in betrayal. It would be true to say that some are martyred and great numbers persecuted, not because of their acceptance of Christ, but because the community at large wrongly think that the new believers are rejecting their own culture and customs.

It is interesting to read a paper on "Reaching Buddhists" prepared by Lakshman Peiris.[3] While the paper is extremely helpful in some aspects, the whole of the content presupposes that one person has come to Christ as an individual, and the author then goes on to deal with the problems arising out of that. In other words, there is the usual Western assumption that we should aim at winning individuals to Christ, rather than groups. Peiris states:

> It is well to recognize that Buddhism is a culture, and national identity to the Buddhists. Since they are born into this system, their own family is a structure that holds them enmeshed in Buddhism. There, it is a great tearing off for a Buddhist to uproot himself from his family and his society (n.d.: 1).

The questions remain:

a. Why did the communicator not wait until there may well have been a group willing and ready to turn?

b. Why should even an individual have to be "torn off" from his cultural and social roots when he or she believes? Again, theological questions should be brought to bear on this subject. For instance:

> 1. Is it not always God's purpose to establish a *body* of believers in a given location, wherever he works? Thus, the "church" (as a group) is anticipated by God to represent him whenever or wherever the Gospel is preached. What would happen it we really believed this?

> 2. That being the case, should we not be looking and waiting for a group or groups rather than individuals to turn to him? John 4 is a classic example. When the woman at the well turned to Christ, he told his disciples to lift up their eyes and look on the harvest, knowing already that there would be a large turning to him in the city of Samaria and that they would say, "It is no longer because of what you have said that we believe, for we have heard for ourselves and we

know that this is indeed the Savior of the world" (John 4:39-42, ESV). From one woman emerges the Samaritan church! There are a number of similar patterns in the Acts of the Apostles, especially the story of Lydia, the first convert to Christ in Europe, and the subsequent turning (see Acts 16:11-40).

The Cultural Factor

The task of separating the *"seed of the Gospel"* from the *"soil of Western Culture"* has been painfully neglected since the emergence of Western mission enterprise. Because Westerners themselves have no "Theology of Culture," their assumption whether consciously or unconsciously has undoubtedly been "the West is best," so the imposition of Western "customs and culture" is taken for granted. Nobody from the West was expected to de-westernize the good news or enculturate it. So whether the mission force has come from Germany, England, USA, or even Korea, little alien subcultures have been formed across the world reflecting, or rather replicating, almost exactly the cultural forms of the sending nation and denomination! The first thing this does is to shout as loudly as possible to the recipient culture: "This Gospel is alien to you, it does not belong to you, and if you accept it you must give up your own ways of doing things and follow..." Follow what? The biblical way? No, the *Western* way! Sadly, while missionaries today are changing radically in their thinking and wanting to contextualize the Gospel in local forms, they had previously done such a successful task of westernization, that now the local church, and especially its leaders, do not want to change. For their security and identity is now bound up in this alien way of doing things that they have embraced. So much has been written on this subject that it is not necessary for the writer to expand on it.[4] Suffice to say—and sad to say—that even in new BW countries that are opening for the Gospel, many of the new churches have not been allowed to have the freedom of the Spirit to worship in their own cultural forms. Graham Kendrick's name as a Western hymn writer will be more familiar to them than any indigenous writers—although there probably will not be *any* of those, since they have not been encouraged by the missionary, who likes his own way of worship and sees no reason why the locals would not like it either. This is cultural imperialism at its worst! It is not enough to brush this off with the excuse that the world is internationalizing, so we do not need to encourage local expressions of worship and witness. Nor is it enough to say that peoples in other countries are so enchanted by the West that presenting the Gospel to them in western forms is more attractive. What will happen if and when the West is suddenly demonized by countries because of political, economic, or religious reasons? Local believers in those countries will find themselves persecuted, and indeed martyred, not because of their belief in Christ, but because they have so allied themselves to the West and all its cultural forms that they can no longer affirm their own culture. Inestimable damage can done, but sadly this issue is still trivialized. J.W. Pickett said:

> The process of extracting individuals from their setting in Hindu or Moslem communities does not build a Church. On the contrary it arouses antagonism against Christianity and builds barriers against the spread of the Gospel (cited in McGavran 1999: 325).

Naturally the same principle applies to the BW.

The Receptor-Oriented Communication Factor

In my book, *Poles Apart,* I relate the story of the enthusiastic young missionary who, desperate to communicate the Gospel but frustrated at his slow acquisition of language skills, concluded, "Woe is me if I do not preach the Gospel." With the help of his language teacher, he memorized John 3:16 to the extent that he had all the tones perfect. After repeating this "gospel in a nutshell" verse scores of times, he boldly went into the marketplace and began to quote it to as many who would listen. Folks did listen—and were amazed at his language facility! The Communicator was expressing in perfect language the substance of John 3:16, but while the Recipients smiled benignly as if understanding, one may confidently state *that they understood the words, but could not interpret the meaning.* The young missionary returned home from the marketplace rejoicing, having satisfied himself that he had effectively communicated the message. In fact, there were other communication factors about which he did not understand at all. More importantly, nor did the recipient. Such as:

a. When the missionary used the word "God" ("For *God* so loved…"), the Receptor could only bring up on his mental computer screen the way that word was used in his cultural and religious framework or context. As far as he was concerned, the word meant the sun, moon and stars, the Buddhist priesthood, Buddha himself, sacred places, and other angelic beings. But nowhere on the Receptor's screen of understanding was there any parallel to the Communicator's biblical God. It would be impossible for the Receptor to understand the Christian concept of God because nothing within his frame of reference came anywhere near the concept.

b. "God so *loved*…" Since love implies attachment and to some extent passion, how on earth could this Christian God love? The goal of Buddhism is detachment, so a God like this would be quite inexplicable—unless, of course, he was like Buddha *before* his enlightenment! This is exactly the conclusion a group of monks came to when the writer was speaking to them about the *love* of God! As Petchsongkram points out,

> Concerning love, there is a Thai proverb "danger comes from what we love" or filth comes from love. Therefore, the Buddhist standard is to eliminate love completely. Any who has severed himself from all love and does not love his

children, his wife, his money, his possessions, not even himself, is on a high level of attainment in Buddhism, but Christian ministers say "God so loved the world." Buddhists hear this and think, "Oh how pitiful; this God is full of unwholesome passion. He is still very sinful" (1975: 21).

c.   "That he sent *his only Son...*" This is a stumbling block of great proportions—as much to the Buddhist as the Muslim.

d.   "That whoever *believes in him...*" This concept of believing or trusting for salvation is totally contrary to the Buddhist concept of salvation, which is achieved, not by trusting anybody else, but depending totally upon one's own merit.

e.   "Will not perish *but have everlasting life.*" The word "everlasting life" used in the Bible is normally understood as "reincarnation" in Buddhism. How could it be good news to be offered the very thing one has been aiming to escape?

In conclusion, just speaking "the Word of God" is not magic. It is not just our task to speak the word of God, but *to ensure that it is understood clearly in terms of the Receptor's understanding.* This clearly has not happened for centuries and is just another obstacle to the Receptor's understanding of the Good News.

Continuity versus Discontinuity: A Reasonable Approach

While our approach to the BW in presenting the Gospel should not be polemic, it must be persuasive. It is certainly a biblical principle to use the "Continuity versus Discontinuity" axis in presenting the Good News. Examples of this method of communication abound both in the ministry of Jesus and in that of Paul.

The element of discontinuity takes the position that the Receptor understands a given subject in one way and that the

Communicator wishes to *reasonably* reject that assumption by replacing it with something new. This process may include making reference to *old forms*, now presented with new meanings. (For instance, extant rites, rituals, and ceremonies can often be invested with Christian meaning. After all, this is exactly what Western Christians have done with the previously pagan rituals of Christmas and Easter.) This would mean that pagan beliefs are shown to be false and replaced with new beliefs—but with there still being a link between the two. Whatever the case, a "reasonable" proposition should always be put forward, with the intention that the Receptor is enabled to see the "unreasonableness" of their present position and be prepared to consider the new proposition as "good news." This method is used in Scripture.

Time and again Jesus states: "You have heard it said…but I say unto you…." The Lord appeals to the receptor's conscience and understanding when he states that when you "look upon a woman with lust," that is already adultery (Matt. 5:27). There is continuity with the theme of adultery but discontinuity as to the previous understanding, and then there is the *reasonableness* of his new interpretation and application of the meaning. Whether this relates to adultery, fasting, giving of alms, prayer, the nature of true righteousness, or whatever, Jesus clearly rejects the contemporary understanding and then goes on to clarify the true nature of things. Who would have been the average Pharisee's neighbor? Certainly not a Samaritan (see Luke 10:25-37). In all of his parables and teachings, Jesus introduces revolutionary concepts, but in the context of everyday life. There is always the subtle use of the continuity/discontinuity axis in his teaching.

Paul's classic message to the Athenians holds very much to this didactic methodology. He clearly shows his understanding of the Athenians concerning their "Unknown god."[5] There is continuity— "the god who you ignorantly worship, I declare to you"—and then discontinuity—this God does not dwell in temples made by human hands. He is creator of all things, he is independent of Creation, he is controller of all things, and our very breath comes from him (Acts 17).

Demolishing Strongholds

In his book, *Talks in the Shade of the Bo Tree*, Wan Petchsongkram points out at the very beginning that in almost all books written by Thais, "We still find the almost unanimous opinion that Buddhism is a religion of cause and effect and that *reason* is considered to be the great thing in Buddhism" (1975: 7).

While others may offer all sorts of solutions to effective communication of the Gospel by emphasizing, for instance, humility, or poverty (vis-à-vis Buddhist priests' lifestyle), or even celibacy, there is no doubt that the battle for the soul of the Buddhist is in his *mind*—his understanding and worldview. Buddhists conclude that their belief is *reasonable*. Instead of presenting the "Good News" as *reasonable,* we apply all sorts of other *methodologies*, hatched in the West, thinking that they will be answers to the questions Buddhists may be asking. The locus for any approach to the Buddhist has to be his *mind and conscience.* John states clearly, "When the Spirit of truth is come, He will convince (convict –'Elengthein' from which we derive the word 'Elenktics') of sin, of righteousness and of judgement" (John 16:7-11). Conviction in this sense is not an emotion; it is an *understanding* of the gravity of the situation.[6] It is necessary to point the two areas covered in the use of the word "sin." The usual emphasis relates to some sort of moral misdemeanor, but in this verse the emphasis is not on moral sin, for the persons referred to could have been morally upright. "Sin" here is *"of sin because they do not believe in me."* This could be termed "directional sin" rather than "moral sin." It relates to the sin of *misunderstanding*, of not recognizing or acknowledging who Christ is and what he has done. The Lord Jesus promised that when the

Spirit comes (in the missiological sense at Pentecost), his task would be to bring conviction of this fundamental sin. Our primary task then is to break open the worldview (belief system) that has no place for Christ, and introduce him as the one to whom all people must bow the knee (Phil. 2:10).

In trying to establish the importance of who Christ really is, the writer often uses the illustration taken from tribal culture where visitors to a village would be welcomed and hosted in the house of the headman for at least three days. On approaching a village the visitor saw two people at the entrance of the village—a young teenager and the headman. The visitor, ignorant of (*misunderstanding*) the appropriate cultural protocol, went up to the teenager and asked permission to stay in the village. Astounding! Impossible! What a loss of face for the headman! Who would possibly do such a thing? The visitor would then point out that demons, which the locals worship, have no real authority. They should be compared to the teenager at the entrance of the village, but Christ, who has all authority, should be compared to the headman. What sort of horrendous mistake was it for the visitor to ask permission from the teenager, and what sort of terrible thing to not recognize who the headman (Christ) is?

The application of this short parable has often had profound effect on the hearers, who suddenly realize that they cannot escape the fact that Christ is Lord—over demons, over all—and that demons after all should not be given the authority and place of honor that tribal people give to them. It could be further pointed out that while the teenager was not deliberately trying to usurp the authority of the headman, demons do deliberately try to hide from humans (*blind their minds*) as to who Christ really is, so that siding with demons is tantamount to setting oneself up against Christ.

The application of the truths found 2 Corinthians 10:1-6 show clearly where we are to focus and how we are to "win the battle" in the BW. Our task is to bring "*every thought* into captivity to Christ" and to "demolish *all arguments*, which are the strongholds." Verse 2 introduces the subject of *mis-understanding*. Paul mentions some "who *think* that we walk according to the flesh." He first acknowledges that a battle is going on but then denies "waging war according to the flesh" (i.e., using earthly methods to resolve the problem). He then focuses first on his weaponry, and second on the strongholds. The weaponry is spoken of as *"divine power;"* its object to *"destroy strongholds."* But what in context are the strongholds? Since this verse is so often applied to the whole area of spiritual warfare and territorial spirits, it must be pointed out that this verse has nothing to do with the location of demons or to any particular geographic location. Instead, it has to do with *"arguments and lofty opinions* raised up *against the knowledge* of Christ" (ESV). Paul's task was to demolish such pretentious arguments, so that every thought (the thinking processes) are brought into *captivity* to obedience to Christ.

Our task is through Christ's power to demolish arguments, reasonings, belief systems, worldviews, and misunderstandings about who Christ is and what he has done. Paul's concern, even for believers, was that somehow *"their minds"* would be "led astray from a pure and sincere devotion to Christ" (2 Cor. 11:1-2). Here we find the locus of satanic activity is in the mind, "lest Satan lead you astray."

Trusting in the power of the Spirit, to own the truth of his word, our primary task is to announce the "kerygma," to proclaim the Gospel without fear or favor, believing that in spite of the devil "blinding the *minds*" of those who do not believe, he who spoke and brought creation into being will also shine the light of his gospel into the lives of those whose eyes will be opened (2 Cor. 4:4-6). And this not by the "foolishness of *preaching*" (as if monologue were the answer!), but by the foolishness of *the message*, which is the power of God to everyone who believes (1 Cor. 1:20), in whatever way it is culturally appropriate to present! The two principal words used by

Luke in Acts concerning the communication of the gospel are "dialogued" and "reasoned."

Some of the Doctrinal Black Holes in Buddhism

The most important question remains: *What are some of the doctrinal or philosophical black holes in Buddhism?* In other words, what are the elements that leave huge gaps in understanding, which may be called "un-reasonable" or unsustainable, and which, in the final analysis, could cause the collapse of the whole belief system?

Most of these could be categorized as those "*strongholds, or arguments that set themselves up against the knowledge of Christ.*" Exposing such inconsistencies will destabilize the thinking processes of those are prepared to listen and thereby prepare their hearts to accept the "Good News." Listed below are some of those areas that could be likened to the Achilles heel of this belief system:

1. Humanbeingness: Bad news for the Buddhist

2. Karma: Futility and fatality for the Buddhist

3. Merit Making: A hope-less goal

4. Nirvana: Who wants to be dissolved into nothingness?

5. Suffering: Is extinction the only way out?

6. Salvation from the Cause and Effect of Sin: Any answers?

We will consider briefly each of the above points with the premise that despite the fact that Buddhists do not acknowledge God, he has not rejected them. Still, the "*image of God*" (however cracked or broken it may be) remains in the soul of every man. This allows even those whose minds have been darkened, when presented with the truth in culturally appropriate ways, to understand, so that when the truth of Scripture is applied to their hearts, there will be a "resonance" and indeed, a longing for release and deliverance from an endless cycle of despair. Two things should happen: (i) the realization that their present system of belief is filled with hopelessness; and (ii) that the Gospel is really "good news" for them.

1. Humanbeingness

Anatta derives from "ana" (without) and "atta" meaning "self." Petchsongkram points out that this concept is "self contradictory" (1975: 15). For if self is just an illusion and without reality, how should one "*depend on self*" in order to gain merit to go one step upwards in the next life? He goes on to say:

> if we depend on self and the self is constantly in flux, as I am when one day I decide on a certain course of action and by the next day I have changed my mind, this is an astonishing kind of dependence, this depending on something which cannot stand up. What will result? The result can be nothing but uncertainty. Most Buddhist are very unsure about belief in the next life – because their source of help is so unsteady.

Selfhood in the Buddhist sense and *humanbeingness* in the Christian sense are quite different. Selfhood results from the collision of five aggregates called *skandas*—Form, Feeling, Recognition, Conscious impression (emotional reaction), and Consciousness (*winnyan*). The moment the *skandas* break up, selfhood disintegrates. The moment they come together, selfhood and suffering begin! The *fact* of existence is the origin of suffering, so the logical thing to do is to extinguish self!

But to extinguish one's self would be to take life, which is forbidden, so one is caught up in an endless cycle. Selfhood, even when the five aggregates have come together, is only illusory or at best temporary, for our personhood at this split second is not the same as it will be in the next split second. It can be likened to standing on a bridge and looking at the fast flowing water under the bridge. In my book, *The Path to Enlightenment*, I wrote:

The water at any second of passing can be called water, but its essential elements are changed at every moment. So while what is flowing under the bridge at one second can truly appear to be the same, it can also be truly said that it is not after all, the same water that flowed a split second later – our "humanbeingness" is therefore simply "water under the bridge" (1997: 59).

Bad news!

The Christian understanding, of course, is that we do not come into existence as a result of an accident or collision of five aggregates or *skandas* that come together to form us. We are each created and each individual has his or her singular identity, in which we can rejoice. Our goal is not to ensure the extinction of our humanbeingness, but to rejoice in it. Of course we recognize our fallen nature, but we know that is both understandable and salvageable. Good news!

One concludes that the biblical explanation, both of the origin of man and the salvation provided for man, is really good news for the Buddhist. Here, surely, is a vital key to presenting the Gospel to our friends in the BW. This is one link in the chain that can break down "strongholds" and false arguments that have bound so many for so long.

2. Karma: Reasonable or un-reason-able?

The Buddhist concept of karma is simple yet profound. It simply means that what you are *now* is because of what you were *then*, and what you are *now* determines what you *will be*! And all of this is based on how much merit was acquired that brought you to where you are now; the amount of merit or demerit you accrue now will then determine your future. In some forms of Buddhism there is confusion at this point. In Theravada, if what one is *now* is the accidental collision of five aggregates, then we are not strictly speaking of "transmigration of souls" (Hindu and Mahayana concepts). Please note that in the previous sentence I mentioned "the accidental collision of five aggregates." Some would say "the predetermined collision of five aggregates." That being the case, how can something be "determined" unless there is a power (rather, a Person) who determines it? To say that karma determined it implies some form of intelligence, which would weigh up the balances of merit gained or lost and then have the power to see that the process is followed through!

The other problem with the concept of karma is an ethical one. If karma is to be just and equitable, then those who make choices must have equal capacity to make such choices; otherwise, karma could neither be effective nor just. Since choices are understood by all to be *moral* choices, one must see here *a massive doctrinal black hole.* How could a mosquito or a mouse, a cat or a camel, have the same capacity of both knowing what is right and wrong, and then making deliberate moral choices to that effect? In other words, while Buddhists see humans as just an extension of the animal kingdom, they must face the fact that we are not the same. This is difficult to establish to the Buddhist mind, for according to one account Buddha himself spoke of over 500 reincarnations he had experienced before his enlightenment.

> Sometimes as a monkey, sometimes as a dog, a bird, a cat, a mouse and in many tens of other ways. He had been a man, a robber, an outlaw. But gradually in these many rebirths he advanced until he became the Lord Buddha. This was the first of the three revelations he received under the Bo tree (1975: 22).

Humans have a conscience. We do not live by the power of instinct, but by our own choices—good or bad. That being the case, what sort of reference or measure can there possibly be, even in Buddhist doctrine, to determine how and when animals could ascend or descend the scale of reincarnations? In other words, how do animals make moral choices?

One must also ask, how are humans predestined—either to ascend to higher planes of existence (rather, non-existence), or descend down the scale to animals? If this is supposed to happen, then it must follow that there is some form of intelligence behind karma, since karma is determined by moral choice. This demands that there be a *moral* Being, capable of ensuring justice is carried out. To affirm that there is a Law of cause and effect must imply *ipso facto* that there must be a Law-giver. How unreasonable to propose that this Karmic Law (cause) came into being by *chance*, but that the results of it (effect), comes by *choice*! There are further ethical problems about women needing to be "reborn as men" before they attain to the state of enlightenment. Winston King vividly describes the fatalistic picture envisaged by the concept of karma. Whatever the case, this belief in karmic inevitability hardly creates a sense of joy and peace!

> To a believer in Karma, death is no escape; it is only a preliminary, to a new series of rebirths—perhaps in Hell for an aeon, perhaps on earth as an animal, as a woman, as a pariah, or as a man whose life is more crowded with disappointment and disaster than that from which death seemed a refuge. If death is no escape from human misery, but merely a portal to rebirth, something must be found to break the chain of cause and effect which makes that rebirth necessary. This, to the Buddha can be done by eradication of 'desire', that is of the will to live, which is the primal cause of birth and continued rebirth' and it can be done in no other way (1963: 115).

Here we have a doctrinal black hole of immense proportions— a state of hopelessness and despair. If this state of affairs is addressed with the "good news," then it is likely that for the person who *understands* their condition as a never-ending treadmill of existences, the Gospel has to be good news. One would anticipate a response similar to a patient with terminal cancer being suddenly told that a cure has been discovered.

3. Merit Making: A hope-less goal

When it comes to merit making, the balances just don't add up. You must depend upon yourselves, but "a boat depends upon water as a tiger depends on the forest." This Thai proverb raises all sorts of problems and shows clearly another doctrinal black hole. One of the best-known statements of Buddha was, "Be a light unto yourselves" or, put another way, "work out your own salvation" (Humphries 1951: 40).

First, there are some ethical ramifications centering round the concept of merit making. For it to be just and equitable, those engaged in making merit need to have equal opportunities. But how can that happen unless we separate animals from humans? Surely no one suggests that animals and humans have equal capacity to make merit?

Nor indeed can one say that all human beings have equal chances of making merit. Then, too, there is the problem of "self-centeredness" or selfishness in human beings. The writer recalls a stocky character outside a café with a begging bowl, asking the owner for money. Without hesitation, the owner gave the beggar a large amount of money, and when he saw that I did not offer anything, he commented about my not "making merit." I asked him why he had given this strong, well-built man money. Was it to help the beggar or to gain merit? Without a flinch, the restaurant owner replied, "To gain merit." The fact that the money would only contribute to making this man lazier than he was did not come into consideration, so it was not the other person's benefit that was the motivation for making merit, but pure self-centeredness. When one sees the multitudinous temples all over Asia, one has to ask what the motives are behind all of this. The same answer would be given about St. Peter's Rome—to gain "indulgences" for the next life!

The other problem with merit making is whether one has to depend solely upon one's self to gain salvation. Why does the Thai proverb contradict this? It states that "A boat depends upon water and a tiger depends upon the forest," the implication being the need for mutual dependence. The whole of life bears out this concept, but when it comes to the most vital issue, our very existence makes it clear that *even Buddha's own followers could not depend upon him, or indeed anything else, for their salvation.* While this dependence upon one's own merit is tempered in Mahayana Buddhism by the introduction of the concept of the "Boddhisatva," there seems little hope in Theravada Buddhism. So dim is the prospect that into this darkness, or hopelessness, gleams of light begin to emerge. Another proverb, used widely in Thailand when it relates to hope in the future is *"Kho Pa Lyang Khyn Sawan,"* literally meaning, "grasping hold of (or depending on) the saffron robe to get to heaven." There, too, is the concept of transfer of merit. All young boys go into the Buddhist priesthood, not to gain merit for themselves, but so that their merit will be transferred to their parents, especially to their mother. The expression "to pay back for Mother's milk" is quite common. All of these concepts can be put together to paint a wonderful picture of the Lord Jesus Christ, more than a Boddhisatva, having more than enough merit to transfer to our spiritually bankrupt account. As "a boat depends upon water and a tiger on the forest" so we depend on Christ, both to transfer his merit to us and to lead us across the sea of suffering to the place he has prepared for us.

4. Nirvana: Who wants to be dissolved into nothingness?

Little needs to be said about this doctrinal black hole. When appeal is made to our instinctive desire for survival, then this dissolution of all identity or personhood is so unattractive to the average Buddhist that he seldom refers to it. In fact, in order to for our humanbeingness to survive, another place is proposed:

> The average Buddhist has no real aspiration to reach Nirvana, because it is generally accepted to belong only to those devotees already ordained into the priesthood, who spend all their time in mediation and good works of merit. In popular Buddhism there is another place called "heaven" (sawan). This is an intermediate state between death and Nirvana, a place of conscious bliss (Davis 1997: 96).

Since there is an "un-reasonable-ness" about the whole concept of nirvana, there is great opportunity to emphasize that in the Gospel, we do not lose our identity, our personhood, but that it is enhanced and developed without the limitations of our present state. Good News indeed! Making a contrast between the biblical concept of heaven and the Buddhist concept of nirvana is very helpful at this point. Heaven for the Christian is not reserved for the elite or even the minority, but for all who put their trust in the merits of what Christ has done for them. Hope for the Christian's future is portrayed by a picture of a great multitude, described as people from every tongue, tribe, people, and language. This is not merely a "state of being," but it is a physical place—being "with Christ." For the Christian, heaven is unabashedly a condition of joy, peace, harmony, love, worship recognition, and attachment,

> a far more attractive prospect than achieving Nirvana and becoming a single drop of dew, dissolving into an ocean of nothingness, a complete evaporation of whoever I was and whoever I would like to have been (Davis 1997: 97).

5. Suffering: Its cause and effect—is extinction the only way out?

It has been said that the main focus in Buddhism is the realization of and escape from suffering, while the main focus in Christianity is the realization of and deliverance from sin. Buddhism teaches that the fundamental root of man's problem has to be recognized in its cause—the cause of man's problems is simply his existence! Suffering is the effect, existence is the cause. King states that "the fundamental root of man's misery is his existence as a personalised individual...the fall of man was his 'fall' into individualised sentient being" (1963: 115). Since the cause of man's suffering is his existence, and the goal of Buddhism is to escape fully and finally from this anchor of existence, then logically the best thing would be to terminate this life as soon as possible. Many monks have desired to do this, so that all attachments to this world are totally severed. It is measured by Buddhist monks that the highest achievement is to get to such a state of not wanting anything, that one no longer "desires" food and has to be spoon-fed in order to be kept alive. However, to take that last step of deliberately dying is wrong. The problems are twofold: first, it is forbidden to take life, and second, if one did take one's own life, since it is breaking the law, then one must inevitably pay the consequence. That would not be "detachment" to nirvana, but further attachment in other future lives—not getting off the wheel of life, but being caught up once again on the treadmill of endless existences. There are some serious contradictions (black holes) in the thinking processes here, which gives opportunity for the light of the Gospel to shine into such dark and sad thinking.

Suffering then, is main focus of Buddhism—following the eightfold path should lead to release. Suffering for the Christian, however, is not something to run away from, but something that can be used to shape our humanity and make it more attractive. It is redemptive. So where does *sin* come into the picture? It is not that Buddhism has no concept of sin in the sense of breaking their law; indeed, they may have even sharper consciences because taking life in any form is "sin." We will look at this in the next section, but there is no sense of sin in the sense of John 16. It is here, at this point that one must return to the biblical emphasis. The reason why 3,000 people were converted on the day of Pentecost was not because they suddenly came under conviction of sin in the moral sense, but in the directional sense. They realized that they had crucified the Prince of Life. Of course they were commanded to repent, but their repentance was in terms of how they had rejected Christ. Most of the messages in the book of Acts center on this aspect, rather than emphasizing the moral aspect of sin. It behooves us to return to the biblical way of presenting the Gospel as we find in Acts.

6. Salvation from the Cause and Effect of Sin: Any answers?

This aspect of truth follows on from the previous section. If one is to communicate the Good News effectively, one naturally needs to refer to the *moral law*, both in the Bible and in Buddhism. Someone has said that the best way to display the beauty of a diamond is to set it against a black velvet cloth. The darkness of the background will reveal the true value and light of the diamond. It is against the dark background of man's sin that the diamond of who Christ is and what he has done lights up. The more one sees the darkness and depravity of one's heart, the more one will realize the need of a Savior.

In Buddhism, the "moral" code is broken up into sections: five laws (universally required), eight laws for the more devout followers, and 252 laws for the ordained monk. To attain to the state of enlightenment, even when has been ordained as a monk, is virtually impossible. Few have ever been said to have attained to such a state. To keep the five laws is also impossible, for not to take life is in itself impossible. While some may add that the real meaning is that to *deliberately* take life is wrong, this has serious ethical flaws. If and when one understands the true nature of things, then what does one do with a rabid dog, for instance, or with mosquitoes that only spread disease, or even with germs themselves that have life? While this may appear pedantic to us, Buddhists are very serious about it and still maintain that taking any form of life is sin.

This whole subject causes problems between the Department of Health and the Department of Religion. The Department of Health insists on putting out poison to kill rabid dogs and spraying houses to kill mosquitoes, but this is deemed sin in Buddhist law.

The whole problem with moral law for the Buddhist is that there are no mechanisms for forgiveness, no assurance that sins have been forgiven. If there is no God, of course, then one could not be sinning against God. This belief cannot satisfy the average Buddhist; he is still aware of wrongdoing and sacrifices are made, not to God, but to demons. Sometimes vows are made and often forgiveness is sought, but Buddhists have no Scriptures to comfort them with assurance of forgiveness, they have no Savior who has paid the price for their sin. Against such a backdrop of darkness, we may be bold to declare that Christ has died for them, that he has paid the penalty for their sin. This concept of substitution, of someone dying on someone else's behalf, is quite understandable to Buddhists. They speak of soldiers dying on their behalf to protect them, and there are histories of famous people who have died on behalf of others. We must make use of these, to make the Gospel appear as *good* news.

Summary and Conclusion

The writer is convinced that exposing the "black holes" indicated is vital as a precursor to presenting the "good news" of the Gospel to those in the BW. It is against the backdrop of the darkness and despair of some Buddhist doctrines that the light of the Gospel will shine into their hearts. We need to re-examine our approaches, our methodologies, and our strategies. There are many other "keys," "eye-openers," or "bridges" that can be used as a means of appealing to those who would listen to the Good News in the BW.

For instance, we need to use drama more. After all most of Jesus' ministry could be summed up with the term "verbal drama." He painted pictures and told stories so vivid and so applicable that his listeners seldom missed the point! He often used well-known historical events or persons to apply a particular point.[7] And Paul often referred to Jewish historical events, even when writing to Gentiles.[8] Such methodologies are perfectly biblical and should be adopted by us, so that there may be a sense of both continuity and discontinuity. The use of "all means" should not merely be an echo from the days of William Carey, or going back even further to Paul. It is our task that "by all means" men and women may be saved, and this may require some real soul-searching for us who are often so bound in our traditions that, rather than helping to make the Gospel relevant, we make it irrelevant.

Finally, perhaps we need to look for some of the black holes in our process of communicating the Good News to those millions in the BW. Such black holes would be our perpetuation of Western theological imperialism, our continuing to expand Western forms of denominationalism, and our concern for "kingdom building." Our ways and methods all need to come under the microscope of Scripture, so that our service for Christ will bring glory to his name throughout the Buddhist World and that millions may own the Good News of the Gospel and bow the knee to him who alone is worthy.

Notes

[1] A term used in astronomy for a massive star that collapses from it own gravity. Colloquially, I have used it to indicate that there are "massive" elements within Buddhism that are not reasonably sustainable and that, by exposing them, the result may be the collapse of this belief system.

[2] This is a quote from McGavran's seminal book, *The Bridges of God.* See the chapter of the same name in *Perspectives on the World Christian Movement: A Reader.* Eds. Ralph D. Winter and Steven C. Hawthorne. 3rd ed. Pasadena: William Carey Library, 1999, pp. 323-338. The whole section deals with this vital subject.

[3] This is a Composite Position Paper of Pre-COWE Group Study. Manila: Unpublished and undated.

[4] But see my book, *Poles Apart: Contextualizing the Gospel in Asia* (Bangalore: Theological Book Trust, 1996).

[5] See an expansion on this theme by Don Richardson. "Finding the Eye-Opener" in *Perspectives on the World Christian Movement: A Reader.* Ed. Ralph D. Winter. Rev. ed. 1992, p. C-67.

[6] The first missiologist to develop this theme was J.D. Bavinck in his book, *An Introduction to the Science of Missions.* Philadelphia: Presbyterian & Reformed 1961. It was picked up and developed by Peter Cotterrell in *The Eleventh Commandment.* Leicester: IVP, 1981.

[7] Note, for instance, Jesus' reference to the Tower of Siloam (Luke 13:1-4), or to Elijah and the widow, and Naaman the Syrian leper (Luke 4:25-30).

[8] See Paul's reference to Israel in the wilderness and his statement that these historic events were for our learning (1 Cor. 10:1-12). Paul even uses Jewish history to instruct Gentiles!

CHAPTER 4

The Value and Limits to Dialogue

Russell Bowers, Jr.

When English speakers describe an infant as "cute," they communicate very little. The adjective has been so stretched by ascribing it to such a variety of objects that it now faces few limits beyond suggesting attractiveness of some kind. If the definition of "definition" is setting limits to meaning,[1] then "cute," with few limits to how it is used, has no definition. The same may be said of "cool," "nice," and a basketful of other words.

An interreligious term similarly tired and stretched nearly beyond definition is "dialogue." Hence "it is not always clear in what sense (or senses) the word is being used, and what are the presuppositions that lie behind it."[2] Sharpe distinguishes four types—discursive, human, secular, and interior.[3] Waldenfels defines the varieties differently—social-political, intellectual-scholarly, philosophical-theological, and ascetical-spiritual.[4] Davies suggests division into parliamentary, institutional, theological, and spiritual dialogue.[5] Daniel Ng considers four Christian models—exclusivism, pluralism, inclusivism, and particularism.[6]

This paper will adopt McGrath's gloss that dialogue represents "an attempt on the part of people with different beliefs to gain a better understanding of each other."[7] Several corollaries devolve from this definition. First, dialogue grows out of respect. Those who engage in it must believe that their partner is worth hearing. Second, it recognizes differences. Various religions are not all saying the same thing. Neusner wisely notes that dialogue must begin with recognizing that there are differences and searching for grounds for communication, rather than with assuming sameness and searching for commonalities.[8] Third, the goal is understanding, and neither syncretization nor "mutual transformation."[9] Proclamation or modification of one's own views may occur within the process, but the primary goal remains understanding. Fourth, dialogue that results in significant new understanding cannot be undertaken casually but requires effort. "Dialogue demands the intellectual, moral, and, at the limit, religious ability to struggle to hear another and to respond."[10]

Values of Dialogue

Discovery of Truth

What then are the values of dialogue? The first is that it aids people in what should be their primary philosophical pursuit—truth. If pressed to choose whether our foundational commitment should be to our religion or to truth, we must answer truth. We adhere to a faith, not because our community does or our ancestors did, but because it is true. We trust in Christ not because he spoke revolutionary, mesmerizing, or loving words, but because those revolutionary, mesmerizing, loving words are true. We are Christians not because, with the existentialists, we felt compelled to define ourselves, and out of all the available worldview options, mindlessly opted for Christianity through a leap of faith. I hope, rather, we are

Christians because we are convinced that Christianity is objectively true, and if it were not we would abandon it.

The Apostle Paul takes this tack while discussing the resurrection. If Christ has not been raised (i.e., if the *facts* of the gospel are not true), then his preaching and the church's faith are useless;[11] Christians are to be pitied above all others;[12] ministry is pointless;[13] wisdom suggests exploiting the present moment.[14] But because Christ's resurrection is true—an historical fact—then death stands defeated and enthusiastic Christian ministry makes good sense.[15] The *preaching* and *practice* of the Christian faith should be abandoned—no matter how comforting they may be—if they are not *true*. Truth takes precedence over received[16] religion.

A foundational commitment to truth is the philosophical orientation we seek in those we evangelize and those with whom we dialogue. When we talk to a Buddhist, we hope that her primary commitment is to know and practice the truth—that she is not so committed *a priori* to her Buddhism that she is unwilling to either examine it or objectively consider the claims of Christianity. If she insists on retaining Buddhism even if that faith were demonstrated to be erroneous and Christianity true—if her primary commitment is to Buddhism (no matter what) and not to truth—we have little to talk about. All our testimony, exegesis, and apologetics will necessarily fall on deaf ears. If, then, we expect our dialogue partner to desire truth above all else, to be willing to examine her faith to see if it is true, then in fairness we must approach discussions the same way. My belief is that Christianity has nothing to fear from a brutal and thoroughgoing commitment to truth.

Even if we reply with presuppositionalists that fallen humans cannot know truth apart from prior acceptance of divine revelation, truth remains the foundational concern. What we seek and putatively obtain by accepting this revelation is truth. If what we received were falsehood or deception, there would be no reason to accept it.

So if both we and others seek truth above all else, we pursue a common quest. We eye the same objective, and steer toward the same goal. Though we may begin from different starting points, ultimately we are not rivals.

A word about truth from the Buddhist perspective. Zen popularizer D.T. Suzuki suggests a general distinction between East and West: "In the West, 'yes' is 'yes' and 'no' is 'no'; 'yes' can never be 'no' or vice versa. The East makes 'yes' slide over to 'no' and 'no' to 'yes'; there is no hard and fast division between 'yes' and 'no.'"[17] More specifically, Buddhism follows a system of two, or perhaps three, truths: "ordinary propositional truth, a kind of propositional truth about sacred realities...; and 'pure religious truth' which transcends not only the scientific truths about the world but also the religious truths contained in the testimony of the seers."[18] The problem is that in the Oriental mind

> the superiority of the higher level of truth is so vast that it, in the final analysis, reveals the lower level of truth to be wholly insignificant; it is but a ladder to be discarded after use.... And this, it seems to me, involves an abrogation of the "reason" that establishes the lower-level truths and hence stands in contrast to them rather than complementing them.[19]

In other words, logic is at best inadequate and at worst deceptive in our search for ultimate truth, which is grasped more by intuition or direct experience than by reason.

The Buddhist is not particularly interested in propositional truth. The laws of identity, excluded middle, and [non-]contradiction do not advance his religious quest. "*Satori* can come only when thought ceases."[20] Even the Buddha's *dharma* is not "true."

> [A] man finds himself at the bottom of a deep well from which he cannot escape on his own. Standing at the edge of the well, the Buddha looks with compassion upon the man's plight and lowers a beautiful golden ladder down to him while urging him to climb to safety. Eagerly the man seizes the bottom rung

of the ladder and rises rung by rung until he reaches the edge of the well where the Buddha waits. As he clasps the Buddha's hand and is pulled to safety, he looks back down into the well, but instead of a beautiful golden ladder, he discovers that he has climbed up a rickety wooden structure that was falling apart beneath him even as he climbed. Springing from the well, he looks upon the Buddha reproachfully and says, "Everything you ever taught me was a lie." To which the Buddha responds, "You are out of the well."[21]

Truth for the Buddhist is existential more than propositional; it is "what works" to turn people from *avidyā*, relieve *duḥkha*, and conduct them from *samsāra* through *satori* to *nirvāṇa*. The means by which that is done need neither be "true"—and the story above admits that it is not true—nor the same for everyone. So even if a Buddhist dialogue partner agrees to value truth above all else, we must first discuss what we mean by "truth." For the Christian truth necessarily includes propositional truth. It need not be limited to but must start with that. In reviewing my book *Someone or Nothing?* Philip Blosser objected to its "disjunctive logic"—"If truth can be 'propositional,' does this mean it can't also be 'existential'?"[22] This critique misses the point that the book does not assert truth *cannot* be existential if it is propositional, only that it must be propositional. The laws of identity, excluded middle, and [non-]contradiction must hold if we are to understand or communicate. The problem is that, for Buddhism in general and Nishitani in particular, truth is only existential and not propositional. Truth is whatever gets people out of the well.

Second, we must bear in mind the principle of *upāya* or skillful means. For the Buddhist the great concern is to escape suffering and rebirth; the means we use to do so is at best a secondary concern. Any number of beliefs or practices, all mutually contradictory, may be used, as long as the desired result of enlightenment is achieved. "[A]ny method of meditation, religious ritual, ethical discipline, or doctrinal formulation can be used to help persons spiritually advance beyond where they are as unenlightened beings toward the final truth of enlightenment."[23] Following the principle of *upāya*, a Buddhist dialogue partner may agree that our Christian doctrine is "true" (in that it nudges us away from *tanhā* toward selflessness) without being "true" (in that its assertions do not, in his view, correspond to reality).

Third, philosophical, historical, or propositional truth will likely take a back seat to other concerns. Schreiter, for example, suggests that in many forums ethical preoccupations such as attempts to save the planet may preempt cognitive clarity and coherence.[24]

So even if our Buddhist dialogue partner agrees that truth is the desideratum of our discussion, he may mean by that a vision that impels us from ignorance and attachment to enlightenment and selflessness, whether or not it is either propositionally coherent or reflects reality. To help him see that truth should be propositional as well as existential, and congruent with external reality as well as internally consistent, will be a great service to him. But regardless of how well we succeed in accomplishing that, dialogue in the sense of "an attempt on the part of people with different beliefs to gain a better understanding of each other" will aid our own search for truth. We want to know what others believe and why, and not simply accept our own intuitions or third-party reports.

Problems result when we don't know the truth about what others believe. Abraham, the friend of God and beneficiary of God's covenant, held an erroneous view of Abimelech's theism and morality. "I said to myself, 'There is surely no fear of God in this place, and they will kill me because of my wife.'"[25] He was wrong on both accounts, and wrong in presuming to know without inquiring. So he lied about his wife, and eventually departed Gerar leaving a less than sterling witness behind him. Honest, receptive, relational, and intensive dialogue in search of the truth about others and what they believe can protect us from similar personal embarrassment and negative testimony.

The Abraham-Abimelech story should silence any evangelical suspicion that today God speaks only to Christians. Old Testament believers, of course, were not "Christians," but at least we can say that Abraham was the believer[26] and covenant partner[27] in this pericope, not Abimelech. God, however, spoke not to Abraham but to Abimelech, and only to Abraham *through* Abimelech. The patriarch's ears were closed to God at present through fear and weak faith. The same could conceivably happen today. Abraham's story is not unique. The godly Josiah, who pledged "to follow Yahweh and keep his commands, regulations and decrees with all his heart and all his soul," and who led his nation so that "[a]s long as he lived, they did not fail to follow Yahweh, the God of their fathers,"[28] determined to fight Neco king of Egypt. Neco rebuffed his challenge, saying "God has told me to hurry; so stop opposing God, who is with me, or he will destroy you." The Chronicler comments that Josiah "would not listen to what Neco had said *at God's command*," but rode on to his death on the plain of Megiddo.[29] Most Judeo-Christian believers would think that God would be more likely to speak to a fervent, godly king of Judah than to a pharaoh of Egypt, but the reverse occurred in this case. The consequences of Josiah's not listening to Neco and learning truth from him were disastrous to himself and his nation.

These specific cases should not surprise us, since God's love for humanity is universal.[30] Hence he speaks in one way or another to all with sufficient force and clarity so that failure to heed is culpable.[31] So it should not surprise us if we could learn truth about God or human life through non-Christians.

This does not mean that the Christian faith is in any way deficient or defective. The God-breathed scriptures are not only accurate but complete, with the result that through them "the man of God may be thoroughly equipped for every good work."[32] We will find neither *necessary* new truth, nor true propositions that contradict the Christian message, in non-Christian people or religions. But we may find that which illumines or fills out biblical tenets, or reminders of what we may have overlooked or forgotten. David Hesselgrave tells of attending a chapel service with his friend Professor Krishna. The speaker was an American youth evangelist.

> The evangelist's leather jacket, festooned with Jesus buttons, constituted a somewhat different attire for a seminary chapel. But it was the message itself that was most unique, punctuated as it was with references to Christ as a "great guy" and "good fellow," and delivered in rapid-fire style with no sense of awe or mystery. After a closing "Amen," I waited for Dr. Krishna to rise, but he just sat there, his head buried in his hands. Aware of his physical problems, I made inquiry. Slowly he lifted his head and, haltingly, said: "I just can't believe it. Is this the way Christians speak of the Lord of the universe?"[33]

It is possible that on this occasion Professor Krishna understood something about worship that would have benefited the evangelist.

Dialogue may not only open our own eyes, but also those of our conversation partners. Misinformation flowing from both "Christian" cults on the right and liberal theologians on the left, as well as misunderstandings benign and malignant arising from within non-Christian faith groups themselves, could be corrected through responsible discussion. Many who denigrate or dismiss Christianity do so not knowing what it is. Moreover, the liberal community that has until now dominated Christian participation in interreligious dialogue (due in large part to evangelical disinterest) seems more interested than in the past to seriously listen to input from even the most conservative of Christians.[34] The evangelical *will* be heard . . . if he or she will join in and speak.

So truth is the first value of dialogue. Truth for us in gaining perspectives we might otherwise have missed. Truth for us in helping us genuinely understanding others. Truth for others in providing them a focused, formal opportunity to hear the historic Christian faith and agenda. The primary and foundational value of dialogue is truth.

Help in Framing Our Message

The Christian message is not spoken into the air but into the ears—of living people from particular mindsets and cultures. Hence that message, while not altered in its *content*, must be adapted in its *presentation* to be understandable to our hearers. Nowhere does this principle emerge more clearly than through comparing Paul's sermons in Acts 13 and 17.

Viewing these sermons side by side shows how similarly Luke describes them. His parallel presentation constitutes a literary device suggesting that he viewed the two as equally valid. The didactic content in particular is similar—starting with God's great deeds, Paul proceeded to touch on the humanity of Christ, announce his resurrection and its significance, quote corroborating sources, and call for repentance. But although the core is similar, the framework is not. God's great deeds in the synagogue sermon focus on Israel's history; in the Areopagus defense on his universal creative work. The sources cited are the Old Testament scriptures versus Aratus and Cleanthes. In the first sermon the resurrection promises justification that the Mosaic Law could not provide, and in the second it forebodes world judgment. The difference in the way the same subject was presented was occasioned, of course, because of the difference of the religions and worldviews of the audiences.

Acts 13 Synagogue	Structural Similarities in Paul's Two Sermons	Acts 17 Areopagus
13:15	invited to speak	17:19
13:16	stood up	17:22
13:16	began with "Men of . . ."	17:22
13:17ff	"The God . . . [describes God's deeds]"	17:24ff
13:22,33–35, 41	quoted sources	17:23, 28
13:30	"raised/raising him from the dead"	17:31
13:24	repentance	17:30
13:23	stressed humanity of Christ	17:31
13:42	leaving	17:33
13:42	invitation to speak again	17:32
13:42	some follow	17:34
13:45	some oppose	17:32

Understanding his audience and adapting to them were not peripheral considerations for the apostle. Paul relates how prior to his speech he "walked around and looked carefully at [their] objects of worship."[35] The original behind "looked carefully" is the compound ἀναθεωρέω, meaning to "look at again and again," hence "examine, observe carefully."[36] In Diodorus Siculus, ἐξ ἐπιπολῆς θεωρούμενος "examine superficially" is contrasted with ἀναθεωρούμενος καὶ μετ᾽ ἀκριβείας ἐξεταζόμενος.[37] Louw and Nida suggest that in the present passage

> ἀναθεωρέω implies considerable mental activity, for Paul was not merely looking at the objects of worship but was undoubtedly thinking about the implications of them. In fact, in some languages it may be necessary to specify the elements of seeing and thinking by translating 'for as I walked around and saw your objects or worship and thought about them.'[38]

Clearly what Paul did before he spoke on this occasion was probe his audience's beliefs and then shape his message based on what he observed.

This study of and adaptation to his audience was not unique to this occasion, but reflects the apostle's underlying strategy outlined in 1 Corinthians 9:19–27 and encountered occasionally in Acts.[39] His objective was to win people, not simply to parrot the gospel. Accordingly, using the freedom he had in Christ,[40] he adapted himself as much as possible to their sensibilities. It is a philosophy he promotes for other applications as well.[41] Paul was consistently uncompromising concerning the *content* of the gospel,[42] but quite flexible in his *communication* of that gospel. Adapting to his audience's beliefs and sensibilities presupposes understanding those beliefs and sensibilities. Hence he "walked around and looked carefully at [their] objects of worship." And hence we today engage in genuine, sustained, and interested dialogue.

In a classic sketch of the miscommunication that occurs when a speaker does not first strive to understand her hearers, John Davis suggests a Thai person's perplexity in his first encounter with John 3:16.[43] There have been tragic results from failure to engage in dialogue as a prerequisite to evangelism.[44] Truth for us and others is the first value of dialogue; help in constructing a framework by which to shape our presentation of the gospel is a second.

Opening the Heart

A third value of dialogue, related to the second, is its ability to open the heart of the listener. Sometimes no opportunity to speak would open unless the one who wished to do so first mastered the thought of his addressee. This was true of Daniel in the Old Testament. Daniel and his friends were uncompromisingly committed to their Jewish faith and practice,[45] yet plunged with such vigor into their study of "the language and literature of the Babylonians" (which doubtless detailed their religions beliefs) that they tested out "ten times better than all the magicians and enchanters in [Nebuchadnezzar's] whole kingdom."[46] Their study, combined with divine intervention in disclosing the king's dream, opened opportunities to present Israel's God to the most powerful potentate of their day. Those opportunities would not have presented themselves had the four declined to learn this new language and literature.

Today the church is charged to make disciples of people from all nations, speaking in the name of a God who is not willing that any should perish. Impelled by the love of Christ, we must exemplify that love. Doing so would include interest in and desire to know the person to whom we speak. Hence we talk and dialogue. Even if he adamantly resists repentance we love him, as does the God who sends rain on the righteous and the unrighteous. But such an interested, inquisitive demeanor that seeks understanding and relationship, regardless of any unlikelihood that our partner will be persuaded to adopt our views, often has the effect of opening the heart and inducing conversion. Discussion and relationship tear down the barriers people erect against challenges to their worldview and self-identity.

I recently visited with villagers from Myanmar. As we discussed the *nats* most Burmese fear, the villagers themselves began to see some of the inconsistencies in their beliefs, and expressed the view that perhaps in another generation they would disappear. Had I come to them simply preaching my view or railing against *nats*, I doubt they would have reacted in the same way.

Limits to Dialogue

Developing a clearer view of truth, constructing a framework for communication, and establishing personal relationships are three values of dialogue. What limits should control the process?

Not a Platform to Promote Pluralism

We have defined dialogue as "an attempt on the part of people with different beliefs to gain a better understanding of each other." Helpful interaction pretends neither that differences do not exist, nor that they do not matter. But with humility that grows from acknowledging one's limited perspective, and with respect for other people, those who dialogue seek 1) to understand, 2) to help the other understand, 3) to be corrected where in error, and 4) to correct the other where she is in error.

Carson suggests that the central thesis of philosophical pluralism is "that any notion that a particular ideological or religious claim is intrinsically superior to another is *necessarily* wrong." Hence "[n]o religion has the right to pronounce itself right or true, and the others false, or even (in the majority view) relatively inferior."[47] For those who hold to such pluralism it would appear that the only thing dialoguers can do is "all happily spend our time congratulating one another on our mutual rightness."[48] By contrast, the position of this paper is that there are differences among religions, that where these differences touch on crucial issues they matter, that some positions are either objectively right or wrong, and that mutually exclusive positions cannot both be right. In dialogue we *do* have something to say and something to learn, and must engage in a great deal more (and other) than happily congratulating one another on our mutual rightness.

Therefore, if a proposed dialogue session requires its participants to embrace and abide by the agenda of philosophical pluralism, the evangelical Christian will probably consider participation unprofitable. There is simply nothing to say in such a session.

Not an End in Itself

Two corollaries devolve from this. The first is that dialogue is not an end in itself. We want to get somewhere; we want to arrive at conclusions and develop new understandings. Endless rounds of "dialogue" that do not aim at or eventually result in decisions and progress may prove a waste of time. The New Testament warns against "myths and endless genealogies" and "meaningless talk," and urges the Christian worker to not "have anything to do with foolish and stupid arguments."[49] It is helpful to recall Sanballat and Geshem's insistence that Nehemiah confer with them on the plain of Ono, and Nehemiah's reply, "I am carrying on a great project and cannot go down. Why should the work stop while I leave it and go down to you?"[50] Good dialogue does take time, including a lot spent in building trust and relationships. None of this should be begrudged. But if prospects for progress appear puny, it may be desirable to decline further discussions and return to more productive work. Dialogue may aid us in fulfilling Christ's great commission, but it does not constitute the essence of that commission.

Not a Reason to Cease Proclamation

A second corollary is that dialogue does not demand that we desist proclamation. The attempt to gain clearer understanding of a different faith does not require that I cease believing and promoting my own. A responsible dialoguer will want to do so enlightened by what she is learning in the interchange, and deferring where possible to the other's sensibilities, but proclamation itself may continue. To desist may in fact constitute faithlessness to one's own tradition and consequent disqualification as a viable dialogue partner. Christians do not cease to be Christian simply because they are talking to Buddhists, nor do Buddhists cease to be Buddhist because they engage with Christians. As Tennent asks,

> How can one have genuine dialogue *without* a faith commitment? How can interfaith dialogue exist without faith? . . . [W]hy can't genuine dialogue involve people speaking persuasively to one another from faith to faith? . . . I fully expect Muslims or Hindus or Buddhists to do their best to convince me that they have more coherent worldviews and clearer visions of God or reality than the Christian faith has. Likewise, I am free to make the best case I can for the Christian gospel. . . .[51]

Not for Every Christian

Interreligious dialogue is a corporate church responsibility, not the responsibility of every individual within it. The "body" metaphor of 1 Corinthians 12 and elsewhere applies to this as it does to other Christian obligations. Some (probably most) of us are not cut out for it, so extensive training in its philosophy and techniques should not rank high among catechetical priorities. I believe all Christians should be taught the twin truths that 1) as Christians we hold to a definite body of truth ("the faith once for all entrusted to the saints") and reject contradictory doctrines, but that 2) we nevertheless respect, relate to, learn from, and share with members of other religions. But that does not mean that every Christian will be engaged in the intricacies of the process.

Specifically, just as there are "strong" and "weak" Christians in regard to ethical questions,[52] so people may prove "strong" or "weak" in debating cultists and non-Christian believers. One who is not grounded, is easily swayed, or is unsophisticated in the niceties of philosophical discussion might not prove the best representative of the Christian case, and may drown if thrust unprepared into the swirling waters of dialogue. Such dialogue, like solid food, "is for the mature, who by constant use have trained themselves to distinguish good from evil."[53] Some will need to be equipped further; while others will never excel in this ministry, just as not all among the Corinthians were apostles, prophets, teachers, or miracle workers.[54]

Therefore, whereas the entire Christian community needs to be committed to the idea that we do not isolate ourselves—fingers in ears—from non-Christian communities, most individuals will probably participate in little or no sustained, formal dialogue. But they can encourage and pray for those who do.

Not for Those in a Rush to Replace Christian Worship

Both the promotion of interreligious dialogue and willingness to change beliefs in the process have come mostly from the West.[55] Netland notes that "Whereas some Christian theologians seem remarkably eager to be transformed by Buddhism or Hinduism, Buddhists and Hindus often do not appear to be nearly as interested in being influenced by Christian faith!"[56] But such people still frequently wish to be regarded as Christians, leading Gross to ask, "If they were so taken by Buddhism, why did they hang on to Christianity?"[57]

The dialogue this paper advocates is undertaken by those who do not enter into the process yearning for change, even though they would be willing to do so if their faith were proven wrong. I am not charging any individual with such a precommitment to change, but simply saying that this is not the impetus for evangelical involvement. We remember the warning of Moses, *mutatis* mutandis: "[B]e careful not to be ensnared by inquiring about their gods, saying, 'How do these nations serve their gods? We will do the same.'"[58] The problem Moses addresses is not inquiry, but a predisposition before inquiry even takes place to either jettison faith in Yahweh for a new, foreign practice, or to syncretize the two.

Not an Opportunity to Supplement Putative Deficiencies in Christianity

While Christianity pretends neither that it contains all truth on all subjects, nor that it has nothing to learn from other faiths and philosophies (see above), it does profess to contain sufficient truth to restore its adherents to right relationship with God and guide them in their earthly lives. The Bible is not exhaustive, but it is enough. The classic text is 2 Timothy 3:16–17, which teaches that all scripture is God-breathed and profitable for teaching and correction so that "the man of God may be competent, equipped for every good work." The word translated "competent," ἄρτιος, was used in classical literature to mean *complete, perfect of its kind, suitable, exactly fitted.* Further, ὁ τοῦ θεοῦ ἄνθρωπος enlightened by these scriptures is ἐξηρτισμένος,[59] *finished, completed; made completely adequate or sufficient; equipped, furnished* for πᾶν ἔργον ἀγαθὸν *every good work.* The use of three words in this verse to express adequacy (ἄρτιος, ἐξαρτίζω, πᾶς) shows that Paul intended Timothy to have confidence that no data outside the scriptures was necessary to fit him for a life and ministry pleasing to God.

That same confidence may secure the mind of the Christian today: in the scriptures that inform our faith we have all that we need. As we dialogue with Buddhists we may discover new vantage points from which to view human experience. We may find ideas with which Christianity agrees (e.g., the inability of material possessions or physical pleasures to ultimately satisfy). We may find truth we have neglected in our own tradition highlighted in such a way that we see the need to adjust our thinking or practice. In these and other ways Christians can find their understanding and faith enriched through dialogue with non-Christians. But we will fail to find outside the Christian scriptures any *necessary* new truth to inform our beliefs or direct our steps.

Not an Opportunity for Voyeurism

Perhaps the following caveat is not required for readers of this paper. Nevertheless, I shall mention it, regretting the need to do so.

Every religion has within its professed ranks sects and practitioners, generally outside the mainstream, that bring embarrassment to the whole. Christianity does. So does Buddhism. Tantric Buddhism promotes various types of ritual sexual practice to attain its goals of enlightenment and Buddhahood. While Christians who dialogue with Buddhists need to be aware of this strand, it is probably unnecessary to exhaustively investigate its details, and certainly wrong to parade them as though they represented the logical consequence of following the *dharma*. The Christian should neither be a prude nor an ostrich, and certainly need not be ashamed of the body or its functions. But there is a point at which in regard to evil we may rest content to be infants, even while striving in our thinking to be adults.[60] "[I]t is shameful even to mention what the disobedient do in secret."[61] The need to dialogue should not be cited as justification to probe the seedier practices of another faith and rehearsing their details.

Conclusion

Jesus was able to talk with the woman of Sychar about her religion, including its weaknesses.[62] He spoke with her the same message as he did with Nicodemus in the previous chapter, but cast in a different form. Paul's message to the Antioch synagogue paralleled that to the Athens Areopagus in content, but differed in presentation. Daniel knew Babylonian literature and thus was able to address Nebuchadnezzar, whereas Abraham didn't investigate Gerar and so fell flat in his witness to Abimelech. Isaiah knew enough about idolatry to enable him to incisively describe its weaknesses.[63] If the church is to grow it must speak not only to itself in words it alone understands. It must also address outsiders, and do so in ways meaningful to them. Dialogue is a part of that. It can aid our humility, enrich our understanding, strengthen friendships with other people, and help us frame the message we wish to share with them.

Glossary and Transliterations

avidyā—the darkness of ignorance

dharma—the universal truth proclaimed by the Buddha. The *dharma* may be found in the *tripiṭaka* or "three baskets" of the *sūtras* (which contain the Buddha's teachings), the *vinayas* (which contain his disciplines), and the *abhidharmas* (which contain commentaries on the *sūtras* and *vinayas* by later scholars).

duḥkha—suffering, uneasiness; in Buddhist thought, the true nature of all existence. *Duḥkha* comes from torment, from the absence of pleasure, and from the necessity of giving up what one loves and has become attached to.

nirvāṇa—perfect tranquility; the state where all human defilement and passion have been extinguished

samsāra—the cycle of birth-and-death

satori—enlightenment

taṇhā—craving, clinging

upāya—the skillful use of any means (meditation, ritual, discipline, or doctrine) to advance people toward enlightenment

ἀναθεωρέω (*anatheōreō*)—*vb.* to look at again and again; examine, observe carefully. The simple verb θεωρέω (look at, observe, see) strengthened by the preposition ἀνά.

ἄρτιος (*artios*)—*adj.* complete, perfect of its kind, suitable, exactly fitted (cognate to ἐξαρτίζω)

ἐξαρτίζω (*exartizō*)—*vb.* to finish, complete; make completely adequate or sufficient; to equip, furnish. The simple verb ἀρτίζω (get ready, prepare) strengthened by the preposition ἐκ.

ἐξηρτισμένος (*exērtismenos*)—nominative masculine singular perfect passive participle of ἐξαρτίζω θεωρέω (*theōreō*)—*vb.* to look at, observe, see

ὁ τοῦ θεοῦ ἄνθρωπος (*ho tou theou anthrōpos*)—"the man of God" (phrase from 2 Tim 3:17)

πᾶν ἔργον ἀγαθὸν (*pan ergon agathon*)—"every good work" (phrase from 2 Tim 3:17; accusative case)

πᾶς (*pas*)—each, every, all (the nominative case of πᾶν in the phrase πᾶν ἔργον ἀγαθὸν, above)

Notes

[1] The Latin verb *finǐo* means to bound, limit, or enclose; hence *dēfinǐo* to bound, mark out, or set limits to.

[2] Eric J. Sharpe, "The Goals of Interreligious Dialogue," in *Truth and Dialogue in World Religions: Conflicting Truth-Claims*, Conference on the Philosophy of Religion, University of Birmingham, 1970; ed. John Hick (Philadelphia: Westminster, 1974), 78. Alister E. McGrath, "The Christian Church's Response to Pluralism," *Journal of the Evangelical Theological Society* 35 (December 1992): 490, laments that "[t]he literature of pluralism is saturated with this word, almost to the point of inducing an intellectual torpor on the part of its unfortunate readers."

[3] Sharpe, "Goals," 82–92.

[4] Hans Waldenfels, "Buddhism and Christianity in Dialogue: Notes on the Intellectual Presuppositions," *Communio: International Catholic Review* 15 (1988): 411–22.

[5] Eryl Davies, "1993," *Foundations* 24 (1990): 16–21.

[6] Daniel Ng, "A Survey of Christian Models in Religious Dialogue," *Regent Chinese Journal* 1 (1993): 8–16.

[7] Alister McGrath, *A Passion for Truth: The Intellectual Coherence of Evangelicalism* (Downers Grove: InterVarsity, 1996), 211.

[8] Jacob Neusner, "Can People Who Believe in Different Religions Talk Together?" *Journal of Ecumenical Studies* 28 (1991): 88–100.

[9] This was often stated in earlier discussions regarding dialogue. See, for example, Heinrich Dumoulin, *Christianity Meets Buddhism* (LaSalle, Illinois: Open Court, 1974), 34–35: "The establishment of a single world religion in which all existing religions would merge and amalgamate with one another is emphatically *not* the goal.... The goals of the dialogue ... are to gain and deepen mutual understanding and cooperation, on the personal level, for the common welfare of mankind." But that definition has changed, starting with John Cobb's *Beyond Dialogue: Toward a Mutual Transformation of Christianity and Buddhism* (Philadelphia: Fortress, 1982), and stated clearly by Abe: "The dialogue [between Buddhism and Christianity] no longer remains merely at the stage of promoting mutual understanding between the two religions. Going a step further, the dialogue is entering a new stage in which the *mutual transformation* of Buddhism and Christianity is seriously being explored." Masao Abe, "Kenosis and Emptiness," in *Buddhist Emptiness and Christian Trinity: Essays and Explorations*, ed. Roger Corless and Paul F. Knitter (Mahweh, New Jersey: Paulist, 1990), 5. This is a revised form of a paper originally entitled "Kenotic God and Dynamic Sunyata" and read at the second conference on East-West Religious Encounter "Paradigm Shifts in Buddhism and Christianity: Cultural Systems and the Self" held January 3–11, 1984, at Hawaii Loa College. An expanded version may be found under that title in John B. Cobb, Jr., and Christopher Ives, eds., *The Emptying God: A Buddhist-Jewish-Christian Conversation*, Faith Meets Faith Series, gen. ed. Paul F. Knitter (Maryknoll, New York: Orbis, 1990), 3–65.

[10] David Tracy, *Dialogue with the Other: The Interreligious Dialogue*, Louvain Theological & Pastoral Monographs (Louvain: Peeters, 1990), 4.

[11] 1 Cor. 15:14 κενός, lit. empty, and thus fig. without content, basis, or truth; 15:17 μάταιος, idle, useless, powerless.

[12] 15:19.

[13] 15:30–32a.

[14] 15:32b.

[15] 15:20–22, 58.

[16] 15:3.

[17] D. T. Suzuki, "Lectures on Zen Buddhism," in *Zen Buddhism and Psychoanalysis*, by Erich Fromm, D. T. Suzuki, and Richard DeMartino (New York: Harper, 1960), 10.

[18] Donald Wiebe, *Religion and Truth: Towards an Alternative Paradigm for the Study of Religion*, Religion and Reason 23: Method and Theory in the Study and Interpretation of Religion, gen. ed. Jacques Waardenburg (New York: Mouton, 1981), 104.

[19] Wiebe, *Religion and Truth*, 145.

[20] Stephen Neill, *Christian Faith and Other Faiths* (Downers Grove: InterVarsity, 1984), 143.

[21] Ben M. Carter, "Evangelical Buddhism," Paper presented at the 54th Annual Meeting of the Evangelical Theological Society, November 20–22, 2002, Toronto, 5.

[22] Philip Blosser, "Review of Russell H. Bowers, Jr., *Someone or Nothing? Nishitani's* Religion and Nothingness *as a Foundation for Christian-Buddhist Dialogue*," *Japanese Journal of Religious Studies* 23 (Spring 1996): 209–11.

[23] Paul O. Ingram, *The Modern Buddhist-Christian Dialogue: Two Universalistic Religions in Transformation*, Studies in Comparative Religion, vol. 2 (Lewiston, New York: Edwin Mellen, 1988), 92.

[24] Robert J. Schreiter, "Interreligious Dialogues: A Hundred Years On," *New Theology Review* 6 (1993): 6–17.

[25] Gen. 20:11.

[26] Gen. 15:6.

[27] Gen. 12:1–3; 15:17–20.

[28] 2 Chron. 34:31–33.

[29] 2 Chron. 35:20–24.

[30] Ps. 145:17; John 3:16; 1 Tim. 4:10; 2 Pet. 3:9; etc.

[31] Ps. 19:1–4; Rom. 1:18–20; 2:14–15.

[32] 2 Tim. 3:17.

[33] David J. Hesselgrave, *Communicating Christ Cross-Culturally: An Introduction to Missionary Communication*, 2nd ed. (Grand Rapids: Zondervan, 1991), 252.

[34] Peter A. Huff, "The Challenge of Fundamentalism for Interreligious Dialogue," *Cross Currents* 50, no. 1/2 (Spring/Summer 2000): 94-102.

[35] Acts 17:23.

[36] BAG, s.v. ἀναθεωρέω.

[37] The passage (*Library*, 12.15.1) reads ὁ δ᾽ οὖν Χαρώνδας καὶ ἕτερόν τινα νόμον ἀποδοχῆς ἀξιούμενον ἔγραψε, τὸν περὶ τῆς τῶν

ὀρφανῶν φυλακῆς. οὗτος δ᾿ ἐξ ἐπιπολῆς μὲν θεωρούμενος οὐδὲν φαίνεται περιττὸν ἔχειν οὐδὲ ἀποδοχῆς ἄξιον, ἀναθεωρούμενος δὲ καὶ μετ᾿ ἀκριβείας ἐξεταζόμενος μεγάλην ἔχει σπουδήν τε καὶ δόξαν and may be translated, "Charondas also wrote another law worthy of approval—one concerning the protection of orphans. If *read superficially*, it does not seem to contain anything out of the ordinary or worthy of approval. But when *scrutinized and examined with care* it evidences careful study and merits high regard."

[38] Louw and Nida, s.v. 24.47 ἀναθεωρέω.

[39] e.g., 16:3; 21:20–26.

[40] Gal. 5:1; cp. 2:4.

[41] Rom. 14:13–16; 1 Cor. 8:9–13.

[42] Gal. 1:6–9; 2:11; 2 Tim. 4:2–4, 7; and frequently throughout his writings.

[43] John R. Davis, *Poles Apart: Contextualizing the Gospel in Asia* (Bangalore: Theological Book Trust, 1998), vi–viii.

[44] William W. Watty, "Evangelization as Dialogue: A Caribbean Perspective," *International Review of Mission* 83 (1994): 429–36.

[45] Dan. 1:8; 3:16–18; 6:10.

[46] Dan. 1:4, 20.

[47] D. A. Carson, *The Gagging of God: Christianity Confronts Pluralism* (Grand Rapids: Zondervan, 1996), 19.

[48] Paul Griffiths and Delmas Lewis, "On Grading Religions, Seeking Truth, and Being Nice to People—A Reply to Professor Hick," *Religious Studies* 19 (1983): 79.

[49] 1 Tim. 1:3–6; 2 Tim. 2:23; cf. 1 Tim. 6:4–5.

[50] Neh. 6:1–4.

[51] Timothy C. Tennent, *Christianity at the Religious Roundtable: Evangelicalism in Conversation with Hinduism, Buddhism, and Islam* (Grand Rapids: Baker, 2002), 14–16.

[52] E.g., Rom. 14; 1 Cor. 8.

[53] Heb. 5:14.

[54] 1 Cor. 10:27–31.

[55] In 1981 Abe stated, "In general, Buddhists are passive (though not necessarily negative) in the dialogue. They take little initiative in seeking dialogical opportunities." Masao Abe in "Buddhist-Christian Dialogue: Past, Present and Future: Masao Abe and John Cobb interviewed by Bruce Long," ed. Winston King, *Buddhist-Christian Studies* 1 (1981): 14. Buddhists are "somewhat self-satisfied with their own religion" (p. 21). "Just because of this, they are not so eager to reexamine and reform their own religious way. I think we Buddhists must change our attitude toward the dialogue. We must become more sensitive and eager to learn from Christianity. . . ." (p. 22). Cobb concurs: "In general the quest for dialogue with other religious traditions has come from the Christian side. . . . On the whole, representatives of other traditions do not feel these needs as keenly, so that although they often respond to the Christian invitation, they rarely initiate the dialogue." John B. Cobb, Jr., preface to *The Emptying God: A Buddhist-Jewish-Christian Conversation*, ed. John B. Cobb, Jr., and Christopher Ives, Faith Meets Faith Series, gen. ed. Paul F. Knitter (Maryknoll, New York: Orbis, 1990), x. Robert Lawson Slater, "The Coming Great Dialogue," in *Christianity: Some Non-Christian Appraisals*, ed. David W. McKain (New York: McGraw-Hill, 1964), 9, observed, "As for the Buddhist world, with the possible exception of some Japanese, most of the Buddhists I have met are more concerned with putting their own house in order and presenting their own faith to the rest of the world than they are with learning what others have to say. . . . Nor, on the basis of Buddhist principles, should one expect anything different. If the only reliable word regarding the Way comes from the Enlightened Buddha, from whom else is it possible to learn?" See also Richard E. Wentz, "The

Prospective Eye of Interreligious Dialogue," *Japanese Journal of Religious Studies* 14 (March 1987), 6–8. Nishitani disagrees: "Why is it primarily the philosophers of Japan who have undertaken to confront the two cultures and two religions with each other?" Keiji Nishitani, foreword to Hans Waldenfels, *Absolute Nothingness: Foundations for a Buddhist-Christian Dialogue*, trans. by J. W. Heisig (New York: Paulist, 1980), v. But he later admits that the "universal mood of interchange in the realm of intellectual culture" is "perhaps as yet little known in Japan." Keiji Nishitani, *Nishida Kitarō*, trans. Yamamoto Seisaku and James W. Heisig, with an introduction by D. S. Clarke, Jr., Nanzan Studies in Religion and Culture, gen. ed. James W. Heisig, (Berkeley: University of California Press, 1991), xxv–xxvi.

[56] Harold A. Netland, *Dissonant Voices: Religious Pluralism and the Question of Truth* (Grand Rapids: Eerdmans, 1991), 284.

[57] Rita Gross and Terry Muck, eds., *Buddhists Talk about Jesus—Christians Talk about the Buddha* (New York: Continuum, 2000), 131, cited in Tennent, *Roundtable*, 9–10.

[58] Deut. 12:30.

[59] A perfect passive participle of ἐξαρτίζω, a cognate of ἄρτιος.

[60] 1 Cor. 14:20.

[61] Eph. 5:12.

[62] John 4:22.

[63] See, e.g., Isa. 44:9–20. These verses certainly do not represent "dialogue," but do document that awareness of another's faith can inform one's own proclamation.

CHAPTER 5

Transfer of Merit in Folk Buddhism

Alex G. Smith

Introduction

Down through the ages the burden of making preparations for adequate care for one's next life, and of inventing ways to store up and transfer merit or other rewards as advance deposits for it, are common on all continents. In many cultures spattered across the globe like colored paints, different peoples have also devised a variegated plethora of ways for making some provision for their ancestors in the afterlife. Around the world a multitude of means for transferring merits to the ancestors by ceremonies, rites, incantations, spirit communications, and other good deeds abound. The concern to show the ancestors proper respect and to help improve their state after death, as well as that of one's own future, is a universal value, as researched in hundreds of anthropological studies. In most Buddhist cultures these practices of creatively making merit and of ingeniously transferring merits to others are frequently found.

A vivid example of transferring merits for the deceased is observed at Chinese funerals where paper money, colorful cardboard cars, elaborate paper houses, and other items are burned symbolically to transfer them to the next world for the ancestors to use. Usually the veneration of ancestors arises from a worldview that includes the "living dead." The deceased are believed to have powers, knowledge, and experience that continue after death, and these can affect and be shared with the relatives still living on earth.

Sometimes a people may hide the secrets behind this belief or deny such practices of preparing ahead for life after death. Occasionally, that is deliberately done. At other times it is subconsciously guarded. When Buddhists are asked about the meaning of certain ceremonies or of the value of specific items used in making merit, they often reply that they do not know. For instance, when the Thai are asked why they offered robes to Buddhist priests at funerals and why they held such elaborate feasts on these occasions, they frequently say, "I am not really sure." If asked whether this is part of transferring merit on behalf of the deceased (*Phae bun too yaat phi nong*), they sometimes initially reply in the negative. Afterward they may revise their perception and explain how the system works in sending on this shared merit to help their dead relatives.

The threefold purpose of this chapter is: (1) to understand the concept of making merit and its possible transfer to others; (2) to illustrate ways in which this is done in various Buddhist cultures; and (3) to make some evaluation and application of these practices.

The Concept of Merit: *Dana*

Primarily the Buddhist idea of *dana* is earning merit (*punna*), which affects one's karma (*kamma)*, particularly in relation to future reincarnations (*samsara*). Merit cleanses the mind and purifies it of "evil tendencies of greed, hatred and delusion" (Dhammananda

2002: 202). Basically, then, merit is the concerted efforts of doing good deeds, which elicit positive effects for the future. This merit is accumulated on behalf of or on account for the maker of the merit. Even the quality of thoughts and motives influence one's karma for good or bad. They are just like deeds, speech, and other actions. Merit is generally considered positive and beneficial, but demerit or negative merit from bad or evil actions is equally potent also and affects karma adversely.

Karma, the absolute and ultimate determinant in Buddhism, is according to Dr. K. Sri Dhammananda, "an impersonal, natural law that operates in accordance with our actions" without any law-giver or external ruling agent (2002: 113-115). It is "the final point of orientation for all other dogmas in Buddhism" (Niles 1967: 33). Since karma is the supreme and primary doctrine behind the system of Buddhism, every action in thought, deed, speech, or act produces a reaction, either positive (*pin/bun*) or negative (*pau/baap*), all of which consequently affects one's own accumulated karma. The classic popular and pithy expression of this is: "Do good, receive good; do evil, receive evil." The Thai say, "*Tham dii dai dii tham chua dai chua.*" Karma is like the shadow that follows you (Pali: *Chayawa anapainie*). This karmic view is not to be confused with the biblical injunction, "Do not be deceived, God is not mocked; for whatever a man sows, this he will also reap" (Gal. 6:7, NASB). In the context of Galatians 6:1-10, Paul focuses on bearing one another's burdens and the responsibility for each one to do his fair share. He refers to accountability in helping carry the load, especially in spiritual matters, rather than in personal fleshly concerns about some kind of "Christian karma." This cannot therefore be equated accurately with Buddhist karma.

Buddhist scholars identify ten major merit-making deeds:

1. Generosity or giving: *Dana*
2. Morality by keeping the precepts: *Sila*

3. Mental culture through meditation: *Bhavana*

4. Reverence or respect: *Apachayana*

5. Service in helping others: *Veyyavaccha*

6. Transference of merits to others: *Pattidana*

7. Rejoicing in the merits of others: *Pattanumodana*

8. Preaching and teaching the Dharma: *Dharma desana*

9. Listening to the Dharma: *Dharma savanna*

10. Straightening one's views or acting with right views: *Ditthijju*

All of these meritorious deeds not only produce benefits for the one making merit, but also give benefits or merits to the recipients of its transfer (Dhammanada 2002: 204).

From my two decades of living and working in Thailand, I learned of three fundamental types of ways by which Buddhists make merit:

1. *Tham thaan*: By giving alms or charity to the living to help alleviate the suffering of their current life and needs.

2. *Tham bun*: By doing good, such as practicing morality by keeping *sila*, or by meditating (*bhavana*), or by giving offerings to Buddhist monks or temples to help one's own cycle of reincarnation.

3. *Tham bun khun*: By giving back in gratitude to someone who has significantly helped or benefited you.

Many means are devised to procure merits, including but not exhausting the following:

1. Participating in various annual merit making festivals such as Viskaha, which commemorates the Buddha's enlightenment (Wells 1960: 117f).

2. Making donations at annual temple fairs and/or presenting food or robes to monks at other times (Wells 1960: 114).

3. Giving offerings to priests on special occasions or celebrations such as birthdays, weddings, housewarming or new office parties, funerals, and other alms-giving.

4. Making oaths administered by a monk on a Buddhist sabbath or on other holy days (Spiro 1970: 98).

5. Involvement in worship with offerings of flowers, incense, perfume, food, and other objects (Beyer 1974: 46-63).

6. Building or repairing temples, schools, orphanages, hospitals, or libraries.

7. Printing and distributing free religious books and literature.

8. Giving alms and other charitable deeds to monks and needy people.

9. Buying and releasing birds, fish, turtles, or other animals.

10. Making pilgrimages to Buddhist shrines and holy places where relics are located.

11. Having a son ordained as a monk or a novice.

12. Purchasing "gold leaf" to stick on the images of Buddha at shrines and temples (Smith 1977: 89).

13. Tibetan Buddhists add merit by saying *mantras*, spinning prayer wheels, fingering rosaries, making magic spells, and walking clockwise around shrines (Tsering 1993: 101-102).

Often these kinds of merit-making activities, among a variety of other forms, can also be employed in transferring merits to others. Both the common level of "*doing* merit" and the deeper level of "*being* through virtue" can be transferred to others (Beyer 1974: 38-41).

Transfer of Merit: *Pattidana*

In Buddhism, according to Dr. Dhammananda, good deeds or merits "bring happiness to the doer in both this world and in the hereafter" and lead "towards the final goal of everlasting happiness" (2002: 393). In this sense all the merit that a person procures in the here and now is transferred to the future incarnation of that person as well as being advantageous to one's current life.

But the concept of *pattidana* usually concerns the transferring of merits to others. "The acquired merit can be transferred to others; it can be shared vicariously with others," either living or departed ones (2002: 393). This merit transfer is only valid for humans, not animals. So purchasing and releasing birds or fish builds merit for the releaser but not for the birds and fish.

James Coleman points out that "The central goal was to acquire merit (good karma), which would then have beneficial effects in this life and in subsequent ones." Coleman continues his discussion by describing the historical development that followed: "Eventually, the idea of the transfer of merit—that the good karma created by one person might be transferred to another—gained great popularity" (2001: 34). Through this concept of transference of merit, Buddhists believe they can share their merit with others (Harvey 1990: 199). The richest fields for such sharing of merit include three groups especially—the priests (*Sangha*) or holy people, one's mother and father, and the needy (Dhammananda 2002: 203).

Origin of the Concept

According to one priest, the origin of Buddhist "transfer of merit" can be traced back to the time of the Buddha. One day King Bimbisana offered food to the Buddhist priests. But during the night he was continuously disturbed by *pretas*, ghosts of his dead relatives, who were wailing in great anguish because they were tormented with hunger. The king asked the Buddha to explain the reason for this.

The Buddha said it was because he had not offered food to the Buddhist priests in the name of his dead relatives who were now bodiless *pretas*, wailing in anguish. He advised the king to offer food to the priests in the name of his relatives. When the king did this, the disturbance of his sleep ceased.

Transfers to the Dead

One of the major ways of merit transfer focuses on departed relatives, especially parents. Peter Harvey writes that

> Compassionate help for others is no less important in death than in life, according to Buddhism. As death approaches, it is the duty of relatives and friends to help a person have a 'good death'; for in a rebirth perspective, death is the most important and problematic 'life-crisis'. The ideal is to die in a calm, aware state, joyfully recollecting good deeds, rather than regretting them, so that the best possible rebirth is obtained, within the limits set by previous karma" (1990: 211).

In *What Buddhists Believe* Dhammananda declares, "If you really want to honour and help your departed ones, then do some meritorious deeds in their name and transfer the merits to them." The Buddha said that the greatest gift one can do for "dead ancestors is to perform 'acts of merit' and to transfer these merits so acquired." Those who transfer merit in this manner "also receive the fruits of their deeds." The merit maker in these instances is not deprived of the merit originally gained by the good deeds. In fact, the "act of transference," being a good deed in itself, enhances the merit already acquired. "In their state of happiness, the departed ones will reciprocate their blessings on their living relatives" (2002: 393-397). Thus doing merit and transferring it to others produces double value to the maker of the good acts. Lynn de Silva writes that by transference of merit to another or by sharing in the merit of another "the original store of merit does not exhaust itself" (1974: 134-135).

Reasons for Transference

Why are transfers of merit to the deceased so vital to Buddhists? The major Mahayana sects are among cultures that are strongly influenced by Confucianism with its strong emphasis on filial piety, particularly throughout Japan, Korea, China, and its satellites. With the consequent ancestral cults among these peoples, the deep concern for transfer of merit to the departed ancestors is not surprising. This veneration is also expected among the Tantric Buddhists from southern Siberia in Russia to Tibet and other similar nearby cultures. When considering this concept in Theravada Buddhism, Tissa Weerasingha of Sri Lanka noted that in the Theravada School "one can only achieve a better life by one's own effort." Thus transfer of merit seems unlikely among Theravadans (1989: 7, 72). However, along with other scholars like S. Tambiah, Hans Schumann declares that transfer of merit is practiced even among the Theravada School in Southeast Asia and Sri Lanka (1973: 92). David Holmberg writes that Theravada Buddhist adherents "work to alter the karmic condition of the deceased by making and transferring merit both in rites directly tied to death and in those that become related to death." He reiterates that some scholars suggest that evil and suffering have both intellectual and emotional dimensions. The adherence to karma solved the intellectual problem of evil, "but the solution was too perfect for emotional comfort" amidst suffering and grief, for which "pre-Buddhist gift giving" became transformed into a symbolic function of "transfer of merit for the deceased" (1989: 207). Sri Dhammananda, a Theravadan himself, explains that this concept of merit transfer is based on the popular belief that when a person dies, that person's "merits and demerits are weighed against one another" and thus destiny is thereby determined, whether for happiness or woe. If assigned to the latter abode especially, they "are always waiting to receive merits from their living relatives to offset their deficiency and to enable them to be reborn in a happy realm" (2002: 395). This shows that the assimilation of concepts from indigenous folk religions is being adapted into Theravada Buddhism and is acceptable to it.

From a Christian and biblical perspective, humans come the into this world from God the creator of life, are endowed with living soul/spirit, are appointed to die once, and following that face the judgment by God who is personal, transcendent Lord over all. He alone provided the grace and means of full salvation by the vicarious suffering of Christ once and for all (Heb. 9:24-28). This is in contradictory contrast to the Monism of Buddhism, and the determination of impersonal karma with its multitudes of reincarnations in the endless cycles of life, escape out of which, according to the Buddha, is totally dependant only on oneself.

Cremation

The Buddhist funeral is a significant, elaborate, and often costly ceremony. A Thai proverb declares: "The dead sell (or eat) the living." (*Khon taaj khaai [kin] khon pen.*) This is because so much money is required to make merit for transfer to the dead that the relatives have to borrow considerable sums and so often go into deep debt (Smith 1977: 92). Dr. S. Tambiah says that the cremation ceremony is one of the chief functions of the Buddhist monk, since they lead the Thai Isaan's deceased *winyan* spirit essence on its way to release by means of their chants. They also add merit to the dead one and provide incantations that protect the deceased from the evil intentions of others, but not from his or her own karma (1970: 179-194). Merit making on the seventh day, the ninetieth day and one year after the death increasingly transfers more merit to the account of the deceased.

Santha Lal De Alwis, a former Buddhist priest, described to me how the average lay Buddhist usually visits the temple four days each month on holy or *poya* days: the days of the full moon, the new moon, and the two quarters in between (*wan phra* in Thai). As they visit the temple on these occasions and especially on the full moon, they bring a tray of flowers, which they offer to the Buddha. They light small lamps and burn incense chanting, "The Buddha I adore with this merit may *nibbana* I attain." By this they transfer merit to their own future existence. The devotees add, "By these meritorious acts may our beloved dead be benefited." The priest then says in Pali: "*Yatha wari wa pura pari purenthu sagaran eva mewa itho dinnm pethanam upa kappathi,*" which means, "Just as the river filled with water by the rain flows into the sea and fills it, so the merit of this offering be transferred or reach our dead." Then the priest says more Pali in a similar fashion, the translation of which is, "Just as the rain water flows from a higher elevation to a lower, may the merit of this offering be transferred to our dead *pretha* relations" (*pretha* means a ghost without a body).

Transfers to Higher Beings

The Buddhist *devas* loosely mean "gods" who experience greater happiness and pleasure in that heavenly state. These *devas* are transitory beings with certain powers beyond those possessed by humans. According to Buddhist belief, in previous existences *devas* were people who had done sufficient merit to gain this high position. The *devas* need to continue to accumulate more merit to keep or protect themselves in that position. If the power of their merit is depleted, they have to go on to the next life according to their karma, which may be good or bad. Thus *devas* are perishable. Some believe their dead relatives may go to this abode of the *devas*, a place similar to a heaven. Merit can be transferred to the *devas*-gods. Significantly these gods are also invoked to bless the Buddhist religion (*sassana*) and all the Buddhist peoples. The well-known Pali *katha* invokes as follows, "May the powerful gods (*devas*) in the sky or on the earth be pleased with this merit and protect the Buddhist religion (*sassana*) for a long time." But invoking the *devas* to help one gain *nirvana* is useless, since that can only "be obtained without any help from an external source" (Dhammananda 2002: 390-391). These gods cannot be equated with the Lord God, creator of heaven and earth, nor are the Buddhist heavens equivalent to the biblical heaven.

Monk Ordination

Another major means of transferring merit occurs at the initiation of the novice or the ordination into the priesthood. "Sons entering temple service pass on considerable merit to their mothers" (Smith 1977: 91). This is like "paying back the cost of mother's milk" (*Chai kha namnom mae*) (Davis 1993: 74). This is a powerful transfer of merit to the mother in particular, though it may be for both parents too. Merit transfer also occurs during the *buat naak* ceremony (literally entering the *Naga*, the mythical multi-headed serpent in Buddhist lore). This rite is conducted the night prior to ordination into the Buddhist priesthood. These ordaining events into the monastery are important social obligations to the community, the extended family and the parents. By them merit is transferred to parents, family, and community, as well as being accumulated for the novice, nun, or priest. They are also vital rites of passage for young men especially, though this seems to be waning in modern Thai society (Smith 1977: 91).

Boddhisattvas

The classical Theravadan School theoretically has no "bodhisattvas" (enlightened beings). But in Mahayana Buddhism the "bodhisattvas," by delaying their own entry into *nirvana*, help transfer merit to individual devotees through the additional accumulated merit they obtain from this postponement of liberation. This kind of self-sacrifice allows others who pray to and follow the boddhisattvas' teachings, to have the opportunity to receive their boddhisattvas' help in order to reach *nirvana*. A popular bodhisattva is "avalokitesvara" (Kwan Yin, known as the goddess of mercy), which is venerated quite widely and can even be found mixed in with Theravada contexts today (Smith 2001: 9). John Davis points out that the Buddha is considered by many of the faithful laity to be "a type of glorified bodhisattva" who is alive and listening to their prayers and "will be equally as generous in extending his merit to them" (1993: 64; 1997: 110). The key to receiving transfer of merit from the various bodhisattvas seems to be linked to the high level of devotion and obedience given to them by the devotees.

Amitabha Buddha

This interesting form of Buddhism was developed from an Indian Sanskrit text translated in China, which gave rise to Amidism probably in the early 6th century AD. It is also known as Pure Land Buddhism. According to David Burnett, "this text taught salvation by faith in Amitabha." It has considerable acceptance in China, Korea, and Japan (where it is known as Amida). "Power inherent in the name of Buddha Amitabha can remove obstacles to salvation and the mere utterance of his name can assure rebirth in the kingdom" of the "western paradise" (1996: 166-168). Thus salvation by faith is stressed by calling on the name of Amitabha, whose grace and compassion, according to this form of Buddhism, assures salvation by entry into the Pure Land at death. Thus a concept of transfer of merits is suggested here, through other beings, who "exercise compassion and, in grace, stand ready to share their merit" (LOC#15 1980: 15).

Spirits, Good and Bad

In the latest 2002 expanded version of his classic text *What Buddhists Believe*, Dr. Dhammananda included more than a dozen new topics, including one on the "Existence of Spirits." He declares that "Buddhism does not deny the existence of good and evil spirits," whether they be visible or invisible beings. Some Buddhists have dabbled into the realm of the spirits out of fascination for the unusual. The Buddha advised his followers to neither worship nor fear the spirits. Significantly and surprisingly, "the Buddhist attitude towards them is to transfer merits and to radiate loving-kindness to them" (2002: 392-393).

Substitutes and Scapegoats

In Buddhist practice in Thailand and elsewhere, devotees who promise offerings to the Buddha when making oaths or contracts, often use substitute offerings following the answers to their prayers. I have seen students pray fervently before images of the Buddha vowing to offer elephants if their request for help to pass an examination is granted. Once they pass, they bring substitutes of wooden elephants, not real ones, to place at the shrine. Other similar items may be substituted, as in the case where a person promised to get a troop of Thai classical dancers to perform. Afterwards only a doll in the form of a Thai dancing artist was presented at the altar, in place of an actual living performance.

I have written elsewhere on the substitutionary sacrifice of the famous Thai Queen Sri Suriyothai, who voluntarily gave her life to save her royal husband, King Chakrapat, during a battle on elephants with the Burmese invaders; and of Phi Ang, who sacrificed his life for the people of Chiangmai by tying his leg to a tree branch under water in order to win a diving contest against the representative of the invading Burmese army, so as to gain freedom for the whole city (2001: 26, 46-47; 2003: 49-50).

Concerning the Tibetan Buddhist world, Marku Tsering notes that the early Buddhist missionaries who introduced their religion to Central Asia were deeply offended by the prevalent blood sacrifices of animals and sometimes humans. They tried to suppress them wherever they went, but the blood sacrifices survived albeit in symbolic forms in many occult rituals in Tibetan Buddhism. He identified four general forms of offerings: substitute, display, physical effort, and redemptive.

The redemptive offerings are of two types. In the *first*, a laboring animal like a horse or a yak is purchased and then set free in a pasture. The redeemed animal is marked with special threads passed through a hole in its ear. It need never work again. Here merit is transferred to both the buyer and to the animal (1993: 108-109).

The *second* kind of substitute offering is the scapegoat. Tibetan Buddhists have a ritual whereby the misfortunes, sins, and demerits of an individual, family, or community are placed upon an image of dough, which is then thrown away in some wild and uninhabited area. Occasionally a domestic animal, such as a goat, is symbolically loaded with the guilt and then it is sent out to wander and be killed by whoever finds it. Another form of scapegoat is "enacted at Lhasa each year by a member of a special class of 'professional scapegoats'." These human scapegoats, often beggars, go from house to house, taking the guilt of the families upon themselves in return for gifts of money. In a special ceremony the scapegoat is driven out of the town into some remote location from which he would not return for several months (Tsering 1993: 109-110). Interestingly, the Laotians also seem to have a sense of a scapegoat tradition (*Phae rap baap*).

Transfer of Demerits

The models of scapegoats discussed in the last paragraph above point out another way that Buddhist karma can be reduced in severity. Besides increasing good merit positively, one can also reduce negative bad merit. This requires mechanisms that take away the evil effects accumulated in life. Scapegoats help do this, and there are other means Buddhists employ to try to accomplish this.

In studying the Buddhist Tamang of Nepal, David H. Holmberg discovered that they focused more on the erasure of demerit than on the transfer of merits. The Tamang did not formalize the positive notion of merit as clearly as they did the negative demerit. They rarely spoke of karma except in relation to mortuary rites. But they frequently referred to demerit or sin using terms like *pap, dikpa, nyheba*, and occasionally *lhayo*, a form of demerit associated with killing. The solution to avoid "sin" was to show respect to the Lamas and to fulfill the ritual obligations. The Tamang, like other Tibetan Buddhists, did recognize the importance of good works, especially as an accumulated way to counter demerits. They also agreed that nothing could be done for those who accumulate great stores of demerits, so at death, a kind of "hopeless send off into the future" was common. "In the ritual context of mortuary rites, Lamas erase the demerit inescapably accumulated during life." The Tamang believe that "without the ritual efforts of the Lamas, proper rebirth is impossible." Throughout the mortuary sequence from cremation on, including the memorial death feasts, "the shadow soul of the deceased is called and fed, and the Lamas apply blessings to erase demerit." The Lamas, grievers, and the circle of kin all work to erase the demerit of the deceased and thereby transfer merits on behalf of the dead (1989: 192-207, 231).

Assimilation in a Variety of Indigenous Models

Since various models and kinds of expression of the transfer of merits are found in a wide range of Buddhist cultures, I have selected a number of them to illustrate the principle of assimilation common to Buddhism. Some of these practices will have more general acceptance. Others are quite diverse and even unique.

Throughout **Southeast Asia**, early morning offerings of food given to the monks on their daily rounds (*tak baht*), produce a transfer of merit from the monk to the giver. While the monk does not thank the donor, the words of blessing he speaks in response passes on merit to the giver of the food which will be shared with the

Sangha community at the Buddhist temple. This is a fairly consistent and usual practice in most Buddhist communities.

Mongolia has its own brand of assimilated Buddhism with mixed influences from Tibetan Lamaism from southern China, Russian Communism from the north, indigenous Shamanism, and other ancient animistic practices. I have learned much from a scholar, who is resident there and whose name I appreciate but withhold anonymously. Several ways of transferring merit have arisen in Mongolia, mostly involving the Buddhist priests though sometimes in ways that seem unlike Buddhism:

1. Names for newborn children are decided after discussing the matter with the Buddhist priest. First a member of the family visits the temple to decide the name with the priest. Even if several weeks pass before a baby has a name, it is important to get the right and appropriate name, which then transfers merit to the child.

2. Certain prayers written by priests for the family in Tibetan, a language that is not understood by Mongolians, are placed under the pillow or beneath the mattress of the child's bed. The purpose of this sacred and magical approach is to change the child's karma, bring good merit to him or her, and protect the child from potential evil.

3. The "open cup" in Mongolian ceremonies expresses blessings, and is always offered uncovered. It usually contains milk tea or mare's milk. Buddhist priests are always present to offer the "open cup" on special holidays and celebrations and at marriages or athletic events. This represents a desire for "the spirits of Buddhism" to bring continuous care, blessing and success in life. The priests offer this "open cup" of blessing to the champions at traditional wrestling competitions. At the same time the priests also offer candies to the winners, who in turn throw them into the crowd to transfer the blessing or merit to the spectators.

4. The annual Mongolian *Naadam* celebration, held for the three manly sports including horse racing, is quite a spectacle. The large crowd, often numbering thousands of people, immediately swarms around the winning horse. They try to touch this horse so as to receive some transference of blessing, good luck, and merit from it. The contesting horses usually wear a piece of silk cloth called a *hadag*, which the Buddhist priest has blessed with merit.

5. Mongolians take death and funeral proceedings seriously, believing that no matter what station one lives in life, everyone is equal at death. Special attention is made to involve all the family and close friends in the funeral process with due care, precision, and protective caution. A family member visits the Buddhist priest or Lama as soon as possible to decide the day for the burial, which can only take place on Mondays, Wednesdays, or Fridays for Mongolian Buddhists. The priest also designates the time for the body to be taken to the burial site and where that will be. The Lama may stipulate any other specific burial rituals to be observed in preparation for the interment also.

Usually a priest or respected relative rides in the vehicle leading the procession. They throw rice out of the window of this vehicle all along the route, from where the body is picked up to the final burial site. This may be a considerable distance of up to twenty-five kilometers. This action is a form of transfer of merit to those who throw the rice out, to the birds or animals who eat it, and who may possibly be reincarnated beings demoted by their karma, and probably also to the deceased on his way to the next reincarnation. Another interesting action occurs as the lead vehicle transporting the corpse approaches any bridges along the road. This lead vehicle slows down so a family member can jump out, run ahead, and place a white silk cloth between the bridge and the vehicle, which then drives over the cloth. This is repeated at each bridge along the route. Mongolians believe this ritual transfers merit from the family to the deceased as he or she travels on to the next life. During the interment, milk tea is offered to the spirits, candy is thrown into the air as offerings, and often a spirit house in the form of a *ger* (the common round felt tent of Mongolians) is placed in front of the headstone. A lighted candle is placed inside this replica of the house to light the way to rebirth. Many times milk tea is placed on the chest of the deceased just prior to burial, as food for the journey on to the next incarnation. Following the funeral, a large meal is prepared for all who attend the ceremony and everyone is fed until they can eat no more. Even the dogs are fed well. These good deeds transfer merit to all the family and to the deceased. Before departing, each person attending receives gifts, which usually have Buddhist significance such as candles, incense, matches, or cups. This action of gift giving earns merit for the family giving the gifts and also for the dead. On the forty-ninth day following burial, the family provides another large dinner, as a memorial to the deceased. This also serves as a means of repelling evil spirits who may be looking to take another person in death. The meal is fed to even more people in the community, to the neighborhood children, and to as many dogs as possible! This process of merit transference for both the dead and the living is called *budaalaga*, meaning "to feed with rice."

In **Thailand** transfer of merit is frequently symbolized by such acts as attaching cotton cords (*dai saai sin*) for blessing or pouring holy water (*nam mon*), as in the ceremony of *buat naak*. Both of these seem to be introduced from Brahmin sources, but are wholly accepted in Thai Buddhism. The merit may be transmitted into prosperity, protection, or happiness in this life (*chaat nii*) or in the next (*chaat naa*). Those who express their faith through giving gifts to show respect and honor, procure an effective transfer of merit.

In **Sri Lanka** the close relatives of the family keep a cup on a plate in front of the Buddhist priests who pour water from a water jug into the cup until it overflows. The priests say, "Through these merits our relatives may get a good life." (Pali: *Idam may nathinam hothu sukitha honthu nathio.*) The repeating of this form after seven days, three months and one year is accompanied by giving food and gifts to the priests, transferring those merits to all the relatives.

In *Cambodia*, the disruption of war in recent decades with the consequent devastating loss of life, has left the Cambodians in a quandary about how to handle proper funeral rites and how to show adequate respect for the dead ancestors killed by groups like the Khmer Rouge. Many of the survivors worry over this and regret the lost opportunity to properly bury or cremate their family members or to transfer merit on their behalf.

The Philippines have a Chinese population of around one million. They are strongly influenced by Mahayana Buddhism mixed with Taoist and Confucian elements. Roman Catholicism also affects many, but the underlying faith that transcends all is ancestor worship (Po-yee 1990: 54). Order and harmony in society, loyalty to family, and ancestor worship are key dynamic values (Spencer 1972: 119). Transfer of merit focuses on burning incense at the family altar, respecting ancestral portraits on the wall, making offerings to the dead, and maintaining grave sites especially at hungry ghost festival.

In *China* an application of merit transfer relates to areas of the occult or magic. The Buddhist priest blesses the image or idol or amulet, infusing it with power. The devotee returns home with the charged item to use in worship or other practices. One can also prearrange a time with the priest, and on the predetermined date, the devotee, though miles away, holds up a glass of water and points it toward the direction of the monk, who transfers power to the glass from a distance. These two illustrations, though practiced within

Buddhism and performed by Buddhist priests, seem to be more related to animism and transfer of power than transfer of merit. However, the principle of operation is the same for both.

Applications in Missiology: Critique and Evaluation

While some brief applications have been observed throughout the above writings, one major issue in Buddhism needs to be re-emphasized again. In fundamental Buddhism, one must depend only on oneself. (Thai: *Tong phyng ton eng thaw nan.*) Even the Buddha cannot help lift someone else's karma. The Dalai Lama stated the Buddhist position clearly: "We must take direct responsibility for our own spiritual lives, and rely upon nobody and nothing. If another being were able to save us, surely he would have already done so. It is time, therefore, that we help ourselves." This fundamental doctrine of Buddhism appears to be categorically contradictory to the possibility of the transfer of merits. This paradox produces a dilemma for Buddhists. The conflict between this concept of transfer and basic Buddhist tenets can only be reconciled by their accepting the syncretistic assimilation that Buddhism has embraced so openly down through the ages. The local indigenous belief structures have been, for the most part, incorporated or adapted into folk Buddhism. This, therefore, produced many variegated faces and forms of Buddhism. Discernment is often a sadly lacking commodity in maintaining spiritual standards and doctrinal purity for precepts and practice in all religions. Accommodation is easily accepted and employed in order to obtain a wider response or a greater adherence from the general populace.

It is nothing new among humans to admit that all have shortcomings, and from birth to death, are not perfect beings. This is defined in Buddhism as present suffering and impermanent existence. Therefore the desire for spiritual growth and the aspiring need for outside help, be it called merit or grace, is evident and even necessary for folk Buddhists. But under these inadequate karma-bound conditions, how can the "merit" that fallible humans make have efficacy to help others, when it is already insufficient to liberate oneself? Or how then can the transfer of one's merits to others be truly "shared vicariously," as Dhammananda suggests, when those merits are ineffective for obtaining one's own full salvation (2002: 393)?

Significant barriers also abound when using the approach of the Cross of Christ as a contextual model for "transferring merits" to Buddhists. As Weerasingha pointed out significant problems arise, which clash with the Buddhists' core values and worldview, such as:

1. Their abhorrence of blood sacrifice as represented by Christ being crucified. This conflicts with their revulsion against killing life in any form.

2. The Buddhist also attributes karma to Christ because of his violent execution on the cross, normally used for criminals. Since the iron law of karma is inescapable, Buddhists hereby suggest Christ must have been less than perfect and insufficient in holiness, because he suffered such an ignominious death.

3. Buddhists categorically reject the claim of Christ's deity as God, as well as any concept that "only God can transfer merit." Jesus is seen as human only.

4. The high concept of the voluntary substitution of Christ is also in question. Taking the place of all humankind, and bearing the sin and karmic consequences of the whole world, are both foreign and also impossible to the Buddhist mind.

These four theological perspectives are serious stumbling blocks to using any model of Christ's "transferring merit" to humans, especially in relation to intellectual Buddhists. Virtually, these concepts are diametrically opposed to the basic tenets of the Buddha.

Furthermore, great care is needed to discern the difference between "grace" and "merit." Grace is not earned; it is inherent in "being;" that is, in the root or the essence, primarily posited in the very character of God. Merit can only be earned by effort and is therefore added to by "doing," comparable to fruit. The action of making merit is a mechanism for human hope, invented out of desperation or fear. Primarily merit is the fruit of human action; grace is the free, voluntary, and selfless giving or sharing of God himself. This grace of God is what is truly transferred, though some might call it merit. Referring to Christ, the Apostle John declares, "The Word became flesh, and dwelt among us, and we beheld his glory, glory as of the only begotten from the Father, *full of grace and truth*" (John 1:14). Paul succinctly claims, "in him all the fullness of Deity dwells in bodily form" (Col. 2:9). Effective help for deep spiritual transformation comes from grace alone not merit, *khun* not *bun*. This issue relates to the quality or efficacy of the agent of salvation.

From a Christian perspective, any transfer of merits to the dead would not be valuable or practical, because humans have but one life, and after death comes the judgment (Heb. 9:27). Nor would it be possible for those living to change that state in death, in spite of the teachings of some groups about prayers for the dead and of purgatory. Remember Lazarus could not help the rich man in his ignominious state beyond the grave, and even any attempts to communicate with the dead were futile (Luke 16:19f). However, from the folk Buddhist perspective, transferring merits is understandable because of endless reincarnations of the "wheel of life." This issue refers to time, especially concerning different conceptualizations of life in the two different worldviews.

In *The Cross and The Bo Tree*, Tissa Weerasingha discussed a model based on transfer of merits in terms of Christ's sacrifice on the cross for redemption of humankind (1989: 72-78). This surely has some value. However, it also raises certain difficult questions.

Does Christ, the fully self-sufficient God of creation, need to "generate merit" for himself, or does he merely offer freely and give to humans out of his infinite riches of grace? What would Buddhists understand by this? Or, more precisely, what would they misunderstand by it?

In common usage, there is a general saying that one is saved only by the "*merits*" of Christ. But in theological parlance, the use of "merits" here means, more accurately, the "*grace*" of Christ. The infinite merits of Christ's love are inexhaustible. There is no need, as Buddhists believe through their transfer of merits, to replenish this by Christ's making more merit for himself. His death was sufficient once and for all, for all humanity in all ages.

Human good deeds are impotent to save one's self. But suppose Christ's positive merit was to be transferred to a person, would that not add to his or her accumulation of merit or good deeds? But what would become of the person's negative demerits or sins? Would they not still remain? Of course in Buddhism this may not be a problem, since the popular view is that the good hopefully outweighs the bad, so that the net karma would likely open the opportunity for a better life in the next rebirth. However, most folk Buddhists of Thailand and Laos, and probably many other groups, (as well as the majority of intellectuals of classical Theravada Buddhism), usually affirm that it is not possible to weigh the good against the bad in trying to balance one's karma. The two sides of merit—the positive *bun* and the negative *baap*—cannot be mixed (*bun ko bun baap ko baap*). The bad karma must be played out first (*Tong chai baap kaam korn*). So using the *pattidana* model for Christ's transference of merit to humans raises serious reservations. By a biblical evaluation, even if Christ transfers positive merits to the sinner, the negative nature and the sinful acts of humans are not thereby dealt with, because the measure of good does not counter balance the measure of evil. There is an answer for this, which will be discussed later.

Another observation indicates that Weerasingha's description of this model seems to have no room for positive human good as only the negative elements are plotted on the right, while Christ's big positives are placed on the left. Since Buddhists believe humans are basically good and only need more education to overcome any seeming shortcomings, this could add another barrier to clear contextual communication. The model does emphasize the inability of humans to help themselves. However, it should also be recognized that even unregenerate humanity has a high capacity to do good as well as evil. Through the faculties of human compassion, mercy, love, kindness, and such like, humans also spread considerable positive and helpful value throughout their world. Since all people are created in the image of God, this potentiality is not surprising. But even in Buddhism the accumulation of one's own good deeds on earth are inadequate to erase one's accumulated negative karma, and is never sufficient to save humans flawed and marred by failure and sin. This principle is true for all, whether they be Buddhists, Hindus, Muslims, or even "Christians."

For this model to work properly, it is necessary to emphasize that the evil demerits be transferred onto Christ at the same time as his positive merits (that is, more appropriately, grace) are transferred to the seeker. Tissa Weerasingha agrees. Otherwise a deficient or unbalanced form of salvation could be misconstrued. This double transfer is not only possible but is already accomplished in Christ, who died for the sins of the whole world. He is the full and sufficient substitute procuring the way of salvation for all. Christ is the supreme scapegoat, the divine substitute "taking away the sins of the world." He is the consummate grace giver to those who call upon him in sincerity and faith. Therefore, experimenting with this approach at the existential and pragmatic levels, with folk Buddhists especially, should be considered, tested, and evaluated. The true measure of any contextual application is determined not through the implementation of the model and its form, but by the outcomes in the actual spiritual understanding, growth, and function of the recipients. Testing the new meanings engendered, and the comprehension of the recipients against biblical credibility as well as cultural acceptability, will measure the real level of effectiveness of these vital applications. This evaluation needs to be done from time to time, not just once, in order to check the stability of meanings and the retention of understanding over extended periods.

John Stott appropriately analyzes three key "notable expressions" that the Apostle Paul used in Romans 4:24-25 to explain the powerful transfer of substitution through the sacrificial death of Christ for sinners. *First* is redemption. God justifies the seeker through the ransom provided by Christ Jesus. *Second* is atonement or propitiation. God presents Christ as a sacrificial covering, which placates and satisfies his holy wrath. *Third* is the demonstration of God's justice. Christ carried the guilt of sinners on himself, openly taking their punishment on the cross (1994: 113-114). This summarizes the key reasons why God can accept repentant humans on the merits of Christ's substitution through his transfer of grace to others.

Another possible avenue for exploring and contextualizing comes from late developments in the northern Mahayana School. A surprising interpretation arose which focused on an unusual kind of transfer. Probable interaction with early Christians in China likely influenced the blossoming of this somewhat unique and popular sect called Pure Land Buddhism. This form was first established as early as the latter sixth century with further developments in the 12th century AD. This Amitabha kind of Buddhism, mentioned earlier as common in China, Korea, and Japan, adapted a concept of transference of grace with its consequent salvation from Amitabha in response to faith in his name (Amida in Japan). Considerable research, careful analysis, and serious study need to be applied to this particular and peculiar form of Buddhism to see what contextual connections might be legitimately drawn upon for presenting Christ to followers of Amidism. This is beyond the scope of this present writing but should provide a valuable approach for another paper.

Conclusion

In conclusion, Christ's transfer of merit (grace) is theoretically acceptable as a possible model for approaching Buddhists, provided that both the negative and positive sides are simultaneously dealt with as well. Also the reality that Christ does not need to make merits for himself in this process must likewise be recognized. However, considerable difference still remains between the Buddhist and the Christian understandings of merit, grace, and substitution. More serious and hard thinking on this matter is needed. Increased efforts in experimentation and application of this model should be undertaken and their results carefully researched, adequately analyzed, and honestly reported. While I have majored in this chapter on trying to understand the Buddhist view of transfer of merits, along with its application, there is also a need to expound more deeply on the Christian theological foundations for and the effects of Christ's transference of grace to the recipients of his loving sacrifice. This would be another rich study.

CHAPTER 6

The Serpent Power and the New Adam:
Religion and Occultism in Tantric and Shakti Traditions

Johannes Aagaard

The Serpent Power and the New Adam

The theme given to me is first and foremost connected with Buddhism in some of its Tantric forms. The key concept is given with the formula "The Serpent Power and the Tantric Traditions." By including "the New Adam" in the theme, it is indicated that what is given is not just history of some forms of Tantrism or Tantric traditions, but the presentation is given in a theological and Christian perspective.

For the person well versed in the Bible it is clear that the Serpent Power indicates the power of the serpent from Genesis 3.

The use of the term "The New Adam" indicates a theological dimension, since the New Adam first refers (in Luke 3) to Jesus as "the son of Adam, son of God," but the relation between the first

Adam, by whom sin entered the world, and Jesus Christ, by whom eternal life entered the world, is the point of the Pauline "Adam-Christ" argument in Romans 5:12-21.

The Serpent Power is not a dominant theme in the Bible, but it is an essential expression of the evil one at work against the New Adam, for instance in the Apocalypse 12 and 20.

The anti-power is not identical with the Old Adam, for he is an expression of humankind, not of the Anti-Christ or Devil or Satan, as is the Serpent Power. The Old Adam is certainly a problematic reality, but one that is not demonized.

Cosmology and Theology

It is an ongoing discussion if theology is part of cosmology or whether the opposite is true. In fact, they relate to one another, but of course *theology is about God, and cosmology is about the cosmos/universe/world.*

It is possible that the question is wrong, and then, of course, any answer would be wrong too. Cosmology writes the obvious context of the theological text. Then, of course, there is an inter-relation between cosmology and theology. Maybe theology is best understood as one of more possible dimensions of cosmology, but not in itself *as* cosmology.

Normally, we find cosmologies in Occult settings! That is simply a fact, and that fact is probably the reason why theology often takes place in opposition to a number of cosmologies, which are more or less Occult or Animist or Spiritualist.

We must admit that theology cannot identify itself with cosmology. It is worth trying to test this proposition critically, and this can best be done by making *an experiment.*

Can one succeed in describing cosmos as an acceptable context for a theology that has its own mission? The many new cosmologies have given us a lot of material, and a large number of modern people seem to find this cosmological trend significant. Can this tendency be taken care of in a theologically responsible way? That is our starting point.

Cosmos and Chaos

Cosmos in Greek means a piece of jewelry, but also order, and indicates something extremely beautifully ordered. The opposite of Cosmos is Chaos, which means ugliness, disorder, and dissolution.

When we try to give an outline of a theologically responsible cosmology, we present an independent experiment in understanding cosmos by means of the material of living spirituality and with Christian theology as the norm and the goal.

This is, however, not the only cosmological possibility. Scientific cosmology is presented as an option by scholars in natural sciences. It is a descriptive understanding, dealing with the given facts. Theology is open to such scientific attempts in cosmology, but theology is not only descriptive. It also relates to that which not yet exists. Theology as a whole deals with the future as a "virtual reality," which is "in becoming," and theology is an attempt to give guidance to and norms for not only the present but also from the future of God as the Truth who "was and is and becomes." Theology is consequently not only descriptive but also fundamentally normative. Therefore theology is both dogmatic and ethic theology.

In order to construct a theologically sound cosmology, it is important to understand the opposite thing which is *the Occult and syncretistic cosmology that is prevalent in Modernism*. In fact, Modernism is historically by nature largely the result of Occult cosmologies. The theologically sound cosmology can use some elements from Occult, syncretistic cosmology, as it is proved by the Bible itself, but the obvious use of such elements from syncretistic movements has to be countered by clear-cut theological guidelines, whereby the center is marked off from the periphery.

All cosmograms or "psycho-cosmograms" may look somewhat like the old Gnostic or Theosophical cosmograms, which does *not* prove that this is what they are. It may be possible to argue by means of the false cosmologies, in order to make the true cosmologies understood. It may be that the theologically sound cosmogram is communicated by denying the false cosmograms from within their own self-understanding. That is, at any rate, the intention of this experiment before you.

It is a surprising fact that modernist attempts towards cosmology—in their reductionism in relation to Christian orthodoxy—still tend to end up in Occultism and Gnosticism. The way this combination works is found already in New Testament texts, in which *"gnosis"* is seen as *an alternative* to true *"epignosis."* The same alternative is seen when libertinism comes up as a conclusion of love (Agape). The operative alternatives often look like the real thing, but without the inner Trinitarian identity.

Dualism and Trinity

Many religious systems operate as dualistic models, which have one concept of man and quite another concept of God or divinity. These two concepts function as poles, having an area of tension in between.

Such dualistic models are also operative in some forms of Christian theology, but a genuine Christian model is not dualistic but Trinitarian. Christ and Spirit somehow constitute the second and the third part. In classical Christian theology Christ is confessed as part of a Trinitarian project for salvation.

But where did man go in this concept? Man himself is also Trinitarian as "body, soul, and spirit." In Christianity the relation between God and man is thus the correspondence between two Trinitarian interpretations of both God and man! That double Trinitarian model is rather complex, because two times three are combined with one another. Thus Christian theology or anthropology or pneumatology are in fact experiments, seemingly complicated for minds that prefer simple, dualistic models.

Historical Observations

The terms "Hinduism" and "Buddhism" are created in modern times by the West. In their own regions a mix of what became Hinduism and Buddhism respectively lived in a sort of co-existence that is itself like the museum in Nepal, where the lack of space and the isolation from the world never allowed the two traditions to separate totally from each other.

The specificity of the rather different traditions were blurred by a common interest in not differentiating. In principle there is *no God and no caste-system in Buddhism,* but in practice both god or gods were part of "practice" whereby cast-ridden traditions functioned and continued to function. That blurred the distinctive difference between Buddhism and Hinduism in especially Nepal, but also elsewhere.

The Brahmanical tradition, from which both Buddhism and Hinduism arose, created a numerous mix of priests and monks (later in Hinduism than in Buddhism), and the clashes between both traditions were found in the often syncretistic practices.

The Sanatha dharma, i.e., the old order of life, is the classical term for the various old traditions that developed into a multitude of Hindu and Buddhist sects and sectors. The tradition of Brahmanism with brahmins and monks created a rich variety of communities and traditions.

But one important and decisive factor from outside must be mentioned: *The Islamic invasion.* It started on a small scale during the 8th and 9th centuries when the Muslims pushed towards the East and crossed the river of Indus, which made them call the area in front of them "Hindustan."

They considered the enormous area ahead of them as populated by heathens. The earlier Christian penetration normally was rather peaceful and undramatic, but the arrival of the Muslims created a new and dramatic situation.

The Muslims saw the Buddhists and Hindus as enemies. These two expressions of idolatry were simply considered blasphemous and had to be done away with. So temples and viharas were ruined and torn down, and mosques were often built on top of the ruined Hindu and Buddhist places of worship. Along the Ganges a lot of centers for Buddhist and Hindu studies were found and put to fire. The burning went on for many months, and invaluable libraries were annihilated.

A Necessary Hypothesis

Buddhist centers and Buddhist monks were special targets for the Muslim aggression. The local Buddhists were often Tantric Buddhists with a lot of icons of various Buddhas and Bodhisattvas and deities and Occult spirits. The centers were plundered and the monks were expelled or killed.

A large exodus to the Northern and Eastern region consequently took place. The refugees fled into the forests and up into the mountains, finding alternative sites in what is now known as Kashmir, Nepal, Bhutan, Sikkim, and even China. These frontier regions where the monks gained an influence have been included in the "Northern Buddhism" known as *Mahayana* and not least *Tantrayana*.

I admit that this exodus theory is still without historical foundation. Little proof exists for this hypothesis, but it is a necessary theory, without which one can hardly explain the fact that loads of ancient manuscripts were brought back from Tibet and the frontier states to India. Many texts were previously lost in India, probably burned together with the centers, but after 1947, some of them turned up again with the refugees from the North! How did these Tantric texts travel southwards in the 20th century unless they had gone northwards in the past? They must have escaped the Islamic pyromaniacs with the refugees, who had access to the secret libraries of Tantric texts. In the mid-20th century, these ancient treasures were saved from the Chinese persecution as they had previously been saved from the Muslim persecution.

Occultism Within

A ghost is passing through the world in the form of occultization. This is not the same as occultism, because the term "occultization" indicates an active, self-promoting disease that can be compared to cancer. Therefore, outwardly it may look as quite innocent Occult religiosity, but it is deadly.

Occultization has a number of forms, because it hides within the "bodies" that it takes over as its outward forms and covers.

There is an old version—or rather, there are a large number of old Hindu versions—of Occultism. And Hinduism can be seen as the womb of such occultizations and arise as a sort of arch-occultism. First and foremost it is seen in the special tantrification that has developed both within Hindu and Buddhist movements. *Tantra is occultization both as Hindu and Buddhist Tantra.*

A general observation in this connection could be that this Tantric occultization in a surprising way is combined with modernization, whereby the classical traditions are dissolved and have lost their ability to resist.

Secularization is implied in modernization. A striking example of this combination is the Vishva Hindu Parishad (VHP), the Hindu World Mission that is spreading modernization and secularization bound up with occultization.

First of all this combination is seen and found by the way in which nationalism and anti-Christian propaganda is combined. But its essential and lasting result is the overall atheistic belief-systems: God is out. God is the looser. God is dethroned, and Hindu dharma is taking over, being offered to people who may confess whatever they like without consequences—if only they confess the Sanatha Dharma.

The Buddhist analogies to Vishva Hindu Parishad are many, but normally not as aggressive as VHP. They prefer softer ways and means, but with a similar agenda, not least because God already is out. There is no god, and there can be no god, in Buddhism—old or new, theravada, Mahayana, or vajrayana.

However, we must go back to the relations between *Islam and the Hindu-Buddhist Tantric coalition against Islam*. Mutual influence can be found, of course, but let us first consider the conflicts and contrasts. The invaders were not assimilated and they did not want to become assimilated. Their god-concentration (Allah only) and their rejection of all gods as idols made the alternative clear. The negation of Allah was understood as a negation of God or an affirmation of gods (in plural) or no god at all. The contrast was absolute and inevitable.

The front resulted in Muslim harassment and rejection of all signs of "idolatry." The opposite and defensive attitude of Buddhists and Hindus was appeasement or escape. Most probably, thousands of refugees "emigrated." That is, the survivors went into the forests, or up into the mountains, or into the wilderness, or abroad, particularly to the frontier states to the north of India. The refugees exercised a strong pressure on the neighboring states and their princes, and it seems that they managed, to some extent at least, to resettle in these northern "frontier states."

The result was a sort of mixed religious civilizations—Hindu and Buddhist—as we clearly see the example in Nepal today. But the result was also a militarization of the monks, both Hindu and Buddhist. We even see the result today. During the great Kumbha Melas it is obvious that both Hindu and Buddhist warrior-monks spearhead their respective armies. The fact is that Buddhist monks are not fully allowed into the Melas because of mutual distrust, but the two parties deal with the tense relationship through rather careful means, and the same thing happens all over the world. But it is not always so peaceful. Recently, the Buddhist patriarch of Thailand blocked the arrangement of a VHP conference in Bangkok after arguments that were not very friendly.

Historically, Buddhist monks have been there centuries before Hindu monks. Buddhism was in fact itself an order of monks. Hindu monks are not just "holy men," i.e., individual seekers for salvation or liberation. Such individuals have been there all the time. Buddha himself (500 years *before* Christ) had monks with him. But Hindu monks are found only a few centuries *after* Christ, i.e., later than Christian monks. According to traditions the great Shankaracharya founded "The Order of the Ochre Robe," a huge Hindu organization, now with more than one million monastic members (divided in a number of subdivisions) and active all over India and worldwide.

Before the real monks came into existence yogis, who performed yoga, had been around. These yogis have become the most important part of Hinduism. Nowadays they offer several different yoga systems worldwide, the most important being the *Rajah Yoga* (the kingly yoga) and the *Hatha Yoga*, which is also called Kundalini Yoga.

The Rajah Yoga was systematized as Patanjali's Yoga Sutras possibly from the beginning of Christianity, but more probably some centuries later. Hatha Yoga, however, comes much later. The development of Hatha Yoga can be understood only from the confrontation between Muslims and Hindus, as just described, about one thousand years after Christ. This timetable can be questioned, however, for Hatha Yoga has older roots, and in some ways it related intimately to Rajah Yoga but is, in fact, quite different from it.

Rajah Yoga is soul-yoga (Atman/Purusha Yoga) and god-yoga, even if the element of divinity is microscopic. Hatha Yoga, though without God or divinity, knows about gods and powers. Hatha Yoga is body-yoga and aims at transforming the bodies into immortal divinities. And that is the point where Hatha and Kundalini join forces, for Kundalini is simply part of the know-how of Hatha Yoga. The Kundalini is, however, not god, but is a religious idiom and teaches how to transform the mortal body to divinity.

A possible theory is that the Kundalini, and thereby the Serpent Power, "wriggled into" Buddhism when the masses of refugees settled in Nepal, in Kashmir, in Bhutan, in Himalaya, and in other frontier areas. Serpent worship is found all over these areas, and snakes and serpents are held in great respect and are worshiped as divinities.

A conclusion must be that occultization in general is at work as a dominant factor in the transformation of religions into Occult systems, which in part they already were from the beginning.

We do not know with certainty what Buddhism and Hinduism in fact were before the escape from the Muslims and before their re-settlements in the frontier areas. Buddhism and Hinduism were already tantrified and thus (in our definition) occultified when they were dominant in the Ganges area and in similar sites before the arrival of the Muslims.

When the hordes of refugees returned to India in 1947 on account of the Chinese persecutions in Tibet and the frontier states, as mentioned already, they brought with them stacks of manuscripts from the libraries that they had saved from the Muslims hundreds of years before, stacks that now were saved from the Chinese Red Army. These were mostly the original texts, but they included some similar texts composed in the in-between period. Research (not least in the West) will eventually find out about that.

Islam, of course, is resistant to the occultization that changes God into secular religion. But the Muslim emphasis on Jihad, which has come to mean a similar Nationalist secularization and modernization, is also based also on occultization. The way in which Islam is abused by many Muslim terror-organizations for Jihad proves the case. Original Muslim trends towards humanism and individuality seem to be swallowed up by a fanaticism that is obviously based on Nationalist occultism (with the U.S. as the great Satan and Jewry as the demonic followers).

But we have to admit some similar trends within fundamentalist Christian groups. Without overstating the issue, one may see in radical fundamentalism (e.g., "The Word of Life/Faith" from Scandinavia) expressions of a wealth-ideology that can be compared to the Muslim Jihad-zealots: Right or wrong, *my* religion! And it is easy to register similarities between Kundalini Occultism and Prosperity Theologies. We have a number of evident analogies.

The key to the system is *analogy*, and analogy is the dominant linguistic model in both Hindu and Buddhist Tantric yoga and homologization. The syncretistic mood from the 4th through the 6th centuries in Asia, especially in India and China, created a proliferation of mystic imaginations by which also the religious iconography exploded into a complexity that comes close to a modern computer-plan diversity, most obvious in the Tantric forms of Mahayana. We shall return to this topic later.

The Erotic and Sexual Alternatives

The computer plans, however, always have a focus that adds the clues of the complexity. This key is the *bodhicitta*, which means both the power of Bodhi and the power of semen, both religious power and sexual power.

The dominant difficulty in interpreting the complexity is the fact that it rarely indicates which of the basic, dual meanings are to be taken seriously. The subtle or yogic power of bodhi or the gross force of semen. The language about these complexities, therefore, ends up as a *twilight-language*, as twisted language, as double-talk, or—with the established term—as *"intentional language!"* This term simply means that there is another and deeper or higher meaning behind the codes. The texts are elaborately worked out in series of analogous digits that conceal the intention from the non-initiated persons. In that sense the signs and codes and figures and digits are twilight-language or intentional language. The meaning is obviously to push the initiates into a series of paradoxes that generate a setting and mentality for a transformation of the new disciples.

In a lot of ways Tantric yoga—Hindu and Buddhist—operates as deconstruction in the modern way of that word! The world and the cosmos and the normal concepts and sense perceptions are not accepted as they are. The so-called reality is made unreal (*maya*) or disclosed as unreal. Yoga is the deconstruction after the experience of disillusion, and the alternative reality is what the discussion is all about.

The deconstruction of the world, as maya, is a transformation "from the unreal to the real." By this, however, is meant a transformation into an alternative sense of the cosmos, in which Occult powers in the guise of thousands of deities and demons and spirits are called for and worshiped.

The "intentional language," therefore, becomes a magical language by which the words themselves are the creative forces that produce an alternative world. In fact, that is what is meant by the term "religion!" Only in this sense can Hindu and Buddhist realities be called "religious" phenomena.

Deconstruction in this way is the same as *apotheosis*. The factual world is dissolved, and in this disillusionment another fictive world comes into existence in order to be worshiped in such a way that the worship itself stands forth as the creative process, the homologization.

The secret is that this analogical fantasy is erotic and often sexual. The whole panorama of erotic signs and codes stand forth in the imagination of icons. The Hindu and Buddhist iconography within the Maha-yana and the Mantra-yana and the Tantra-yana (all yanas are part of the same transport to Tushita, which means the heavenly refuge in Paradise) represent a flight or evasion from the suffering and disillusionment of this world to the heavenly Tushita. The iconography transfigures the world of maya into this alternative world.

The integration or fusion between Buddha-dharma and Hindu-dharma seems primarily to have coincided with the development of the movement of *Yoga-chara* and its first expressions through *Mâdhyamika* and its great Yogachara-philosophers such as *Asanga* and *Vasubandhu*. They became "canonical" authorities in nearly all sorts of Buddhisms. Mâdhyamika (one of the major consequences of the Buddhist Mahasanghikas) was first and foremost formed by "the second Buddha," called *Nâgârjuna* (150 AD) who is regarded as the founder of, and formative expression of, the Mâdhyamika schools (from the extreme Zen Buddhism to Tibetan Buddhism). These schools became important because, in a timely way, they were the expression of a universal Buddhism. In Mâdhyamika and Yogachara the foundation was laid for a Northern Buddhism, and indeed, even for an international Buddhism.

Some very important, but not well-known, basic texts for this "Buddhism of a new era," must be mentioned. They will not, however, be drawn into the analysis, because they are too complicated for this purpose:

1. *Guhya-samaja*, of which the Buddha himself is seen as "the author," and in which the *Five Dhyani-Buddhas* and their "New Era Icons" are given reality. In this book the five *Kulas* (or Kulashas) are promulgated as expressions of the five Skandhas. This text is called the beginning of the Mantra-yana, since mantras are used as important expressions of Occult Buddhist technology and seeming to have been at the center in both Hindu and Buddhist Tantra in this formative and fertile first Mahayana period.

2. Another important Buddhist Tantra from this period (the 1st Christian centuries) is *Hevajra-tantra.*

3. Finally, we must not forget the very Occult *Kala-chakra,* a much later text.

Kula Kundalini and Shakti Kundalini

It is now becoming generally accepted that *Tantra* is dominant in both modern Buddhism and in modern Hinduism in a large number of different versions. But it is still not generally accepted that it is the *Shakti Tantra* that is prevalent and decisive. And it is normally not registered that the Shakti form of Tantrism is bound up with a more or less massive Kundalini Yoga, often in the form of *Kaula Shaktism.* So in the indexes you often have to look for Kaula Shakti or Kula Shakti to find the most important information. A Pandora's Box opens when you find the entrance to the secret knowledge.

Shakti, of course, is female, and so is Kaula Shakti. But there are various perspectives on "female." Thus Kundalini is found in different versions, but naturally as female: Mother Kundalini, Virgin

Kundalini, Prostitute Kundalini, and Witch Kundalini are just a few of the most popular Kundalini forms of Shakti. They all can be experienced as the Shakti, and they all express the general "Bhakti of Shakti."

Is Kundalini as a form of Shakti divine or human? Does it represent Atman or Brahman? Purusha or Prakriti? Shiva or Shakti? Of course Kundalini represents Shakti, she *is* Shakti! She is, however, also Shiva and Purusha and Brahman. The reason is that the traditional dualism somehow has evaporated. But still in Shaktism, there is no God the Almighty or god or divinity as Rudolf Otto's concept of "the entirely other one." There is no "other one.!" There is only oneness. That is why this trend fuses so elegantly with atheistic Buddhism, even if it stems from Hinduism.

But it could be an important signal that when Brahman is lost, Param-atman comes in as a substitute. Why? The answer seems to be that Param-atman Shakti, Kundalini and Kaula Kundalini, functions in order to (or as means to) evade the God-issue. In Brahman, in Purusha, and in Shiva there is still a "smell of God," but even that is evaporating with Shaktism in all its variations. The reason must be *tantrification* in its effective forms as Shaktism, Kundalini Tantra, and Kaula Shakti.

But the important addition has to be made that this transformation away from the divine to the human has some special characteristics:

1. *"Human"* does no longer get its meaning from divine, because the divine has gone. So "human" is a very unclear concept.

2. *"Human"* by necessity tries to become divine, tries to transcend itself, tries to find its meta-size or meta-calibre. This tendency is found in our modern cultures in the West when prefixes as *trans-* and *meta-* are added to secularized realities to give also them "a smell of the divine." Do we find the same tendency in the

prefix of *param-* in front of atman? Is this an indication of an aspiration to go beyond while remaining within?

Rajah Yoga, Hatha Yoga, and Tantrification

The fact that the sounds of "Tantra, Mantra, and Yantra" rhyme with one another could be important, for all three words are of ancient origin. We shall not deal with the yantras in this presentation, but we will have to look at mantras, for they are decisive for the tantrification, especially in the form of Shaktism.

Tantrification can be compared to petrifaction or fossilization, because the external forms are often kept but all processes of life stop and become stony.

It can be uphold that there is *no Tantra*, but *a lot of different results of tantrification*. And the instruments for this process are not least the mantras. By *mantra-japa*, life is tantrified and becomes "stony." By *mantra-japa*, rituals are changed from worship into magic manipulation. By *mantra-japa*, the devotees learn to take and steal the powers from the gods. By *mantra-japa*, the believers try to go divine by going out of their mind. By *mantra-japa*, they get control of one another and of people in general.

Mantras were used during classical Brahmanical worship and they are still used during the morning fires in the homes. But the Tantric mantras are first of all instruments for gaining power, both in personal relationships (for love-making, for instance) and in social and political relations, for controlling and overcoming. The study of mantras has become a science in itself, and manuals for mantra-japa are numerous. But these manuals do not agree with each other! As in Western Occult astrology, the contradictions and denials of the mantras prove the illusory essence of the project. But even as illusions and self-contradictory fantasies, these Occult ways of thinking take effect!

Siddhis have to be understood in connection with mantras and yantras, but what *Siddha Yoga* as such implies is both a complex and an unclear question. Already in *Rajah Yoga* we observe siddhis as supernatural feats. In fact, what Rajah Yoga implies is contained in the concept of siddhi: supernatural powers and abilities. In the Yoga sutras of Patanjali, a vision is given that makes Rajah yogi the king of the universe with all sorts of supernatural abilities, as already mentioned. The Rajah yogi is strong as an elephant and flies as a bird. He is invincible as a superman and can make himself invisible, when needed.

In recent time, Transcendental Meditation (TM) has revived these pretensions and offers such fantasies and phantasms as means for their business-minded program for progress. Modern drug-businesses also hold on to these promising perspectives, which—if they were realized—would make the front pages of the newspapers look quite different from the daily news of today.

Hatha Yoga entered the scene much later, at any rate some centuries later, but it legitimized itself by a conscious attempt to create a united block with Rajah Yoga, thereby mixing all Yogas into one Occult front. It is probably important that this seems to have been happening coinciding with the active Occult revival in especially the frontier-states.

The predominant characteristics of the medieval Hatha Yoga were its emphasis on the *divine Guru*. Gurus are old as Hinduism and older than Buddhism, but they changed their nature from being spiritual guides and teachers to become divine masters beyond all human limitation. By yogic influence, especially by means of Hatha Yoga, Gurus went beyond the gods and changed gods into means for the guru-powers. The old gurus were Gnostic teachers; the new gurus were Occult masters.

Two Occult Masters and their Consequences

Two fantastic masters in particular were behind the double movement of *nathas* and *siddhas*, the masters who took upon themselves to "take the kingdom by force," i.e., not to meditate themselves to salvation, but to take their salvation "by storm." This is my description of *Matsyendra-nath*, with his *Sahaja-yana*, and *Gorakh-nath*, with his *Hatha Yoga*. They laid the foundation of a fantastic religiosity on the roof of the world, i.e., the frontier states.

From the same setting 84 Siddhas came forth with their often grotesque behavior and their turning religiosity upside down. The Kulas or Kaulas seem to belong to the same religious environment. And most probably important parts of the *Vajra-yana* iconography relate to this stormy period when the Siddhas in the "dress up" from the mountains went ahead and demonstrated what it meant to be Siddhas: drinking, adulterating, lying, blaspheming, eating human flesh, etc. Some of these men seem to have been very talented, but others were just provoking without any serious message.

Behind both Gorakh-nath and Matsyendra-nath, a first "nath" seems to have been operating, but he may be a sort of affirmative "forefather." He was called *Adi-nath*, meaning "the original nath." He is supernatural and out of time. Whereas the nature of Gorakh-nath seems to be well-described in an understandable way, the reality of Matsyendra-nath is quite dubious. But these two men seem at any rate to have existed, and they created a sort of "Janus-faced" movement, together promoting a revival movement, first in the frontier states and later all over India, and became very influential worldwide. The fact that drugs and alcohol are parts of the presentation of these peculiar "saints" should not be forgotten, like the fact that their notorious sexual behaviour is extravagant, even seen from our modern times.

It is important to note the suffix *-nath* and *-nathis* in both Gorakh-*nath* and Matsyendra-*nath*, and for that matter, also in Adi-

nath. The syncretism between those two schools characterizes the "order of the nathis," who make their presence much felt on the Kumbha Melas. These monks are both Buddhists and Hindus—or rather, they are neither Buddhist nor Hindu, but represent the Kaulas and the Yogini Kaulas from, for instance, Kamarupa in Assam, which is probably the hottest of all the Shaktistic centers.

To find the link from this weird Occultism to the many orders of Buddhism is not easy and is perhaps not a realistic possibility.

The Alternative Way—The Christ Way

The New Adam is offered as an alternative to the Old Adam who in Genesis 3 gave in to the Serpent Power. In the setting of what the Serpent Power has come to mean, the New Adam means Jesus Christ who had cast out the Great Dragon and the Serpent by means of Michael and his angels. That is the short story of the Apocalypse. That Great Dragon is called (Apoc. 12:9) the Old Serpent, and is also called the Devil and Satan, and his angels were cast out with him. Thus the Serpent Power is the same power as the Great Dragon, the deceiver, and is the apocalyptic alternative to Jesus Christ.

The great war went on and goes on against the Satan and his army that was cast out of Heaven onto Earth. This Occult power is not a problem in Heaven any more, but it has become the decisive problem on Earth. That is why the church prays: "Your will be done on Earth as in Heaven."

The blunt conclusion (v. 12) is that the devil has come down to Earth having great wrath, "because he knows that he only has a short time." In reality the time of evil has already run out! That is the perspective of the whole New Testament. The Dragon is fighting a lost war, but he goes on fighting against the remnant of the seed of the woman, i.e., "the faithful who keep the commandments of God and have the testimony of Christ" (v. 17).

In our contemporary theological way of talking it could be interpreted like this: There is a cosmic spiritual war going on. It started in Heavens, but the Dragon or the Serpent and their angels— i.e., their messengers—could not stand the might of Michael and his messengers. Finally, they were cast out of Heavens and arrived as a defeated army on our world. That is the situation of the church today in this world up against the already defeated army of Occult powers.

The messengers of Michael are fighting a war that has already been won! The messengers of the church, with Christ as the winning Lord and Master, know that the time is short for the loosing, demonic and satanic forces of the Evil One. Their time is short, and the short time is in "the time of the church" and its missionaries!

To use the well-known metaphor form World War II. Victory Day (V-day) is not yet a reality, but D-day as the day of invasion is already having its way and promises the full victory, "for the devils has just a short time!"

That theological vision has been an operative reality in 2,000 years. The witness of the disciples has been communicated to the defeated army of the Occult powers that are headed by the Old Dragon, the Old Serpent. They are part of the defeat.

The vision of this war as a spiritual battle against evil Occultism stands with the same urgency after 2,000 years. The war is on, but the war is already decided. The New Adam has come into power: Christ is risen!

Different interpretations are possible in relation to the theme of this presentation, which is *The Serpent Power* and *The New Adam*. If we take the Serpent Power to include that part of Tantrism that we name Shaktism, and when we take the Kundalini-ideology as a pointer towards the general Shakti-emphasis that is registered worldwide as a growing trend within both Hinduism and Buddhism (and even in parts of modernist Christianity), then we have made a limitation in the perspective that makes some generalizations and conclusions possible and necessary.

The Serpent Power is a key to the fully naturalistic realization of religiosity whereby faith in God is eliminated. There is no God but Shakti who is the guru!

This "creed" makes it clear that the Christian faith and the Shakti-religion stand against one another as Yahweh stood against Baal in the days of Elijah (1 Kings 17). And Paul saw "the powers and principalities" as the beaten army of the evil forces, and the church of Christ as the army of the victor. But Christ is not really like a victorious general! Christ is the suffering servant, not at least when he is victorious.

CHAPTER 7

An Exploration of the Book of Ecclesiastes in the Light of Buddha's Four Noble Truths[1]

Michal Solomon Vasanthakumar

Christian mission, however one defines it, needs contextualized messages.[2] Unless the mission considers its local context seriously and formulates its missiology accordingly, it will not be effective and relevant to the people to whom it hopes to bring the message of Jesus Christ. It has been often pointed out that in many countries Christianity is still an imported "potted plant" and not a "transplanted plant"[3] in the local soil. Since the traditional Christian Missiology[4] is typically Western, it is irrelevant to the non-Western countries to a great extent. Therefore, various attempts have been made in recent decades to contextualize the Christian message, and consequently several indigenous theologies emerged in the Third World. In such contextualized theologies, the context of the people is considered as the decisive factor in formulating missiological concepts.[5] In fact, such contexualizations are extremely vital and valuable since our living contexts are different to that of the contexts of the Bible and traditional Christian Theology. This essay is an attempt to contextualize the Christian message to the Buddhists, using the book of Ecclesiastes in the light of Buddha's Four Noble Truths.

Since traditional Christian missiology begins with the subject of God, Buddhists find it difficult to comprehend its fundamental message, for the simple reason that their mind is not ready to accept theistic notions of Christianity at once.[6] Hence the starting point of Christian missiology in Buddhist contexts should be anthropological and not theological. As God had contextualized himself and became a man to reach the human beings, Christian missiology must incarnate itself in Buddhist conceptual spheres in order to relate to them in a meaningful way. In this respect, the book of Ecclesiastes could become a bridge which would take the Christian message to the Buddhist mind in a meaningful way, for this Old Testament wisdom literature deals with a familiar subject to the Buddhists, even though it proposes a different solution to the human predicament.

(A) The Methodology of Buddha and Qoheleth

The Buddha and Qoheleth (author of the book of Ecclesiastes) have employed similar methodologies to analyze human existence and propose solutions to its predicament. The Buddha explained the Four Noble Truths after his enlightenment in consequence to his intense meditation on human life, which he had personally experienced, observed, and analyzed. Likewise, Qoheleth's depictions are based on his own experiences and observations. Hence, both have discovered similar facts about human life, but analyzed and proposed solutions differently according to their religious and cultural contexts. Since the Buddha has denied the existence of God and human soul, his doctrines do not have any reference to these concepts. Qoheleth, however, due to his Hebraic religious background had made references to these aspects.

Nevertheless, the Buddhists could appreciate and comprehend Qoheleth's writings, due to their familiarity of the similar analysis of the Buddha.

The Buddha had experienced and observed the pleasurable as well as the pathetic aspects of human life. His youth was filled with pleasure and extravagant luxury. He was protected from seeing pain and suffering, and spared contact with death and decay. Nevertheless, his satisfaction from the earthly pleasures enjoyed in his luxurious palace decreased as time went by, and he began to search a deeper meaning to his existence, instead of just enjoying the pleasures and being satisfied. When the Buddha was twenty-nine, he went beyond the protecting walls of his palace and for the first time saw the real life in the form of four people—old, sick, dead, and ascetic. This shocked him and he was extremely sorrowful over what he saw. Hence, he renounced all the pleasures of the royal life, left his wife and son, and traveled to various places studying under various Brahmanic sages. Yet his studies did not provide satisfactory answers to his quest concerning the meaning of life. Then he practiced the extreme forms of asceticism of the Jains. He surpassed the ascetics in self-mortification, but was unable to find answers to his spiritual quest. After six years of this wandering ascetic life, he went to Bodh Gaya and meditated under a Bo tree for seven weeks until he was enlightened.[7]

The initial discourse of the Buddha after his enlightenment, known as the Four Noble Truths, contains his discovery of the condition, cause, and cure of universal suffering. In fact, the Buddha's meditations concerning human life are based on his observations and experiences of life. Even four weeks after his enlightenment the Buddha meditated on the truths he had discovered. Hence, to a great extent, the Buddha used his mind to discover the facts of human existence that were based on his personal experiences and observations.

As the Buddha has observed and contemplated on human life, Qoheleth too has used his eyes and mind to analyze the human predicament. He too, like the Buddha, has discovered the realities of human life, subjectively by experiencing it in his own life and objectively by observing and investigating the lives of other human beings. His analysis and depictions are the product of human research similar to that of the Buddha. In fact, "he does not appeal to revelation or any kind of special insight into God or the world."[8] On the contrary he constantly remarks, "I have seen" (Eccles. 1:14; 3:10; 5:13; 6:1; 7:15; 10:5, 7), or similar expressions such as "I saw" (Eccles. 2:13; 3:16, 22; 4:4, 15; 8:10, 17; 9:13), "I see" (Eccles. 2:24), "I looked and saw" (Eccles. 4:1), and "I realized" (Eccles. 5:18). Qoheleth's expression, "I applied my mind" in 8:9 refers to using his mind to evaluate his observation. It "serves to introduce a reflection."[9] Qoheleth uses this expression to "indicate his focused, deeply personal, disciplined pursuit of the object of his study."[10] Hence it is similar to that of Buddha's meditation.

Regarding his method of discovering the state of human dilemma Qoheleth remarked, "I devoted myself to study and explore by wisdom all that is done under the heaven" (Eccles. 1:13). The expression "by wisdom" indicates that Qoheleth's discovery is "characterized and guided by wisdom."[11] The two words that he employs to describe his method of investigation point to "the exhaustiveness of his study."[12] These words, study (*lidros*) and explore (*tur*), though "near synonymous"[13] have slightly different meanings. The first term means, "to penetrate to the root of the matter"[14] or "search deeply into something."[15] The second word means "to search thoroughly over the widespread"[16] or "to investigate it from all sides."[17] Hence the two verbs refer to the "deepness and wideness of the search."[18] Qoheleth, like the Buddha, has used his mind and wisdom to investigate the human predicament thoroughly. The phrase "all the things that are done under the sun"

(Eccles. 1:13) indicates the comprehensiveness of Qoheleth's observations and investigations.

(B) The Discoveries of Buddha and Qoheleth

The Buddha has depicted his understanding of human life as *dukkha* in Pali language, and Qoheleth had expressed the same thing in Hebrew as *hebel*. Both *dukkha* and *hebel* have wide range of meanings but fundamentally agree in their basic connotations. Therefore, the Buddhists could comprehend what Qoheleth is saying about human life.

The analysis of the Buddha concerning the human life is summed up in the concept of *dukkha*. In fact, "everything he had taught is related to *dukkha*. For him the entire teaching is just the understanding of *dukkha*… and the understanding of the way out of this unsatisfactoriness."[19] Thus his inaugural address after the enlightenment expresses this aspect of human life. In it the Buddha depicts the human condition as follows:

> Birth is *dukkha*, ageing is *dukkha*, sickness is *dukkha*, death is *dukkha*; sorrow, lamentation, pain, grief and despair are *dukkha*; association with unpleasant is *dukkha*, dissociation from the pleasant is *dukkha*, not to get one wants is *dukkha;* in short, the five aggregates of attachment are *dukkha*.[20]

According to the *Samyutta-Nikaya*, the Buddha saw that "the world is established on *dukkha*, is founded on *dukkha*."[21] For him the human existence is nothing else other than *dukkha*. In fact, life according to Buddhism is *dukkha*; it dominates all life, and it is the fundamental problem of life.

The Buddhist texts divide *dukkha* into three aspects. They are ordinary suffering (*dukkha-dukkha*), sufferings caused by changes (*Viparinama-dukkha*), and suffering as conditioned states (*samkhara-dukkha*). Birth, old age, sickness, death, association with unpleasant persons and conditions, not getting what one desires, grief, lamentation, distress—all such forms of physical and mental suffering, which are universally accepted as suffering or pain, are included in *dukkha* as ordinary suffering.[22] Sufferings caused by changes are the vanishing pleasant feelings or impermanent condition of happiness.

> A happy feeling, a happy condition in life, is not permanent, not everlasting. It changes sooner or later. When it changes, it produces pain, suffering, and unhappiness. This vicissitude is included in *dukkha* as suffering produced by change.[23]

The third aspect is the most important philosophical definition of *dukkha*. A person or a being according to Buddhism is a composite of five *skandhas* (matter, sensations, perception, mental formation, and consciousness) and, according to the Buddha, these five aggregates themselves are *dukkha*.[24] Therefore, "*dukkha* and the five aggregates are not two different things; the five aggregates themselves are *dukkha*."[25] Since the combination of these aggregates constitutes a being, *dukkha* is fundamental to all existence.

Though the First Noble Truth points out that *dukkha* is inherent in the fabric of life, Buddhist scholars insist that Buddha's doctrines are not totally pessimistic and opposed to the joys of human life.[26] Yet they admit that according to the Buddha happiness, too, is included in *dukkha*. Buddhism "does not deny the existence of happiness in the world… but it does emphasise that all forms of happiness (bar that of *Nibbana*) do not last."[27] Hence, according to the Buddha, human life is totally characterized and conditioned by *dukkha*.

Life according to Qoheleth is *hebel*, which is the "central keyword in the book of Ecclesiastes"[28] and generally rendered in English as "vanity." The NIV translates it as "meaningless." It occurs thirty-eight times in the book,[29] slightly over half of the number of times it appears in the entire Bible.[30] Qoheleth applies this term to a number of areas of human activities and shows that there is no meaning and value in them. The book begins and ends with the declaration "vanity of vanities, all is vanity" (Eccles. 1:2; 12:8). The word "all" in these verses literally means "the whole." Hence "all earthly experience, seen as a unit, is subject to vanity."[31] According to Qoheleth, vanity characterizes all human activities. Hence he says, "I have seen all the things that are done under the sun: all of them are meaningless, a chasing after the wind" (Eccles. 1:14).

Qoheleth leaves nothing out. He cannot find meaning in anybody or in anything. Hence he asks, "What does man gain from all his labor at which he toils under the sun?" (Eccles. 1:3). Such rhetorical question is a typical feature of this book. The question is repeated in 3:9 and 5:16. Variants of the phrase (containing the word for profit, *yitron*) are found in Ecclesiastes 2:11, 2:13, and 10:11. "It often tends… to suggest a negation: there is no profit from one's hard lot, the toil inherent in human existence."[32]

The term translated as "gain" (*yitron*) is also a key word in the book of Ecclesiastes. It occurs nine times in this book and nowhere else in the Old Testament (Eccles. 1:3; 2:11, 13; 3:9; 5:9, 16; 7:12; 10.10, 11). It derives from a verb (*ytr*), which means "to be left over" or "remain."[33] It is a commercial term, signifying "profit," that is, what is left over after expenses are met.[34] Accordingly, in this earthly life there is no profit left over for people's work. Since the earthly realm is subject to vanity, "there is no hope of finding ultimate gain or satisfaction from its resources."[35] "However much we acquire, in the end we are left with nothing at all."[36] Hence Qoheleth concludes that work, with which human beings are occupied in this world, is meaningless and gives no satisfaction.

In 2:18-23, Qoheleth states another reason for work being unable to satisfy human beings. People are not in a position to enjoy their earnings, for death forces them to leave their wealth to others. He realized that all his efforts and earnings might be wasted by others. Hence work did not bring real satisfaction to Qoheleth.

Qoheleth tried to find meaning and lasting satisfaction in pleasure. He set out to test its possibilities but found nothing that could bring real enjoyment. Hence he says, "I thought in my heart, come now, I will test you with pleasure to find out what is good? But that also proved to be meaningless" (Eccles. 2:1). Qoheleth sought to find joy in drink, music, and sex. He used his wealth to build houses, gardens, and enjoy all luxurious comforts (Eccles. 2:2-9). His wealth and all the pleasures that money could buy did not bring lasting satisfaction. Hence he says:

> I denied myself nothing my eyes desired; I refused my heart no pleasure. My heart took delight in all my work, and this was the reward for all my labor. Yet when I surveyed all that my hands had done and what I had toiled to achieve, everything was meaningless, a chasing after the wind (Eccles. 2:10-11).

Human endeavors, as well as pleasures and comforts, did not bring real enjoyment or lasting satisfaction. Hence Qoheleth sought to find meaning in wisdom, but that too disappointed him (Eccles. 2:12-17).

He sees the relative value of wisdom in comparison to folly in much the same way that he admits the reward of material pleasure. Further thought, however, leads him to contemplate the benefits of wisdom in the light of his impending death. Death renders all things, including wisdom, meaningless.[37]

Since both wise and fool share the same fate, Qoheleth regrets that he couldn't find meaning in wisdom (Eccles. 2:15-17). In Qoheleth's analysis of human life, death plays a major role. According to him the fact of death often reminds him the meaninglessness of this life. In fact, Qoheleth's "thinking was affected by his fear of death."[38] Since both wise and fool die, Qoheleth has concluded that pursuit of wisdom is meaningless (Eccles. 2:12-17). Similarly, considering the death of human beings and animals, since both die, Qoheleth has asserted that human beings have no advantage over the animals (Eccles. 3:19-21). According to Qoheleth the human existence is characterized by *hebel*. Hence he depicts life in this earth as "all the days of this meaningless life" (Eccles. 9:9).

(C) The Meaning of *Dukkha* and *Hebel*

Since the Buddha and Qoheleth have depicted human life in their respective languages, it is necessary for us to know the exact meaning of the terms they have employed in order to comprehend their messages in the correct perspective. The Buddha's depiction of human life as *dukkha* is generally understood as life filled with suffering or pain. But *dukkha* is one of the Pali words that cannot be translated adequately into other languages. No single word in English covers the wide range of meanings of *dukkha*. The common rendering of it as suffering or pain, "is an inadequate description of Buddha's general outlook."[39] In fact, it is "highly unsatisfactory and misleading."[40] "The word *dukkha* is defined variously as ill, suffering, pain and so on, which may be correct in certain contexts. But in other contexts… the term is used in wider senses."[41] *Dukkha* "represents the Buddha's view of life and the world, [and] has a deeper philosophical meaning and connotes enormously wider senses.[42]

From Buddha's description about happiness we can comprehend an important aspect of *dukkha*. Since Buddha saw happiness as *dukkha* because of its impermanent nature, it could be deduced that according to Buddha, *dukkha* means impermanence. When Buddha said that human life is *dukkha*, he explicitly pointed out that the five aggregates that constitute a person are *dukkha* for the basic reason that they are constantly changing and not permanent. Since the aggregates themselves are *dukkha*, it is evident that *dukkha* means impermanence too, for the aggregates are not permanent in themselves.

The changing, unstable nature of life is such that people are led to experience dissatisfaction, loss, and disappointment or frustration. Thus another aspect or meaning of *dukkha* according to the Buddha is unsatisfactoriness. In fact, Buddhist scholars refer to *dukkha* as unsatisfactoriness.[43] They point out that "where it is said that the five aggregates of grasping are *dukkha*, the term is used in the wider sense of unsatisfactory."[44] Referring to the Buddha's sermon on the First Noble Truth, they remark "here the word *dukkha* refers to all those things which are unpleasant, imperfect, and which we would like to be otherwise. It is both suffering and the general unsatisfactoriness of life."[45] It is admitted that the term *dukkha* in the First Noble Truth contains, quite obviously, the ordinary meaning of suffering, but in addition it also includes deeper ideas such as imperfection, impermanence, emptiness, and insubstantiality.[46] Thus in addition to suffering and pain, Buddha's understanding of *dukkha* includes impermanence, unsatisfactoriness, and insubstantiality. In fact, the Hebrew term employed by Qoheleth to depict human predicament has all these connotations.

The Hebrew term *hebel* is generally translated in English as vanity. Like the Pali expression *dukkha*, there is not a single word in English that will capture the full meaning of this significant Hebrew term. Different words are suggested by biblical scholars, such as "useless,"[47] "emptiness,"[48] "meaningless,"[49] "absurd,"[50] "futility,"[51] etc. The term "vanity" goes back to the Authorized Version's equivalent of Latin *vanitas*, which connotes emptiness and futility.[52] It is important to note that the modern use of the word vanity in the sense of empty pride or conceit was not in the original term. The Hebrew term literally means "breath" or "vapor."[53] Hence it could mean "without substance or reality."[54] Always it points to "something which is insubstantial or transitory or in some sense futile... It can refer to any activity which seems to be pointless."[55] Biblical commentators explain this term as "a wisp of vapor, a puff of wind, a mere breath—nothing you could get your hands on; the nearest thing to zero. That is the 'vanity' this book is about."[56] And "whatever is left after you break a soap bubble is vanity."[57] Hence whatever disappears quickly, leaves nothing behind and does not satisfy is *hebel*, vanity. In Ecclesiastes, "it is used for things that do not last, cannot be grasped, or are not worthwhile."[58]

Generally the word *hebel* has metaphorical use of that which is evanescent and unstable, hence in this book "meaningless," "frustration," or "futility."[59] *Hebel* occurs approximately thirty-two times outside the book of Ecclesiastes.[60] In thirteen passages it characterizes the idols,[61] hence these passages attribute "uselessness or meaninglessness to the idols."[62] In remaining passages, too,[63] *hebel* means meaninglessness and in some instances it connotes "temporary" or "fleeting."[64] In the book of Ecclesiastes these ideas, meaninglessness and transitoriness, are conveyed by the term *hebel*. A comparison with its use elsewhere makes it clear that Qoheleth knows and uses all its nuances.[65] The Septuagint consistently translates it by one Greek word *mataiotes*, which means emptiness, futility, purposelessness, and transitoriness. "The verdict of vanity in the book of Ecclesiastes includes brevity, unsubstantiality, unreliability, frailty, futility and deceit."[66] Hence, according to Qoheleth all is untrustworthy and unsubstantial. No endeavor will in itself bring permanent satisfaction, for the greatest joys are fleeting; everything is meaningless and impermanent. This clearly captures the meaning of the term *dukkha*, used by the Buddha to depict human existence.

Qoheleth also uses the phrase "chasing after the wind" to describe the term *hebel* in some instances.[67] In the old versions, this phrase has been translated as "vexation of spirit."[68] For *ruah* in Hebrew could mean "spirit" or "wind." Hence the meaning would be "frustration by the insoluble (vexing of spirit), or ambition for the unattainable (striving after wind)."[69] Yet the contexts of this phrase in the entire book favor the second meaning. "Since the wind, changeable and invisible, yields nothing, even were it to be caught."[70] Hence it describes the utter futility and foolishness in trying to find meaning and satisfaction in this life. For the Buddha and Qoheleth, human life is filled with frustration, suffering, unsatisfactoriness, impermanence, and insubstantiality.

(D) The Cause for *Dukkha* and *Hebel*

The Buddha and Qoheleth not only discovered the realities of human existence, but they had also sought the root cause or reason for the human predicament. According to the Buddha it is the human desires or cravings that bring *dukkha*. The Second Noble Truth in Buddha's initial sermon states this as follows:

> The noble truth of the origin of *dukkha* is this: It is this thirst (craving) which produces re-existence and re-becoming, bound up with passionate greed.[71]

Desire or craving, the cause or the origin of *dukkha*, is described in the Pali texts as *tanha*, which literally means "thirst" and "clearly refers to demanding desires or drives which are ever on the lookout for gratification."[72] *Tanha* includes not only desire for, and attachment to, sense-pleasure, wealth, and power, but also desire for and attachment to ideas, views, opinions, theories, conceptions, and beliefs. According to the analysis of the Buddha, all the troubles and strife in the world, from the little quarrels in families to the great wars between nations, arise out of this selfish thirst.

Like the Buddha, Qoheleth also sees human desires as the root cause for the human predicament. Though he does not express it in such phraseology, his description resembles to the explanation of the Buddha. According to Qoheleth's Hebraic orientation, human cravings or desires are nothing other than human will or selfish motivations in opposition to the divine will. Instead of constantly seeking and living according to the will of God as the Bible admonishes, people live as the way they want, thus bringing sorrow and unsatisfactoriness into their lives. This type of life could be described in Buddhist way of thinking as life conditioned by cravings. It is a life conditioned and characterized by human desires only. Qoheleth describes such a life in reference to 'under the sun', a phrase that occurs nowhere in the Bible except in the book of Ecclesiastes.[73] Like the term *hebel*, this expression is an important concept in the book of Ecclesiastes, used by Qoheleth twenty-nine times.[74] Qoheleth thus restricts his remarks to terrestrial human activity and work. Qoheleth's "frequent use of the phrase 'under the sun' highlights the restricted scope of his inquiry. His worldview does not allow him to take a transcendent yet immanent God into consideration in his quest for meaning."[75] Hence Qoheleth's approach and that of the Buddha were almost the same. Both have tried to find out meaning in human life without considering God's dealings in human affairs. For the Buddha human desires bring sorrows and frustrations and for Qoheleth human desires are godless self-oriented motivations.

(E) Proposed Solutions to *Dukkha* and *Hebel*

The fundamental difference between Buddha's and Qoheleth's theses lies in their proposed solutions to the human predicament. According to the Buddha, one has to eliminate the cause of *dukkha* by his or her own effort, in order to get rid of it. This is clearly stated in Buddha's Third Noble Truth, which is that of cessation of *dukkha*. This is the ultimate goal of the Buddhists, known as *nibbana*. Hence *nibbana* is known also as "extinction of *tanha*."[76] According to the Buddha, *nibbana* is the cessation or the extinction of craving.[77] Since *dukkha* originates from cravings, the extinction of cravings brings an end to *dukkha*. "With the giving up of craving one also gives up suffering and all that pertains to suffering. *Nibbana*, therefore, is explained as the extinction of suffering."[78]

According to the teachings of the Buddha, in order to extinguish the cravings and experience *nibbana* one has to follow the path Buddha has prescribed. It is generally known as the Middle Path[79] or the Noble Eight-Fold Path, which is composed of eight categories: right understanding, right thought, right speech, right action, right livelihood, right effort, right mindfulness, and right concentration. The Buddha's entire teachings more or less depend on this Path. These eight categories of the Path should be followed simultaneously and not one after the other. They are all linked together, and each helps the cultivation of the other. The Eight-Fold Path aims at promoting and perfecting the three essentials of Buddhist training and discipline. These are ethical conduct (*sila*), mental discipline (*samadhi*), and wisdom (*panna*).[80]

The Eight-Fold Path is a way of life to be practiced and developed by each individual. It requires self-discipline in body and mind, self-development, and self-purification. It is a path leading to the realization of Ultimate Reality, to complete freedom and peace through moral, spiritual, and intellectual perfection.[81]

According to the Buddha, one has to follow the Eight-Fold Path to emancipate from *dukkha*. Qoheleth, on the other hand, admonishes people to bring God into their lives to end *hebel* and enjoy life. In fact, he has divided the human life into two spheres as realms of God and man. "God is in heaven, and you upon earth (Ecc. 5:2) is an underlying assumption throughout the text."[82] Earthly life without reference to God is depicted in terms of "under the sun" in the book of Ecclesiastes. Hence according to Qoheleth, "life will never be meaningful 'under the sun' until we make contact with the One who is above the sun."[83] Under the sun life is characterized by *hebel*. Therefore human beings gain nothing "under the sun" (Eccles. 1:3); the "earth," which is dominated by futility "goes on for ever" (Eccles. 1:4); no new thing can take place "under the sun" (Eccles. 1:9-11). Qoheleth sought out what was done "under the sun" (Eccles.1:13) and evaluated what resources could be found "under the sun" (Eccles. 1:14). His quest for pleasure, likewise, found no hope of gain "under the sun" (Eccles. 2:11); what is done "under the sun" was grievous to him (Eccles. 2:17).

When Qoheleth describes the life under the sun, which is *hebel*, God is out of his account. But when God was introduced everything changed. Instead of frustration and meaninglessness there is a joyful life for human beings from God. Hence "the hand of God" (Eccles. 2:24), "the joy of man" (Eccles. 2:25; 3:12; 5:18, 20; 9:7; 11:7-9), and "the generosity of God" (Eccles. 2:26; 3:13; 5:19) are dominating themes in Qoheleth's thesis. On seven occasions Qohelet has declared that human beings have a joyful "portion" from God (Eccles. 2:10, 21; 3:22; 5:18, 19; 9:6, 9), and on twelve occasions God is depicted as a giver of joyful life (Eccles. 1:13; 2:26 3:10, 11; 5:18, 19; 6:2; 8:15, 9:9; 12:7, 11). Intermingled with its pessimism, Qoheleth's thesis contains "invitations to a different outlook altogether, in which joy and purpose are found when God is seen to be 'there' and to be characterised supremely by generosity."[84] Hence Qoheleth has described God as the giver of good gifts (Eccles. 2:26), sovereign over everything (Eccles. 7:13-14), and the creator to whom people owe everything (Eccles. 12:1, 7).

(F) Qoheleth's Conclusion and the Buddhists

Qoheleth's conclusion may sound strange to the Buddhists for he has a twofold theistic advice to offer. One is to fear God and the other is to follow God's commandments. He also mentions the judgment of God.

> Now all has been heard, here is the conclusion of the matter. Fear God and keep His commandments for this is the whole duty of man. For God will bring every deed into judgment, including every hidden thing whether it is good or evil (Eccles. 12:13-14).

(a) The Buddhists and the Concept of God

"Buddhism has no God to whom it can refer as Creator, Lord, Saviour etc, who can be described as omniscient, omnipotent, etc."[85] Hence Qoheleth's admonition, "fear God," may seem difficult to comprehend by the Buddhists who rationalize and reject the existence of God. Nevertheless, since according to Qoheleth's background the fear of God is also the beginning of wisdom (Prov. 1:7; 9:10),[86] the Buddhists should be exposed to the fact that divine wisdom is necessary for experience a meaningful and eradicate *dukkha*. According to Qoheleth, it is human wisdom that is meaningless, but the wisdom of God is essential for human beings to enjoy a meaningful life. The Buddhists, on the other hand, give much emphasis to wisdom, which according to them guides people in their path to eradicate *dukkha*. Hence, Christians must show the Buddhists that human wisdom is not enough to achieve their ultimate goal and that all human beings are in need of God's wisdom (cf. 1 Cor. 1:16-21). Further,

> the fear of God is the realisation of His unchanging power and justice (Eccles. 3:14)… [which] delivers from wickedness and self-righteousness (Ecc. 7:8) and leads to a hatred of sin (Eccl. 5:6f.; 8:12f.).[87]

This will enable the Buddhists to extinguish the evil desires, for which they strive by their own efforts.

The necessity of God could be explained to the Buddhists in relation to their doctrine of *anatta*. Lynn de Silva has correctly pointed out how this doctrine could help the Buddhists to understand the necessity of God. It is his contention that Christianity "carries the doctrine of *anatta* to its logical conclusion."[88] Thus de Silva argues, "if *anatta* is real, God is necessary; it is in relation to the reality of God that the reality of *anatta* can be meaningful."[89] De Silva points out the awareness people have towards the Transcendent Reality[90] and remarks; "this transcendental quality is to be found in man's relationship to God."[91] To substantiate his thesis, de Silva highlights the apparent difficulties in Buddhist concept of *anatta* and supplements it by his Christian understanding of it, and says that "the Biblical understanding of ... *anatta* can enable us to understand what the term God means."[92] Thus de Silva brings God into the picture and expects the Buddhists to realize the need for God within the Buddhist philosophical system.

Buddhism, while denying the self (this is the crux of *anatta*), teaches that a man must depend on himself for his own deliverance. For de Silva, this is "one of the deepest dilemmas in Buddhism."[93] So he asks, "What is the self that denies the self and at the same time asserts that it alone can save the self?"[94] The ultimate goal to which Buddhist morality is directed is *nibbana*, and that is achieved by self-effort. According to Buddhism people have the power to achieve this goal. Therefore, de Silva says, "to deny the self and to affirm self-sufficiency is a contradiction."[95] According to him it is the Bible that takes the doctrine of *anatta* seriously and points out the inability of human beings to save themselves. Thus he remarks,

> In fact it can be shown that the Bible takes what is implied in the doctrine of *anatta* more seriously than Buddhism does, for the Biblical teaching is that man is nothing by himself and can do nothing by himself about his salvation. The doctrine of *anatta* therefore points to the truth that man cannot save himself by his own efforts and is in need of saving grace.[96]

As De Silva positively affirms, "it is in relation to the unconditioned (God) that the full depth and significance of *anatta* can be understood."[97] That is, in view of *anatta*, God becomes indispensable. Thus by emphasizing *anatta* Christians could make an attempt to convince the Buddhists the necessity of divine help in attaining the ultimate goal in religious pursuit.[98] There is no doubt that Qohelet's conclusion could be communicated to the Buddhists by explaining the full implications of the doctrine of *anata*.

In contemporary Sri Lanka, the Buddhists' ultimate goal of *nibbana* is considered as a present living experience. According to them "*nibbana* is a state to be attained here and now; in this very life and not a state to be attained only after death."[99] A person can attain *nibbana* "even while alive, by rooting out lust, hate, and delusion."[100] Accordingly, when a person totally eradicates lust, hate and delusion he is liberated from the shackles of *samsara*, from repeated existence.[101] Hence *nibbana* becomes a "living experience," characterized by four special attributes: happiness, moral perfection, realization, and freedom.[102] Likewise, life with God according to Qoheleth has the same happiness, joy, and freedom. Hence he concludes his thesis with the twofold admonition of fearing God and following his commandments. Since the Buddhists in Sri Lanka go behind the gods for a prosperous and peaceful life, Christians can introduce Jesus Christ to them who came to give humanity a meaningful life.

Jesus Christ is the ultimate answer to Qoheleth's conclusion of meaninglessness under the sun. Jesus emptied himself of his divine prerogatives to subject himself of the world "under the sun" in order to free us of the chaos to which God subjected the world after the fall into sin (cf. Rom. 8:18-27 and Gal. 3:3).[103]

(b) The Buddhists and the Laws of God

Qoheleth's second admonition to keep God's commandments is not a difficult advice for the Buddhists, for they too have similar commandments in the Eight-Fold Path, which the Buddha had enumerated in his Fourth Noble Truth. God's commandment in the book of Ecclesiastes is not restricted to the Mosaic Law but they refer to "all that is known to be God's Will."[104] God has revealed his will both in human conscience and in his word. Ecclesiastes 3:11 speaks about the divine work in human hearts. Romans 2:14-15 explicitly states that God has written his commandments in the hearts of people who do not have the Book of Law which was given to the Jews.

Indeed, when Gentiles, who do not have the law, do by nature things required by the law, they are a law for themselves, even though they do not have the law, since they show that the requirements of the law are written on their hearts, their conscience also bearing witnesses, and their thoughts are accusing, now even defending them (Rom. 2:14-15).

Hence, the non-Christians, "although they do not have the law in their hands, they do have its requirements in their hearts, because God has written them there."[105] The Bible clearly teaches that God has revealed himself to all human beings,[106] which is theologically known as General Revelation.[107] Thus, God's existence and some of his attributes are known to all human beings, and "the basic requirements of the law are stamped on human hearts."[108] Therefore it could be concluded that the moral teachings of the Buddha were related to this phenomenal and mysterious work of God in human hearts despite his denial of God. By explaining the nature of the ethical teachings of the Buddha via general revelation, Christians can communicate the commandments of God to the Buddhists. It could be done by pointing out the similarities of the ethical teachings of the Buddha and those that are found in the Bible. In fact, many have seen the similar teachings of both religions but wrongly concluded this phenomenon as Buddhist influence on the biblical writings.[109] The similarities were not necessarily due to such influences, but were mainly due to the general revelation of God.

Conclusion

According to the Bible, all religions are nothing other than human responses to divine revelation and human attempts to reach God, even though they do not conform to the Judeo-Christian standards.[110] They are "a mixture of human response and divine revelation."[111] As the Bible declares, and human experience demonstrates, people are religious because of the intuitive awareness they have regarding the divine. This innate knowledge is due to the divine image within the constitution of human beings,[112] and the divine self-disclosure in the human conscience.[113] Human religions do have diabolical and immoral aspects, but they are due to the sin, ignorance, and fallibility that are inherent in human nature. Nevertheless, people with all their errors and evils seek God in response to divine revelation, and it is the responsibility of Christians to recognize this religious instinct without condemning it and attributing everything in other religions to Satan. In this respect, Paul, the greatest apostle of Christianity, set an excellent example in Athens. Although that city was full of idols, and idolatry was condemned by God, and whilst Paul was greatly distressed by the religious practices of the people (Acts 17:16), instead of condemning them, he commended their religious observances (Acts 17:22). Paul was not endorsing or sanctioning idolatry, but neither was he approaching the non-Christians with a polemical mentality. In Paul's approach, "we have a respectful recognition of religious endeavors,"[114] for it was "a cultured compliment to the distinguished audience."[115] Such a positive attitude and broadmindedness are vital when encountering the people of other faiths.[116] With such an attitude the Christians can use the book of Ecclesiastes to help the Buddhists to find an answer to their spiritual quest.

Notes

[1] Originally, an extended version of this essay was presented by the author in 1999 at Dharma Deepika Missiological consultation, held in Madras, under the title *A Missiological Manifesto for the Sri Lankan Buddhist Context*. The present version is extensively revised for the SEANET conference 2003.

[2] Defending the contextualized messages does not mean that the central and essential aspects of the Christian gospel need changes. On the contrary, it is indigenizing the gospel in terms of making it relevant to the context. In other words, it is taking the context of the listeners seriously and being sensitive to their ethos.

[3] This famous dictum of Daniel T. Niles is cited in Douglas J. Elwood, *Asian Christian Theology: Emerging Themes*, Philadelphia. Westminster, 1980, p. 27.

[4] Traditional Christian Theology, or Missiology and Traditional Christianity in this essay refer to the western theology we have received from the missionaries of the colonial period.

[5] Interpreting the biblical text in the light of the contemporary context does not mean that the original context of the text is ignored or forgotten. On the contrary, it is being faithful to the biblical text and becoming flexible to the contemporary context at the same time. As John Stott has admonished "we are called to the difficult and even painful task of double listening. That is, we are to listen carefully both to the ancient Word and to the modern world, in order to relate the one to the other with a combination of fidelity and sensitivity" (*The Contemporary Christian*, Leicester: IVP, 1992, p. 13).

[6] As far as the Buddhists are concerned, traditional Christian Theology is irrelevant to their contexts and insensitive to their ethos. It does not make sense to the Buddhist mind since the fundamental tenets of both religions differ greatly. Traditional Christian Theology depends on divine initiative

in human salvation. God's self-revelation to humanity and divine substitutionary activities in relation to redemption are stressed. Christianity also highlights the depravity of human nature to the extent that people cannot achieve salvation on their own, without divine aid. Buddhism, on the other hand, while rejecting the existence and activities of God, focuses on human beings and their ability to achieve redemption from the sufferings that relate to the existence of living beings. According to Buddhism, people are inherently good and have the ability to achieve salvation without help from God. It rejects the theistic position of Christianity and the constitutional nature of human beings as taught in the Bible.

[7] Bhikkhu Bodhi, *The Buddha and His Dhamma*, Kandy: Buddhist Publication Society, 1999, pp. 3-8.

[8] Tremper Longman III, *Ecclesiastes: The New International Commentary on the Old Testament*, Grand Rapids: Eerdmans, 1998, p. 81.

[9] Roland Murphy, *Ecclesiastes: Word Biblical Commentary*, Waco: Word Books, 1992, p. 11.

[10] Longman III, *Ecclesiastes*, p. 78.

[11] *Ibid.* 79.

[12] Michael A. Eaton, *Ecclesiastes: Tyndale OT Commentaries*, Leicester: IVP, 1983, p. 62.

[13] Longman III, *Ecclesiastes*, p. 79.

[14] Robert Gordis, *Koheleth – The Man and His World*, New York: Schocken Books, 1968, p. 209.

[15] Eaton, *Ecclesiastes*, p. 62

[16] *Ibid.* p. 62.

[17] Gordis, *Koheleth*, p. 209.

[18] E. W. Hengstenberg, *A Commentary on Ecclesiastes*, Evansville: Sovereign Grace, 1960, pp. 61-63.

[19] Piyadassi Thera, *The Buddha's Ancient Path,* Kandy: Buddhist Publication Society, 1996, p. 38.

[20] The Buddha's first sermon, the *Dhamma-cakka-pavattana-sutta* (Discourse Setting in Motion the Wheel of Truth) is recorded in the *Samyutta-nikaya* LVI. This is believed to have consisted of a brief statement of the Middle Way, the Four Noble Truths, and the Eight-Fold Path and delivered to his first five disciples in the Deer Park near the ancient city of Benares.

[21] *Samyutta-Nikaya*, I

[22] Piyadassi, p. 43. "It refers to the uninvited models of physical pain... It also accommodates the span of daily anxieties and apprehensions that are a permanent feature of life in a complicated and perturbed world" (Matthews, *Craving and Salvation*, p.7).

[23] Walpola Rahula, *What the Buddha Taught*, Oxford: Oneworld Publications, 1959, p.20.

[24] Piyadassi, p.44.

[25] Rahula, p. 20.

[26] Piyadassi, p. 42; Rahula, pp. 17-18.

[27] Peter Harvey, *An Introduction to Buddhism,* Cambridge: Cambridge University Press, 1992, p. 48.

[28] R. C. Van Leeuwen, "Vanity" in *The International Standard Bible Encyclopaedia Volume Four*, ed. G. W. Bromiley, Grand Rapids: Eerdmans, 1993, p. 966.

[29] Cf. 1:1, 14; 2:1, 11, 15, 17, 19, 21, 23, 26; 3:19; 4:4, 7, 8, 16; 5:7, 10; 6:2, 4, 11, 12; 7:6, 15; 8:10, 14; 9:9; 11:8, 10; 12:8.

[30] Murphy, p. lviii.

[31] Eaton, pp. 56-57.

[32] Murphy, p. 7.

[33] Longman III, p. 65.

[34] M. J. Dahood, "Canaanite-Phoenician Influence in Qoheleth" in *Biblica* Vol. 33 (1952), p. 221.

[35] Eaton, p. 57.

[36] Stuart Olyott, *A Life Worth Living and a Lord Worth Loving: Ecclesiastes & Song of Solomon*, Hertfordshire: Evangelical Press, 1986, p.18.

[37] Longman III, p. 94.

[38] *Ibid.* p. 94

[39] Bruce Matthews, *Craving and Salvation: A Study in Buddhist Soteriology*, Canada: Wilfrid Laurier Press, 1983, p.6.

[40] Rahula, p.16.

[41] David J. Kalupahana, *Buddhist Philosophy: A Historical Analysis*, Honolulu: University of Hawaii Press, 1976, p. 37.

[42] *Ibid.* p. 17.

[43] Piyadassi, p. 38.

[44] Kalupahana, p. 37.

[45] Harvey, p. 48.

[46] Rahula, p. 17.

[47] This is the rendering of the Good News Bible.

[48] New English Bible uses this word.

[49] New International Version has this word.

[50] Michael V. Fox argues for this term ("The Meaning of *hebel* for Qohelet" in *Journal of Biblical Literature*, 105 [1986], pp. 409-427) Albert Camus insists that this is the exact equivalent of hebel (*Qohelet and His Contradictions*, Sheffield: Almond Press, 1989).

[51] Revised English Bible and New Jerusalem Bible employ this term.

[52] Leeuwen, p. 966. New Revised Standard Version and New American Bible prefer this term and scholars such as J. L. Crenshaw (*Ecclesiastes: Old Testament Library*, Philadelphia: Westminster Press, 1987), R. Gordis, *Koheleth: The Man and His World. A Study of Ecclesiastes*, New York: Schocken Books, 1968), R. E. Murphy, (*Ecclesiastes: Word Biblical Commentary Volume 23*, Waco: Word Books, 1992), and C. L. Seow, (*Ecclesiastes: Anchor Bible Commentary*, Garden City: Doubleday, 1997) also employ this traditional word.

[53] Hence R. B. Y. Scott uses this term in his commentary (*Proverbs and Ecclesiastes: Anchor Bible Commentary*, Garden City: Doubleday, 1965).

[54] L. O. Richards, *Expository Dictionary of Bible Words,* Basingstoke: Marshall Pickering, 1988, p. 608.

[55] Robert Davidson, *Ecclesiastes and Song of Solomon,* Edinburgh: Saint Andrew Press, 1986, p. 9.

[56] Derek Kidner, *The Message of Ecclesiastes*, Leicester: IVP, 1976, p. 22.

[57] Warren W. Wiersbe, *Be Satisfied*, Wheaton: Victor Books, 1990, p. 15.

[58] R. Murphy and E. Huwiler, *Proverbs, Ecclesiastes, Song of Songs: New International Biblical Commentary*, Peabody: Hendrickson, 1999, p. 181.

[59] J. Stafford Wright, *Ecclesiastes: The Expositor's Bible Commentary*, Grand Rapids: Zondervan, 1991, p. 1152

[60] Longman III, p. 63.

[61] Deut. 32:21; 2 Kings 17:15; Pss. 31:6; 57:13; Jer. 2:5; 8:19; 10:8, 15; 14:22; 16:19; 51:18; Jon. 2:8; Zech. 10:2.

[62] Longman III, p. 63.

[63] 2 Kings 17:15; Job 9:29; 21:34; 27:12; 35:16; Pss. 31:7; 39:6; 62:9; 78:33; 94:11; Prov.13:11; Isa. 30:7; Lam. 4:17.

[64] Pss. 39:4-5; 144:4; Job 7:16; Prov. 31:30.

[65] Kiel K. Seybold, "hebhel" in *Theological Dictionary of the Old Testament*, ed. G. J. Botterweck and H. Ringgren, Grand Rapids: Eerdmans, 1978, p. 318.

[66] Eaton, p. 56.

[67] Eccles. 1:14, 17; 2:11, 17, 26; 4:4, 6, 16; 6:9.

[68] See Revised Standard Version and the Authorized Version.

[69] Eaton, p. 63.

[70] Murphy, p. 13.

[71] This explanation is found in many other discourses recorded in the early Buddhist scriptures.

[72] Harvey, p. 53. While elucidating the nature of *tanha* the Buddha identifies three aspects of cravings. Thus in the *Mahavagga* of the *Vinaya* the Buddha has said: "It is this *tanha* which produces re-existence and re-becoming, and which is bound up with passionate greed, and which finds fresh delight now here and now there, namely, thirst of sense-pleasure (*kama-tanha*), thirst for existence and becoming (*bava-tanha*), and thirst for non-existence (self-annihilation, *vibhava-tanha*)."

[73] It is, however, conceptually similar to the expressions "under heaven" (Ex. 17:14; Deut. 7:24; 9:14; Eccles. 22:3; 3:1).

[74] Eccles. 1:3, 9; 2:11, 17, 18, 19, 20, 22; 3:16; 4:1, 3, 7, 15; 5:14, 19; 6:1, 12; 7:11; 8:9, 15, 17, 9:3, 6, 9, 11, 13; 10:5.

[75] Longman, p. 66.

[76] Rahula, p. 35. Etymologically *nibbana* (*ni+vana*) means "freedom from cravings," a "departure from craving," or in Sanskrit *nirvana* (*nir+va*) means "to cease blowing" or "to be extinguished" (Piyadassi, p. 67).

[77] *Majjhima-Nikaya* 28th *sutta*.

[78] Piyadassi, p. 68.

[79] It is middle path because it avoids two extremes: "one extreme being the search for happiness through the pleasures of the senses, which is 'low, common, unprofitable and the way of ordinary people;' the other being the

search for happiness through self-mortification different forms of asceticism, which is 'painful, unworthy and unprofitable.' Having himself first tried these two extremes, and having found them to be useless, the Buddha discovered through personal experience the Middle Path 'which gives vision and knowledge, which leads to Calm, Insight, Enlightenment, Nirvana" (Rahula, p. 45).

[80] Ethical conduct is built on the conception of universal love and compassion for all living beings, which includes right speech, right action and right livelihood. Right effort, right mindfulness and right concentration are included in the mental discipline. The remaining two factors, right thought and right understanding constitute wisdom.

[81] Rahula, p. 45.

[82] Eaton, p. 44.

[83] Selwyn Hughes, *Ecclesiastes: The Search for Meaning*, Surrey: CWR, 1993, p. 5.

[84] Eaton, p. 45.

[85] Chandima Wijebandara, *Early Buddhism: Its Religious and Intellectual Milieu*, Kelaniya, Sri Lanka: The Postgraduate Institute of Pali and Buddhist Studies, 1993, pp. 108-109.

[86] Psalms 110:10 also has the two aspects of Qoheleth's conclusion.

[87] Eaton, p. 156.

[88] Lynn de Silva, "Good News of Salvation to the Buddhists," in *International Review of Missions*, LVII (Oct. 1968), p. 450.

[89] Lynn de Silva, "Emergent Theology in The Buddhist Context," in *Asian Christian Theology: Emerging Themes*, ed. D. J. Elwood, Philadelphia: Westminster Press, 1980, p. 226.

[90] Lynn de Silva has dealt this in detail in his *Why Believe in God,* (Colombo: Christian Study Centre, 1970).

[91] Lynn de Silva, "Emergent Theology in The Buddhist Context," p. 228.

[92] Lynn de Silva, "Emergent Theology in the Buddhist Context" (booklet), Colombo: Ecumenical Institute for Study and Dialogue, 1979, p. 58.

[93] Lynn de Silva, "Good News of Salvation to the Buddhists," p. 450.

[94] *Ibid.* p. 450.

[95] *Ibid.* p. 451.

[96] *Ibid.* p. 451.

[97] Lynn de Silva, "Emergent Theology in the Buddhist Context" (booklet), p. 58.

[98] Lynn de Silva has elaborated this concept in more detail in his book, *Why Can't I Save Myself: The Christian Answer in Relation to Buddhist Thought* (Colombo: Christian Study Centre, 1967).

[99] Lily de Silva, *Nibbana as Living Experience,* Kandy: Buddhist Publication Society, 1996, p. 2.

[100] Piyadassi, p. 70.

[101] *Ibid.* p. 71.

[102] Lily de Silva, *Nibbana as Living Experience,* p. 2.

[103] Longman III, p. 284.

[104] Eaton, p. 156.

[105] John R. W. Stott, *The Message of Romans*, Leicester: IVP, 1994, p. 84.

[106] Cf. Romans 1:19-20; Psalms 19:1-4; Acts 14:15-17; 17:22-31.

[107] General Revelation is defined as "God's communication of himself to all persons at all times and all places... It refers to God's self-manifestation through nature, history and the inner being of the human person" (Millard J. Erickson, *Christian Theology*, Grand Rapids: Baker, 1988, pp. 153-154).

[108] Everett F. Harrison, *Romans: The Expositor's Bible Commentary Volume 10*, Grand Rapids: Zondervan, 1976, p. 31.

[109] For instance, Anagarika Dharmapala thought that Jesus' Sermon on the Mount was adopted from Buddhist sources. He remarked that the beatitudes harmonises with the Eight-Fold Path (A. W. Guruge, ed., *Return to Righteousness: A Collection of Speeches, Essays and Letters of Anagarika Dharmapala*, Colombo: Ministry of Education & Cultural Affairs, 1965, p. 696). Likewise, Holger Kersten, whose writings are popular among the Sri Lankan Buddhists, insists that "the Buddhist thought is found in Jesus' teaching" (*Jesus Lived in India*, Dorset: Element Books, 1995, pp. 99-102). According to him the Sermon on the Mount is a condensed version of Buddhism" (Kerston with E. R. Gruber, *The Original Jesus: The Buddhist Sources of Christianity*, Dorset: Element Books, 1995, p. viii). It is his contention that the Q source in the synoptic tradition as well as the Gospel of Thomas were the oldest material containing the original teachings of Jesus and that they are highly influenced by Buddhism (*Ibid.* pp. 111-112). Particularly, he asserts that Dhammapada and an extended collections of teachings based on Dhammapada is found in the Q source (*Ibid.* pp. 123).

[110] According to Romans chapter 1 idolatry and immorality are the natural consequences of the total or partial rejection of the divine revelation.

[111] C. Wright, *Thinking Clearly About the Uniqueness of Jesus.* Crowborough: Monarch Publications, 1997, p. 109.

[112] The Bible explicitly states that human beings are created in the image of God (Gen. 1:26-27). Though the Fall has affected the divine image to a

considerable extent (Gen. 3), it is not totally destroyed by human sin but distorted because of it. Even after the fall human beings are depicted as possessors of the divine image (Gen. 9:6, James 3:9).

[113] According to Psalm 19:1 and Romans 1:18-20 God has revealed himself both in creation and in human conscience. Paul says that the non-Jewish communities had divine laws inscribed in their hearts (Rom. 2:14-15). The similarities between the ethical precepts of Moses and Hamurabi were also due to this phenomenon.

[114] W. J. Larkin, *Acts: The IVP New Testament Commentary*. Downers Grove: IVP, 1995, p. 255.

[115] J. D. G. Dunn, *The Acts of the Apostles: Epworth Commentaries*. Peterborough: Epworth Press, p. 234.

[116] In Acts 17:22, the Greek word translated as "religious" (*deisidaimonesterous*) could be used either in good or bad sense. The KJV rendering "Ye are too superstitious" implies criticism. Hence "it is an unlikely way to start an evangelistic speech" (A. Fernando, *Acts: The NIV Application Commentary*, Grand Rapids: Zondervan, 1999, p. 475). F. F. Bruce, however, citing an ancient writer Lucian, says, it cannot be a complimentary expression, for "it was forbidden to use complimentary exordia in addressing the Areopagus court, with the hope of securing its goodwill" (Bruce, *The Books of Acts: The New International Commentary on the NT*, Grand Rapids: Eerdmans, p. 355). Nevertheless, we cannot be certain on how far Paul was abiding by this prohibition and the NIV rendering is more positive. Moreover, the Athenians' reputation for religious piety is well attested (W. J. Larkin, *Acts: The IVP New Testament Commentaries*, p. 255). Hence Paul was expressing commendation in his address, as K. Grayston has pointed out, "to provide a way into his address that would engage the attention of the audience" (Quoted in I. H. Marshall, *Acts: Tyndale New Testament Commentaries*, Grand Rapids: Eerdmans, p. 285).

CHAPTER 8

A Contextualized Presentation
of the Gospel in Thai Society

Alan R. Johnson

Introduction

Protestant missionaries first came to Thailand in 1828 and have worked without interruption to the present. However, the response to the message of the Gospel has been disturbingly slow when contrasted to the amount of time missionaries have been in the country and to the amount of effort expended in bringing the Gospel to the Thai people. There is no doubt that the Church in Thailand is growing. The latest edition of *Operation World* by Patrick Johnstone estimates adherents to Christianity to be 1.62% of the population now.[1] This breaks down to .42% Catholic and 1.18% Protestant. This is a significant community of almost 1 million people in a total population of just over 61 million. However, a large number of the Christian population is found among tribal peoples meaning that the actual percentage among Thai people is still quite low. Alex Smith found the following comment from a missionary to Thailand nearly one hundred years ago to be expressive of the feelings of many who have struggled to make Christ known in this land, "I believe there is no country more open to unrestrained missionary effort than Siam, but I believe that there can hardly be a country in which it is harder to make an impression."[2]

Reasons for this difficulty in gaining a response to the Gospel have been discussed in detail by Smith in his book *Siamese Gold*, which focuses on the history of the Christian movement in Thailand to the end of the 1970s through a church growth lens.[3] Smith points out that the obstacles include not only problems related to the Thai religion and culture but also to missionary methods and practices. Tom Wisely, in his doctoral dissertation at Fuller Theological Seminary, reviews the work of a number of the researchers on the growth of the church in Thailand and concludes that Protestant Christianity is a struggling religious minority and that "one of the major factors for its slow growth and its continuing struggle is its westernity"[4] Inevitably, however, discussion regarding the resistance of the Thai to the Gospel returns to the fact that Thailand presents unique difficulties since it is

> one of the few countries where Theravada Buddhism has traditionally been all but *de rigueur* and Buddhist concepts inform the speech and thought-forms and feelings of the great majority, if not all of Thai society.[5]

Although there are a number of factors involved in creating the feeling among the Thai that Christianity is foreign and the religion of the white man, the tremendous influence of Theravada Buddhism undoubtedly carries a great deal of weight in the matter. It becomes obvious that if we are to avoid, as Frances Hudgins calls it, "reciting conundrums" to our Thai listeners, then we must endeavor to contextualize our message so that the mind steeped in Buddhist thought and culture can begin to understand.[6]

The Need for Message Contextualization

I came to Thailand in 1986 excited to learn the Thai language so that I could begin to share the Good News with my newfound Thai friends. It did not take long for me to realize that even though I was speaking Thai, and people for the most part were polite and respectful as we talked, creating understanding involved a great deal more than simply encoding words in the local language. Even when we know intellectually that people think differently, the temptation to assume that our listeners are making the same meaning of our words as we intend exists.

Although there were a number of experiences over time that helped to bring the reality of the complexity of communication home to me, one stands out in particular. I was conducting an English lesson with a couple of Thai high school students and we were working through Luke 5 in the English text. We came to the point where I wanted to discuss the meaning of the passage and some of its implications, and since they were unable to converse easily in English, I said that we would switch into Thai. I asked the question, why did Peter fall on his knees and say that he was a sinful man? Without a moment's hesitation the young man said, "Because he killed all of those fish!"

I have to admit that his response caught me totally off guard. He was reading the text through his "Buddhist eyes" of the principle of not taking life. It made me realize in a much clearer fashion that the worldview, beliefs, values, and assumptions of my listeners were causing them to make different meanings than what I was intending, even when those understandings did not surface in conversation.

This started me on the process of trying to understand the meanings that people would be making in their minds from the terms and concepts that we use when we share the Gospel. It became clear to me that Thais were not simply rejecting the Gospel or Christianity; in reality, the situation was much more complicated. At least part of their lack of response is a rejection of the linguistic and stylistic wrapping in which missionaries and local Christians have presented the message. When the "wrapping" makes no sense, it keeps them from ever getting to the gift of the Good News inside.

Learning to wrap the message in a way that makes sense to local people is a part of the broader task known as contextualization. Hesselgrave and Rommen define contextualization as the attempt to communicate the message of the person, works, Word, and will of God in a way that is faithful to God's revelation and that is meaningful to respondents in their respective cultural and existential contexts.[7] This is both verbal and nonverbal and has to do with theologizing, Bible translation, interpretation and application, incarnational lifestyle, evangelism, Christian instruction, church planting and growth, church organization, worship style, and all the elements of what it means to be a community of faith in this world. This contextualization model takes seriously the message of the Bible as well as that of culture, and attempts to communicate the supra-cultural message in a way that is relevant to the hearer. Stephen Bevans calls this the "translation" model, which is an application of the principles of dynamic equivalence translation theory to the doing of theology.[8]

Endeavoring to do this kind of dynamic equivalence theologizing is an arduous task, which must be undertaken by a wide variety of workers both local and expatriate over an extended period of time. The purpose of this paper is to make a small contribution to this broader task in the specific area of contextualizing the communication of the Gospel message.

The material developed here grows out of hundreds of conversations with Thai people for over 16 years and reflects my interest in training Thai Christians in sharing their faith with their Buddhist neighbors. There are two assumptions that guide me in the development of this project. The first is that in sharing the Gospel, we need an approach where dialogue can take place, questions can be asked, and answers attempted. This is because, in my experience, a large part of the sharing of our faith is first the correcting of misunderstandings before one can move to the heart of the message. A canned approach that consists of a monologue may be politely listened to, but it does not create room for building true understanding. Second, it is my conviction that local Christians need to have a flexible track to run on when sharing the Gospel. This track provides a coherent sequence whereby a person can present and illustrate key points of the Gospel in a single conversation or over many meetings. The track allows for multiple entry points, the chance to ask questions and yet provides a way to share the message in a way that makes sense and has logical consistency.

I will begin with an examination of the religious context of Thai society consisting of a brief overview of classical Buddhism, a look at the broad religious context of Thailand, and a discussion of how Buddhism is integrated into Thai life. I then illustrate what the Gospel message sounds like to the ears of a Thai Buddhist listener. The final section develops some starting points to share the Gospel and the looks in some detail at each of the major points of the Gospel message.

The Religious Context of Thai Society

This section will begin with an examination of the major tenets of Theravada Buddhism, and then look in overview fashion at the belief systems present in the country and some of common conceptions people have about religion. The final part will study the actual practice of Buddhism in Thailand.

The Basic Tenets of Theravada Buddhism

The essence of Buddhism is found in the four Noble Truths, which Siddhartha Guatama discovered when he received enlightenment.[9] The term "Buddha" is a title and means one who is enlightened. Following the three principal transmission routes as Buddhism expanded out of India, there are today three major streams of Buddhism. The form of Buddhism followed in Sri Lanka and Southeast Asia is known as Hinayana (The Smaller Vehicle) or Theravada (The Way of the Elders). It is considered to be the stricter version that aligns itself most closely with the teaching and practice of the Buddha during his lifetime.

The First Noble Truth

The first of these truths concerns suffering or *dukkha*. All existence is marked by suffering, the cycle of birth, death, and decay. All unpleasantness, sorrow, pain, and being separated from the pleasant is *dukkha*.[10] In order to better understand the nature of suffering, we must look at the nature of reality as explained by the Buddha. There are three characteristics of all existence: *anicca*, which speaks of impermanence, *dukkha*, and *anatta*, which means no soul or no self.[11] Thus in Buddhist thinking, all sentient beings are merely bundles of aggregates, *khanda*,[12] that are impermanent and constantly changing. "To the Buddhists, separate individual existence is really a fiction."[13]

The Second Noble Truth

This background then leads to the Second Noble Truth concerning the cause of suffering, which is desire or *tanha*. *Tanha* is the desire for existence, the desire to preserve self (which really does not exist), and the desire for things.[14] This desire is caused by *avijja*, or ignorance. When people are ignorant of the nature of reality as expressed in the three characteristics of existence and ignorant of the First Noble Truth, then a desire for existence arises, and this desire creates karma (Thai-*kam*).[15]

Karma is a rather complicated concept that is variously understood within the framework of Buddhism. However, in its most basic sense, karma means action, which can be good or bad or neutral, but which produces a reaction.[16] Wan Petchsongkram notes that karma causes one to be born, it reinforces by making good deeds better and evil worse, it acts as a barrier by standing in the way either positively or negatively of the apparent course of one's life, and it can cause reversal of one's circumstances.[17] Thus it is karma that causes one to be caught in an endless cycle of rebirths and the consequent suffering. As an unchanging law of cause and effect, karma cannot be escaped; one will always be paid back, for both good deeds and bad, at some point in this life or in future lives.

The Third Noble Truth

The Third Noble Truth has to do with the cessation of suffering. When one is freed from the cycle of rebirths and of suffering by extinguishing desire, one enters Nirvana (Pali: *nibbana*; Thai: *nippaan*). "Nirvana is cessation, extinction, and detachment, but not only that, it is unconditioned and uncompounded, and it is stopping or eliminating causation."[18]

The Fourth Noble Truth

The Fourth Noble Truth deals with the path to salvation, the cessation of suffering. Known as the Noble Eightfold Path, this consists of right understanding, right intention, right speech, right action, right livelihood, right effort, mindfulness, and concentration.[19] This state is attainable by one's own efforts through renouncing the world and following this path. Meditation plays an important role in following the path and in renouncing the world. As it is practiced, there are two stages: *kammatthana* and *vipassana*.[20] The first form helps in creating detachment and understanding the impermanence of everything, while

> From *vipassana* arises wisdom...and when this wisdom comes
> we are able to relinquish our grasp on everything. We can cut
> ourselves off from the world for we are not any longer
> intoxicated with it.[21]

In this state, ignorance and desire have been destroyed and attachment has been broken so that one can enter *nibbana*.[22]

Overview of Religion in Thailand

A. Thomas Kirsch points out that there are three basic subsystems that make up what he calls Thai religion.[23] This consists of Theravada Buddhism, Brahmanism, and animism.[24] Kirsch notes that these three subsystems are, "functionally specialized so that they mutually support each other and rarely conflict."[25] John Davis says that Asian Theravardians

> see no inconsistency between an organic Animistic world
> view with its multitudinous gods and spirits, and a mechanistic
> Buddhist world view; they marry conveniently and live
> harmoniously together.[26]

In addition to these three subsystems, there is a continuum of practice within Buddhism itself.[27] There are intellectual Buddhists who emphasize the philosophical aspects, liberal Buddhists who try to conform Buddhism to modern life, folk Buddhists who practice traditional Buddhism in its modified animistic form, and nominal Buddhists, who consider themselves Buddhist by virtue of being Thai but do not participate in Buddhist practices or ceremonies.

For those who practice Buddhism at least to some degree, it is useful to think in terms of a continuum with *nippanistic* Buddhists on one end and karmatic Buddhists on the other. *Nippan* is the Thai term for Nirvana, the state that one enters upon breaking out of the cycle of rebirth. There are relatively few *nippanistic* Buddhists who are seriously endeavoring to follow the Eightfold Path of classical Buddhism. The majority of the practitioners can be considered karmatic Buddhists for whom the essence of their religious practice is the collecting of good merit in order to be reborn into a better state in the future. Here the focus is not so much upon the actual practice of Buddhism as on the ritual elements of making merit. For these people, the goal of liberation from their karma to reach Nirvana is too difficult and impractical, given the demands of daily life. The goal of bettering their karma through making merit via a variety of means becomes the core of their practice. This is the orientation of the folk Buddhist, mixing both Buddhist and animistic practice without any sense of incompatibility.

In discussing with a Thai Buddhist monk this issue of the compatibility of animistic shrine behavior with classical Buddhist doctrine, the explanation was couched in terms of the "strength" of a person's belief and understanding of truth. A strong person can walk up steps without any help, but a weaker person needs to use a railing. For those who can see the truth of the *dhamma* there is no need for animistic practices, but for other people who are not yet at that point to be able to understand the truth, the "railing" of spirit shrines and such beliefs is helpful.

There are two final points that are important to consider when looking at the religious context of Thai society. First, the Thai equate being Thai with being a Buddhist. They make a connection between nationality and religion. This is a major factor in their view that Christianity is a foreign religion and a stumbling-block in their understanding of the Christian religion. Their assumption is that all "white" people, like Europeans and Americans, are Christian and that everything they see in tourists and through media represent Christian values and behavior.

A second point is that Thais maintain the view that all religions are equally good because they teach us to be good people (*thuk sasana di muan gan sawn hai rao ben khon di*). Nearly every witnessing conversation I have ever been involved in has begun and ended with this saying. What is interesting is that although this is verbalized frequently when Thais come into contact with people of other religions, they do not mean by it that they completely believe in the true relativity of all religion. First, this saying seems to be a way for them to politely respond to the encounter with those of another religion in a face-saving and calm manner that avoids any tension of opposing beliefs. The reality is that they do not want their children or a relative or their own people to change their religion to another supposedly equally good option. Equality of religion is espoused, but it does not mean people feel that they should be able to choose freely among the different options. To be Thai is to be a Buddhist. Second, I have both read things written by monks and spoken with people who will use this saying and at the same time show their belief that Buddhism is the "real" truth by reinterpreting Christianity in Buddhist terms.

The Practice of Buddhism in Thailand

As can be seen from the discussion in the previous section, there is a wide range of belief and practice among those who call themselves Buddhists. In this section I want to examine how Thais in general approach their Buddhist faith.[28] These remarks are of necessity an oversimplification and generalization, but they are indicative of broad patterns found in Thai society.

The first point that must be made is that Thais on the whole have a limited knowledge of philosophical Buddhism.[29] I have seen a government study that came out some years ago indicating that 75% of the people in Bangkok have never been to a temple. Suntaree Komin's research on Thai values showed that people in the city showed increased activity at spirit shrines and less of a connection to temple activities.[30] Secondly, as mentioned above, there is a strong animistic influence in Thai religion. In a practical sense, this means that the chief concern of many is not how to follow in detail the tenets of philosophical Buddhism, but rather how to properly relate to the spirit world so as to gain help, peace, power, and other tangible benefits in the present life. Third, a survey has shown that for Thai farmers, their main concern was about money and personal security and not religious perfection.[31] Another survey done among converts in central Thailand showed that for 53% the love of God was a significant factor in their conversion (with 25% making it the primary cause).[32] This shows that for a large number of people, the deep human needs of love, acceptance, and security take precedence over the doctrinal considerations, which make the love of God a stumbling block for the strict Buddhist.[33] Finally, the hope of Nirvana is for most people very far off and not a practical reality.[34]

What then precisely are the "core" beliefs that Thais in general understand from their Buddhist background? Most would probably agree that playing a central role are the concepts of karma, merit (*bun*), and particularly the making of merit (*tam bun*) in order to improve one's lot both in this life and in following existences.[35] Kirsch also argues that reincarnation is a key concept as it relates to the concept of karma with its accumulation of rewards and punishments that are worked out over many lifetimes.[36] If many people do not completely understand the Four Noble Truths, they do probably understand (from their own personal experience) that life has suffering and that there is a cause and effect relationship in all of this. The common man also has some concept of the necessity to keep the moral precepts, which are a part of the Buddha's teaching. In the lower level of the *dhamma*,[37] these precepts are embodied in the five prohibitions (*sil ha*).[38] These prohibitions are certainly not always kept, but at the least they provide a common moral framework, which everyone understands, and give people an understanding of wrongdoing that centers on the actual committing of an evil deed or act.[39]

In a practical sense, people are interested in bettering their present lives or succeeding ones by the collection of merit and the avoidance of demerit (*baab*). The other-worldly aspects of true

Buddhism, though expressed through Buddhist ritual[40] and understood at least to a degree by the general populace, tend to be pursued only by those who are older and who have the time to expend in religious pursuits. Those who have families and jobs are tied to this-world concerns and often only have time to give to the gaining of merit through ritual means.

Hearing the Gospel through Thai Buddhist Ears

As I began to understand the influence of Buddhist thought in the decoding of the Gospel message as we typically encode it in the Thai language, I realized that even though my Thai friends were not usually voicing their objections or misunderstandings, every point of the Gospel would raise questions or create confusion based on their worldview. This is why often times a Gospel presentation is a "reciting of conundrums" to the Theravada Buddhist.

In this section I want to illustrate briefly what the traditional points of the Gospel message as encoded in Thai "sound" like to a Thai Buddhist listener.[41] For the purpose of this example I will use the format popularized by the Four Spiritual Laws tract, a style that has been translated and used widely in Thailand in numerous different witnessing tools. I am not picking out every possible objection or point of confusion; rather, I am simply highlighting major areas that are most definitely issues.

"God loves you"

There are two issues that come to the front immediately when we start to talk about God and his love for us. First, there is the whole concept of God. Buddha did not deny there could be deity; rather, he indicated that it was not an important consideration. The worldview behind this is that all beings are part of a karmatic continuum and thus all are in need of being freed from the karmatic cycle. In Thai we have difficulty because there is no single word that expresses the idea of God who is creator and over all. Normally we use two terms put together, *phra* and *jao*. *Phra* is a word with a wide range of use and is used as a prefix for numerous words. By itself, the term can mean lord, god, priest, and Buddha image. As a prefix it can be used in a conferred title, as a title placed before kings, things associated with royalty, divinities, objects of worship, and sacred places and things. Thus there are numerous common terms with the *phra* prefix: *phrajan* (moon), *phraatit* (sun), *phrasong* (monk), *phrajaopaendin* (the king). The term *jao* means a prince, ruler, or holy being. Today when Thais hear the compounded term *phrajao*, the common understanding is that this refers to the *phra* (god) of the *farang* (white people). So the word *phrajao* does not popularly convey the idea of the living creator God of the universe.

The second problem comes when we talk about God loving us. The Four Noble Truths remind us that the path to being freed from suffering is to extinguish all desire. Thus it is a value to be cool-hearted, and the separation of the monk from all worldly things is seen as the ideal. For God to love means that he is hot, involved and still connected with the desire that keeps the cycle of rebirth happening. This means that God is *awicha* (ignorant), because he does not understand that suffering is caused by desire.

"Man is separated from God because of sin"

The concept of sin in Scripture takes on its meaning in the context of a relationship with the living, personal God who is our maker and to whom we are responsible and owe our obedience. The Thai word we must use at this point is *baab*, which carries the idea of sin in the sense of demerit. There is no sense of guilt because there is no one to be guilty toward. *Baap* contrasts with *bun* (merit), and the goal becomes to have more *bun* than *baap*.

Thais, for the most part, see sin as embodied in an evil deed or act. *Baab* also is used in contrast to merit in the sense of demerit and does not carry as strong of a connotation as the biblical concept of sin as being an offense against God. Nor is there anything in Buddhist belief to convey the idea that we commit sin because we are sinners, born with sin. The typical idea is that sin can be expressed through the body and the heart, and that if it is not an overt act, then it does not really count as sin.[42]

There is also no concept of a sin nature, where people commit acts of sin because they are sinful by nature. Thais will say that humans are basically good but it is through *awicha* (ignorance), lack of education, and bad models that they become bad. There seems to be the general feeling that if people had the right opportunities in life they would be good and moral and follow the *dhamma*.

"Jesus died on a cross to forgive your sin"

In a worldview with karma—the law of cause and effect—at the center, and where all evil deeds will be inexorably paid back in some life, a person who is given the cruel death of crucifixion by the government at a young age is very suspect. It is obvious to a Thai person that Jesus must have committed serious wrong in a previous life in order to have that happen.

"Put your faith in Christ"

When we conclude by saying the wonderful gift that God has given us, eternal life, is received by faith, this again creates tension with Buddhist doctrine. In the first place, in the Buddhist worldview, people *have* eternal life and are trying to break out of the suffering that it entails to the state of nirvana where there is no more rebirth. Secondly, the Buddha said that one must *pungtuaeang* (depend upon yourself). There is no other who can help you.

Conclusion

This brief exercise reveals why we so often do not make any sense to Thai listeners when we share the Gospel. The terms that we are compelled to use have a radically different meaning than what we are intending. There are vast conceptual differences as well, relating in particular to the idea of a living and personal God versus impersonal karma. We cannot assume simply because people listen politely and do not object that it means the same understanding is being created in the receptor as in the message sender. When we take into account the worldview, beliefs, and assumptions of Thai listeners it demands that we contextualize the message in order to create an understanding that is in line with the biblical message.

A Contextualized Gospel Message for Thai Buddhists

The previous section shows that the Gospel as it is usually explained has a very foreign ring to the Thai listener. I now want to make some tentative suggestions as to how we can work to reduce this sense of foreignness and weave into a presentation of the Good News answers to some of the questions that are naturally raised by our listeners. In this final major section I will examine entry points for sharing the Gospel and look in detail at each major point with suggestions on how to use terms and illustrations are meaningful to Thai listeners.

One of the primary sources that I have utilized in this is Wan Petchsongkram's *Talks in the Shade of the Bo Tree*. Wan spent eight years as a Buddhist monk before becoming a Christian. He currently serves as the senior pastor of the Rom Glao Church. The book was developed from the translation of taped lectures in Thai to a group of Christian leaders back in 1972. The purpose was to look at popular Buddhism and suggest "guidelines for presenting the Christian message to the Thai Buddhist in terms which he would find intelligible."[43] As a new missionary, Wan's material helped me both understand Buddhism and see new ways to experiment with sharing the message in Thai society.

Two principles are foundational to the process of message contextualization. The first is that if we are going to make the Gospel presentation itself more understandable we have to be able to "hear" what they hear from our communication and build into it in advance answers to objections and questions that naturally arise. My experience has been that very rarely will Thais voice their objections or questions in the context of a witnessing encounter. The fact that they do not verbalize these things does not mean they are not there. So the goal here is to anticipate the problem areas where the Christian message, as couched in the terms available for us in Thai, creates some sense of confusion or question in the minds of the listeners. Rather than bringing these points of difference out in a confrontational fashion, it is better to provide the clarification right in the presentation itself.

A second point is that this process of message contextualization can only take place if we are willing to utilize Thai terms and concepts and invest them with new and higher meanings. The justification for doing this can be found in the New Testament itself, where Greek words like *agape* and *euanggelion* were taken from the local context and invested with new meaning to show what God had done through Christ. Filbeck argues that in the process of communication, there is something behind and deeper that forms the foundation for the giving and receiving of messages than just encoding, transmitting, and decoding. This deeper foundation concerns the way in which the society of both communicator and receiver is organized.[44] He makes the point that we must realize the particular sociological foundations of our listeners if we are going to communicate in a way that can be understood.[45] The words and concepts used within a given society designate certain mutually agreed upon realities and are expressive of both worldview and social organization. If we choose to communicate in words that are not a part of the normal concepts commonly understood by people, we make it very difficult for true communication to take place. Conversely, if we use words that already have a range of meaning within that society, then our listeners are going to naturally decode them and make meaning based on their understandings and not on the ones that we may intend.

I am arguing that in order to create a successful "environment" for communicating, we must be willing to take words that are used by Thai Buddhists as our starting point and accept the fact that there may be an initial gap between the biblical meaning and what they are understanding. The point is that we are already being "misunderstood" in our traditional presentation of the Gospel, and we seek to correct those misunderstandings through constant clarification and explanation. I am simply suggesting that by using terms and concepts that are familiar to local people as a starting point and investing them with new or intensified meaning, we can lessen the tendency for the message to feel completely foreign. At the same time, the ongoing process of clarification and explanation in dialogue must happen to move towards full biblical meaning.

Entry Points for Sharing the Gospel

The approach that I am taking for sharing the Gospel is based on the idea of a core "track" that provides a logical presentation of the message, modularity of concepts, and the use of illustrations to clarify each major point. The idea of modularity means that each of the major concepts about man, God, Christ, and faith that we share in a Gospel presentation can be compared to a self-contained unit with its own points and illustrations. Depending on where you engage a person you can begin with a different module, but the point is that there is always the "track" to get back on so that your listener has a connected line of thought rather than random chunks of information.

In order to get on to the "track" of Gospel content, it is necessary to find an entry point for beginning a conversation and securing permission to be able to share with another person. In this section I will look at two types of entry points that help open the door to share the basic content of the Gospel. I have observed that for many people, the hardest part in sharing the Christian faith with another person is not the actual content, but in finding an entry point into such a conversation. My contention is that entry points vary depending on the local context. What is meaningful in one place will not be meaningful in another. Typical starting points in Western contexts such as God's plan for our lives, God's love, and asking what happens after you die are meaningful there but not in the Thai context. The two major types of entry points that I have found to be most helpful concern the concept of the performance gap and common objections that Thais will have about the Christian faith.

The Performance Gap

It is my personal opinion that in most instances, it is best to start talking about man's predicament before attempting to talk about God. As was noted in previous discussion, the average Thai is familiar with the *sil ha* (the five prohibitions) and with karma, and is probably involved in making merit (*tam bun*), both ritual and otherwise, that hopefully will help to improve this life or a future existence. On the other hand, he or she probably has little or no conception at all of a living, personal God. It is thus better to start with what is known in terms of their own human experience than to talk about God, which is an unknown concept. Joseph Cooke has pointed out that for most Thais, there is hardly ever a great sense of guilt because of wrongdoing.[46] Their culture is oriented towards shame and not guilt. This is in part a consequence of the fact that the Thai Buddhist incurs guilt (in the legal sense of wrongdoing) only in one dimension—the manward side—since he has no belief in God.[47] However, Cooke notes that in this single dimension, it is quite probable that those who take seriously the following of *sil ha* and other precepts, find themselves with a performance gap.[48] In other words, the behavior that they are able to produce and what they want to produce, is not the same, creating a gap. What follows are several ways in which we can use this idea of the "performance gap" to open the door for sharing the Good News about Christ.

Starting with Suffering

Keeping in mind what Joseph Cooke has said in regard to the lack of a sense of guilt that the Thai have concerning wrongdoing, it seems that rather than trying to create a sense of wrongdoing, we should begin where they are, with an understanding of *dukkha* (Thai: *thuk*), which is suffering. By using one of the three key terms that mark human existence in Buddhism, we can zero in on what the Thai commonly understand and experience—the frustration, suffering and difficulties of life—and we can begin to steer them in the discussion to see that this *thuk* arises from problems that are within us, rather than external to us.

There are a number of ways of dealing with this area and illustrating it. Brasert Gusawadi has an excellent illustration about a tree and its fruit. A mango tree that produces sour-tasting fruit cannot change itself, but in order to get sweet fruit, we must obtain a variety or species that bears sweet fruit and plant those seeds.[49] In other words, to solve man's problem of the performance gap, we cannot change on our own but need the impartation of new life.

Starting with Karma and Ignorance

A missionary with the Overseas Missionary Fellowship has developed a Gospel presentation called "The Way to Freedom—The Way to a New Life," which has a similar starting point of dealing with man's problems.[50] It looks at life in three concentric circles from family and friends out to the hostile spirit world. It characterizes life using two key terms which the Thai Buddhists are familiar with: *awicha* (Pali: *avijja*) and *kam* (Pali: *kamma* or karma). Here man is seen as locked in *awicha* (ignorance), and also reaping what he sows, which is the law of *kam*. This approach has much to commend it because it ties the human condition into two common key Thai word-concepts that also have a contact point in Scripture.

Another method that starts off from the concept of karma is to use the introductory two questions of the Evangelism Explosion presentation modified for people with a karmatic worldview. Rather than asking if one would go to heaven after they die, you ask if they would be liberated from the law of karma (*pon jaak got haeng kam*). The follow-up question is to ask how they think that people are able to be freed from their karma.

Starting with a Thai Proverb

Another place to begin from in dealing with the performance gap is to use the Thai proverb, *kwamruthuamhua aowtuamairawt*. This means that though knowledge floods one's head, he cannot use it to save himself. After setting the stage by showing how many problems occur both in society and personally, and by zeroing in on the listener's own perceived difficulties, this proverb can be helpful in showing that, although we may possess lots of knowledge about what is right, we still cannot actually follow through on it and do it; we need power to act, not just knowledge. In this regard, the illustration of the man drowning and having someone try to teach him to swim and having another pull him out of the water is very helpful.[51]

Starting with a Common Saying on Good and Evil and the Desire Concept

Another possible place to begin in talking about man and his problems is to use the well-known phrase, *thamdii daidii thamchua daichua.* This saying about the law of karma means, "do good, receive good; do evil, receive evil." We can use Galatians 6:6–8 to show that this principle of retribution is one that God uses in governing the world. The question can be asked, what happens if you do both good and evil? What do you receive then? This draws upon the fact of their experience that no one consistently does good. At this point, I think it is permissible to use the word *tanha* (desire) or *kileedtanha* to speak of the sin principle in man rather than the word *nuanang* (flesh) as is used in the Thai Bible. *Nuanang* is two words meaning the flesh or skin (*nua*), and hide (*nang*) compounded together. Just as the English translation of the Greek *sarx* as "flesh" is not understood by a first-time reader of Scripture as referring to the sin principle inside of humanity, so is the case with *nuanang*. It has to be explained, and its meaning is made clear through its use in context. However, *tanha* is a religious word that is well-known, and the concept that we cling to life and commit acts of sin because of *tanha* is well-recognized by the common man. Thus in Galatians 6:8, we can show that because of *tanha*, we consistently do not do good and cannot break the cycle of karma in which we are caught. However, the text says that if we sow to the Spirit, we reap eternal life. This can become the bridge for showing how we can break out of *tanha* and karma. We need new life, life from God's Spirit.

Common Objections as Entry Points

Apart from issues that relate to the performance gap, I have also discovered that the common objections one hears frequently relating to Christianity can become entry points for sharing the content of the Gospel. One lesson that I learned from my witnessing encounters over the years is that in Thailand, before you can really share the message, you must first correct misunderstandings. There are a number of relatively "stock" phrases that represent some local beliefs about the relationship of Buddhism to the evangelism of the Christians. Rather than this being seen as a negative factor, it can serve as a bridge for entering into a conversation about the message of the Gospel. In this section, I examine four major objections and methods for answering them and moving on to share Christ.

"To be Thai is to be Buddhist"

There are a couple of ways of handling this concept. One is to note that the Thai were not always Buddhists, and that the religion traveled to their region. We explain that just as not all Americans are Christians, so not all Thais are solid practitioners of Buddhism. People are not simply born into their religion; they must chose to practice it on a daily basis.

"We must follow our ancestors"

Sometimes Thai believers are accused of selling their nationality. In a village setting, when something goes wrong the Christians will be blamed because they have left the path of the ancestors. I have dealt with this by trying to get people to think about how much change has been introduced into Thai society. Years ago there were no modern medicines, no school system, or vaccines. All of these are things that the Thais did not have in the past but have readily accepted them into their society because they bring some kind of benefit with them. Thais have had a remarkable adaptability, because if something seems beneficial to them they will take it and use it for the good of their country. You can make that point that the ancestors themselves changed and adopted new things and thus today, we of this age can do the same.

"I do not sin"

The first time I heard this objection, it stumped me. After thinking about it I found that the perfect illustration for dealing with this had to do with the concept of filial piety. This is where love, loyalty, and obedience must be expressed to one's parents. I set up the following scenario, which is readily understood. I ask them to remember their parents who worked so hard to facilitate their education. Then I ask them how their parents would feel if they were to walk down the street, randomly pick out someone, and call them their parents and *graabwai* them (prostrate themselves and put their forehead to the ground and make the *wai* position with the hands to the forehead and then on the ground). This is shocking to a Thai, for whom showing filial piety and gratitude (*katanyu*) is so important. I then tell them that this is precisely what all of humankind has done. We have rejected God who is our maker and worshiped things that are created rather than the creator himself. We are *akantanyu* to the one who made us and this is the cardinal sin, to have other gods before him. So no matter how ethically moral our life is, if we have broken that commandment, we have sinned.

"All religions are equally good"

The best answer that I have ever heard to this dilemma comes from Pastor Wirachai Kowae. When someone tells him this he affirms that statement, but then goes on to make the following argument. Suppose you were out working or playing and got your face all dirty. When you come into the house you go to the mirror and it shows you the state of your face, how dirty it is. The mirror itself cannot help you. At this point, you need outside help to clean up. In the same way religion, like the mirror, cannot clean us up either. Religion will help to show the state of our heart, just as the mirror shows the state of our face. Trying to keep the commandments of any religion will reveal that we have trouble doing so; the religion and the commandments show us the state of our hearts. However, just like the mirror, the religion itself cannot cleanse us from our sin. It takes help outside of us, from Jesus Christ, to be able to remove sin from our lives.

The Major Points of the Gospel

In this final section, I will examine the major points of the Gospel message and make suggestions as to both terms and illustrations that can help facilitate understanding, with a view towards building answers in advance to the kinds of objections that a Buddhist listener would have.

Concepts about Man's Dilemma and the Problem of Sin

Many of the entry points for sharing the Gospel begin the discussion in light of the performance gap, the problem that people have between what they hold as an ideal and how they really live. Buddhism and its concept of suffering begins with man's dilemma. I personally have found it most easy to engage Thais in talking about man's problem using the fruit tree illustration of Brasert Gusawadi that was noted above. Wan Petchsongkram talks about the common word *tujarit*, meaning "dishonesty," as actually meaning "evil action." When compounded, it can be used to speak of evil physical action, evil speech, and evil in the heart (*gaaytujarit*, *wajitujarit*, and *manotujarit*, respectively).[52]

These words can be used in addition to *baab* to show concrete expressions of sin in our lives. In the fruit tree illustration, the sour fruit of our lives is expressed as evil physical actions, evil speech, and evil in our hearts. It all has its start in the seed, the sour species that produces sour fruit. Using *tanha* as previously mentioned to refer to something like the sin principle (biblical "flesh"), we can show that we commit evil deeds because from within we have a problem, the *tanha* problem, and that man is in desperate need of a change deep from within if he is to truly change his actions.

The advantage of using these starting points and then talking about man's dilemma is that it can be done by connecting with a variety of terms and concepts such as karma, suffering, ignorance, or proverbs and sayings that are familiar to Thais. This has the effect of making people feel you are "talking their language" and understand where they are at, and it opens the door for further conversation.

Concepts about God

Once we have established that man indeed has a serious problem that stems from within, we can then set it in its larger context as being a separation from a real, living, personal God who made us and who is interested in our lives. Wan Petchsongkram notes that the question of God's existence and the creation of the world are the key hurdles; people who can say yes to those two questions usually are much more willing to see Jesus Christ as the Son of God.[53] This is a very difficult area, for we are moving from the known (man's experience in the world) to the unknown and unseen. Tissa Weerasingha suggests that since "Buddhist doctrine does not deal with the issue of a First Cause,...the biblical doctrine of creation would fill a crucial cosmological deficiency."[54]

One of the common objections about God being the creator is that the world is in such a sorry state that if someone did create the world, he must be *awicha* (ignorant), and a perpetrator of evil.[55] When one does talk about God as creator, there must be an emphasis that what God made was good and whole, and that it was the entrance of sin through man's disobedience that ruined things. Petchsongkram has a fascinating way of relating the Creation story in which he shows how both *awicha* and *tanha* sprang up in man's heart and that this is the source of the world's problems.[56]

Also, in dealing with arguments for the existence of God, it is good to be conversant with concepts and evidences that point to the existence of a creator. Dealing with the First Cause, the argument from design, and the argument from human personality and morality are all profitable ways to begin.

Due to the fact that in Buddhism the ultimate reality is impersonal, Joseph Cooke recommends that we stress the personhood of God, since this is one of the essential differences between Buddhism and Christianity.[57] He suggests that this can be done by emphasizing the personhood of God in creation, using the realities of relationships in Thai society to develop analogies, and by demonstrating our own relationship with God.[58] One way that I have found to talk with people about the personality of God as a starting point is to talk about the term *singsaksittanlaituasakonlok*, which refers to all the powerful sacred things in the universe. *Sing* carries the idea with it of a "thing" and I will remark that this concept is almost right, but there is actually a *phu* (a person) who is the Most High Sacred One. This often opens the door to discussing the nature of God and then other parts of the Gospel.

Once we have established that God exists, it is then necessary to talk about what he is like and to show that he is truly interested in us. This Good News is that God, whom we cannot see, has revealed himself to be a God who is interested in us, who has not thrown us away, and who wants to restore us to the fellowship with him that he intended us to have. In a Western presentation of the Gospel, these points are explained in terms of the love of God that brings us salvation. However, as noted above, the love of God can be a concept that is a stumbling block to an educated Buddhist, and the word used in the Bible and Christian circles for salvation, *kwamrawt*, does not carry much meaning for the average person. Fortunately, several other concepts can be used to convey these truths.

We can talk about the mercy and compassion of God using the term *metta*. This is a very high word in Buddhism, and can be translated as beneficence or grace.[59] The word used for grace, *phrakun*, is also important. These words can be used and illustrated to show that even though we ruined our lives through sin, and even though we have turned our backs on the One who made us, he is still seeking us out and does not abandon us. Joseph Cooke notes that this theme of grace and love that does not abandon us even when it is awkward or inconvenient or when we fail to measure up, would most likely be very important to a Thai.[60]

One illustration from Thai life that is helpful is the practice of the king's releasing prisoners on special occasions. In the Thai language this is expressed as occurring *doy phrakun*, or "through the grace of the King." We can show how through our own efforts at doing good and making merit we cannot get rid of our evil heart and evil actions, but God through his grace, even though we do not merit it, brings us release and forgiveness, just as the king releases prisoners who deserve to be in prison.

Concepts about Salvation in Christ

The idea of salvation from sin is essentially foreign in terms of the common terminology used in the Thai language. It is probably more fruitful to use the concept of being released from the cycle of karma and sin (*lutponjaakkamlaebaab*). Another option would be to use the term *vimutti* (Thai: *wimutti*) in order to talk about salvation. Wan Petchsongkram notes that this Pali word means to "liberate or free" and could appropriately used of Christian salvation.[61] However, in my experience, this word is not widely known by Thais; they have heard of it, but unless they have studied religion in some detail, they are prone not to know what it refers to right off. Since it is not well known or understood, it does not have much advantage over using the term *kwamrawt* (salvation) and explaining it.

When speaking of the substitutionary death of Jesus, it is necessary to emphasize the free and voluntary nature of his sacrifice as we see in John 10:18. As noted above, there is a tendency to think that because Jesus died a violent death as a criminal, he must have had very bad karma in his past life. There must be positive teaching at this point and illustration of sacrificial acts that stem from a desire to help another. Alex Smith has pointed out a key historical story concerning the Thai queen Phranang Srisuriyothai.[62] The substance of the story is that she disguised herself as a warrior to help her husband in the fight against the Burmese. As the Thai king was about to be killed in the battle, the queen rode her elephant between the two fighters and was killed, but her husband was spared. This type of true story, which illustrates vicarious sacrifice, can be helpful in conveying the meaning to the Thai listener who has no background in his religious beliefs for such an act.

In speaking of the death of Christ and using the terminology that his sacrifice enables us to be delivered from the effects of karma, we must also emphasize the broader scope that is included in his death and resurrection. This includes his victory over sin, over death, and over Satan and evil spirits. In this way, we can make practical applications to the actual place that people live in. Christ's resurrection brings us power for living the new life, not the deadness of mere precepts and prohibitions, as good as they may be. It also frees us from the tyranny of death, and for the many who are tormented or afraid of evil spirits, Christ's victory over the enemy and his power to cast out demons, is very important. In a similar vein, the inbreaking of God's kingdom rule, which was inaugurated in the ministry of Jesus and which is carried on by his people, saw the demonstration of God's mercy in miracles of healing. All of these aspects must be given in order to show that the victory Christ has purchased for us through his shed blood touches every area of our daily lives.

One question that the Gospel communicator is sure to face, when trying to explain about salvation by grace through faith and not through our works, concerns merit (*bun*). People are so accustomed to the merit/demerit system and the law of karma paying them back good for good and evil for evil, that the idea of being freed from the weight of our evil deeds without doing anything seems foreign. I have experimented to a degree with using the concept of merit transference as a way of conveying this idea. It has to do with explaining the idea of our being justified by faith through Christ's death in the category of Jesus being our *bun* (merit).

The idea came to me while attending a Thai funeral. Prior to the cremation, there was a whole sequence of offering cloth that I did not understand. I asked a Thai friend sitting next to me what was happening and he said that it was making merit. Then the question became, making merit for whom? Was it for the person giving the cloth or to the deceased? He replied that the offerings of cloth were to make merit for the person who had died. I realized then that although Thais do not talk about the transference of merit commonly, they do believe in it and it is found in rituals like this. So I have tried using that concept in the following way.

I ask the question, "Why do you make merit?" The answer usually involves some concept of trying to gain merit for a better life both now and in the future. I then make the point that that *bun*, either through ritual or through good actions, is done for a reason, and therefore there is some ultimate direction that it points toward. At this point, I make the case for the fact that our own *bun* is simply not enough, because when we look closely at our lives we realize that we have more demerit (*baab*) than merit. In this way we can never, through our own actions, deeds, and *bun,* ever escape from our *kam* (karma), or make our way into heaven, or be accepted into fellowship with the God who made us.

The verse I use comes from the language of Paul in Ephesians and Colossians, where he says that in Christ we were made alive, even though formerly dead in trespasses and sins (Eph. 2:5; Col. 2:13). Jesus, who committed no sin, was a perfect sacrifice and has become *bun* for us. He has wiped out karma and delivered us from death and made us pure in God's eyes. We do not acquire his *bun* by our deeds but by trusting in him, and as we do so he transfers to us all the benefit of his *bun*.

It is obvious that the biblical term we are dealing with here is righteousness. The difficulty is that since there is no concept of God and sin that breaks a relationship with God, there is not a sense of need for righteousness. The forensic sense of justification developed by Paul is not a motivating factor for a Thai Buddhist. The issue of merit, on the other hand, is right at the front of the average person's current thinking and experience, and it provides a starting point for talking about what Christ has done in his work on the cross. Further research needs to be done on this to see if explaining Christ's work in terms of transference of merit will create understanding and build a bridge to grasp the biblical meaning of the cross and justification.

Concepts about Man's Response to God's Gift

We have looked at some possible ways to approach talking about man and his problem, about God and his character, and about the redeeming work of the Son, but man must make a response through faith if he is to enter into the blessings of a relationship with the living God. I want to make two suggestions for this area. The first concerns the use of vocabulary in explaining the concept of faith.

In the Bible, saving faith has cognitive, emotional, and volitional elements. This can and should be explained in Thai. However, I have noticed that there are a number of words which express the idea of believing in the verb form and faith in the noun form: *chua, sattha, luamsai,* and *waiwangjai.* More detailed study could reveal that, in terms of their current usage, one of these words could fit the idea of volitional commitment better than mere cognitive belief in the facts. As an instance of this, I have heard people, when referring to losing a sense of faith and trust in another because of their poor behavior or example, to say that they are *"mot sattha"* and not *"mot kwamchua."* Perhaps *chua* is the broader term that includes and emphasizes cognitive assent, and *sattha* carries more of the idea of trusting or giving yourself to another. Further research in this area may open up a new way to communicate the fullness of saving faith.

I have heard some bemoan the fact that in Thai there is no clear word for commitment, thus making it difficult to express the concept of "commitment to Christ," which we use so frequently in English. However, I do not view this as much of a problem on two grounds. The first is that we do not find the word "commitment" in the New Testament, but rather the concept, stated and illustrated in many different ways. We should seek to develop these biblical categories that include the Synoptic Gospels and leave our sole reliance on John's language of belief in order to get a broader and more accurate picture of what it means to follow Christ. The second reason is that there are other phrases like *mawbhai* (to give oneself over), and *jamnon* (to surrender) that can be used to convey the concept in Thai without having to have a word that specifically means commitment in the English sense.

In talking about saving faith, it is not enough to use correct vocabulary; we also must talk about the practical development of the life of faith. It is often difficult for people who are so indoctrinated into the works concept found in the merit and karma system to conceive of living a life "free from the Law," so to speak. They often feel that if there is no compelling reason to do good, then why should you do it? Hearing about salvation by grace through faith raises the same line of questioning that Paul addresses in Romans 6, and the Thai is prone to think that it is all "too easy."

However, I think there is a helpful analogy to be found in the thinking of Thais as it relates to respect for and gratitude towards parents. Showing gratitude to a parent (*jaikatanjuu*) is very important, and the child who does not show gratitude by sending money and taking care of his parents as they grow older is looked down upon. Our parents have sacrificed for us, and we should sacrifice for them. We can use this concept to great benefit when talking about the practical outworking of the Christian life. We are saved and delivered by grace (*phrakhun*), but we are to live our Christian life by showing gratitude to our heavenly Father (*doysadangjaikatanjuu*). He has sacrificed his own Son that we might be restored to fellowship with him, and it is our duty to show gratitude by living our lives to please him.

Conclusion

The preceding material has made it clear that there is no one "right" way to share the Gospel to Thai people, and that the reasons for the slow response of the Thai over the many decades are multiple and complex. In my opinion, the contextualization of the message is a critical and overlooked element in bringing Thai people to respond to the Gospel. However, I want to acknowledge that it is a part of a complex of several important elements that I believe must be brought together to effectively present Christ to the Thai people.

One of the major elements has to do with our presuppositions about communicating the Gospel. I believe that we will be more effective if we move towards dialogue and a sense of process rather than emphasizing a point-in-time decision where people have not really been able to assess the implications of a decision to follow Christ. A second set of elements concerns methodology. Two of the critical components here are putting discussion of the Christian life and discipleship upfront so that the listener can have some idea of what life as a follower of Christ will look like, and making room for God's power in the witnessing relationship. Bringing prayer for a person into the encounter opens the door for God to reveal himself in some way through healing or answer to a felt need. Finally, there are important structural issues about the way we "do church" that must be addressed. The Gospel message is put in context through relationships, and I believe there needs to be a rethinking of how to structure church life so that believers can spend quality time with people in their personal networks, so that they can have a base of trust from which to talk about Christ.

The material presented in this paper is a work in progress. It has grown out of reading and interacting with others who have approached this subject and from many personal experiences in attempting to share the Gospel in one-on-one and small-group contexts for over 16 years. The act of thinking through these issues highlights the need for further research to answer the many questions that grow out of this line of inquiry. It is my hope that the material here will be able to receive thorough examination and criticism from both missionaries and Thais, and lead to the development of helpful tools to use and pass on to others as we work together in endeavoring to bring the Gospel message to the Thai people.

Notes

[1] Patrick Johnstone and Jason Mandryk, *Operation World: When We Pray God Works* (Paternoster Publishing, 2001).

[2] *Missionary Review of the World*, Vol. 43, quoted Alex Smith, *Siamese Gold* (Bangkok: Kanok Bannasan [OMF Publishers], 1981), p. 274.

[3] Smith, pp. 271-278.

[4] Tom Wisely, *Dynamic Biblical Christianity in the Buddhist/Marxist Context: Northeast Thailand.* (Ph.D. dissertation, Fuller Theological Seminary, 1984), p. 163.

[5] Wan Petchsongkram, *Talks in the Shade of the Bo Tree*, trans. and ed. by Frances Hudgins (Bangkok: Thai Gospel Press, 1975), p. 7.

[6] Ibid.

[7] David Hesselgrave and Edward Rommen, *Contextualization: Meanings, Methods and Models* (Pasadena: William Carey Library, 1989).

[8] Stephen Bevans, "Models of Contextual Theology," in *Missiology: An International Review XIII* (April 1985), p. 190.

[9] For an excellent and concise overview of the key concepts of Buddhism see Hong-Shik Shin, *Principles of Church Planting as Illustrated In Thai Theravada Buddhist Context*, (Bangkok: Kanok Bannasan [OMF Publishers], 1989), pp. 226-231.

[10] Phra Sasanasobhana, *Phraputtajao Song Soon Arai* [What did the Buddha Teach?], trans. and ed. Phra Khantipalo and Phra Nagaseno (Thailand: The War Veterans Organization of Thailand, 1967), p. 5.

[11] Ibid., p. 15.

[12] Petchsongkram, p. 208.

[13] Ezra Mothanaprakoon, "A Critique of Buddhist Soteriology From a Biblical Perspective," paper presented for Seminar in Asian Theological Issues, Far East Advanced School of Theology, 12 January 1987.

[14] Ibid.

[15] Ibid.

[16] Petchsongkram, p. 129.

[17] Ibid., pp. 129ff.

[18] Shin, p. 229

[19] Sasanasobhana, p. 6.

[20] Petchsongkram, pp. 102–122.

[21] Ibid., p. 115.

[22] Ibid.

[23] A. Thomas Kirsch, "Notes on Thai Religion," in *Clues to Thai Culture*, ed. Central Thai Language Committee (Bangkok: Overseas Missionary Fellowship, May 1981), pp. 146–147.

[24] Ibid., p. 146.

[25] Ibid., p. 147.

[26] John Davis, *Poles Apart: Contextualizing the Gospel in Asia,* (Bangalore: Theological Book Trust, 1998), p. 45.

[27] Alex Smith, *Strategy To Multiply Rural Churches: A Central Thailand Case Study* (Bangkok: OMF Publishers, 1977), p. 88.

[28] For much more detailed work in this area see Davis, chapter 3; Nantachai Mejudhon, *Meekness: A New Approach to Christian Witness To the Thai People,* (D.Miss. dissertation, Asbury Theological Seminary, 1997), pp. 21-46; and Wisely, chapter 3.

[29] Smith, p. 88; Petchsongkram, p. 35.

[30] Suntaree Komin, *Psychology of the Thai People: Values and Behavior Patterns* (Bangkok: National Inst. of Development Administration, 1990).

[31] Mary Cooke, "A Thai's Attitude Toward Religion." Bangkok: Overseas Missionary Fellowship, p. 2. (Typewritten lecture notes).

[32] Smith, *Strategy*, p. 174.

[33] Petchsongkram (pp. 15–16) shows how the Buddhist ideal of detachment makes the concept of God's love problematic because it means that God is full of passion and attached.

[34] Shin, p. 230.

[35] Ibid. See also A. Thomas Kirsch in "The Thai Buddhist Quest for Merit," in *Clues to Thai Culture*, ed. Central Thai Language Committee (Bangkok: Overseas Missionary Fellowship, May 1981), p. 121.

[36] Kirsch, p. 121.

[37] Petchsongkram (pp. 38–42; 124–128), notes that within the framework of Buddhism there are actually three categories of teaching or *dhamma* and that this can be broadly divided into two parts: those precepts dealing with an ordinary or mundane level of life (*lokiyadhamma*), and those which specifically deal with the Four Noble Truths leading to ending the cycle of rebirths (*lokuttaradhamma*). Most people are only really familiar with and attempt to practice to a degree the teaching that has to do with the more mundane level as it is embodied in the five precepts or prohibitions.

[38] The five prohibitions are as follows: Do not destroy life, do not steal, do not commit fornication, do not lie or speak falsely, and do not drink intoxicants. These five precepts are considered to be universally applicable, and form the basic understanding of morality for the common people.

[39] Petchsongkram, p. 141.

[40] Kirsch, p. 126.

[41] The material here I got primarily from John Davis in his introduction to *Poles Apart*, pp. vi-viii.

[42] Petchsongkram, pp. 141–145.

[43] Ibid., pp. 8-9.

[44] David Filbeck, *Social Context and Proclamation: A Socio-Cognitive Study in Proclaiming the Gospel Cross-Culturally* (Pasadena: William Carey Library, 1985), p. 3.

[45] Ibid.

[46] Joseph Cooke, "The Gospel for Thai Ears," July 1978, p. 3. (Typewritten).

[47] Ibid., p. 7.

[48] Ibid., pp. 16-17.

[49] Brasert Gusawadi, "Witi Atibaay Tang Hang Kwam Rod Doy Chai Ruub Wongglom Sung Maaythung Gaay Jai Lae Winnyan [A Method of Explaining the Way of Salvation Using Concentric Circles with the Meaning of Body, Mind and Spirit]" Bangkok: Overseas Missionary Fellowship. (Typewritten.)

[50] "The Way to Freedom—The Way to a New Life," Bangkok: Overseas Missionary Fellowship. (Typewritten.)

[51] This illustration is found in the language study book *Practical Communications* by Overseas Missionary Fellowship.

[52] Ibid., p. 141.

[53] Ibid., pp. 99-100.

[54] Tissa Weerasingha, "A Critique of Theology from Buddhist Cultures," in *The Bible and Theology in Asian Contexts*, ed. Bong Rin Ro and Ruth Eshnaur (Taiwan: Tai Shin Color Printing Co. Ltd., 1984), p. 304.

[55] Petchsongkram, pp. 84–85.

[56] Ibid., pp. 85–89.

[57] Joseph Cooke, p. 20.

[58] Ibid., pp. 20–21.

[59] Petchsongkram, pp. 152–153.

[60] Cooke, pp. 13-14.

[61] Petchsongkram, pp. 139–140.

[62] Smith, pp. 276–277.

CHAPTER 9

The Ritual of Reconciliation in Thai Culture:
Discipling New Converts

Ubolwan Mejudhon

Introduction

A Thai pastor complains, "When our church gets one weak Christian, we get two hundred strong enemies from the new convert's social networks."

What this Thai pastor says is a plain fact. In Thailand, a Thai becomes a Christian in secret. The church and the seeker do not let the parents know about the searching, being afraid that the parents will stop the seeker from attending the church. Then, one day, out of the blue, their son or daughter announces his or her conversion to Christ. Having no emotional shock absorber, the parents are enraged. The conversion brings shame to them. The neighbors gossip that they did not bring their child up well. The convert challenges their authority by making an important decision without acknowledging them or asking for advice. The parents worry for their child. They have no idea about the new social network their son or daughter is having fellowship with. They know nothing about Christ. The announcement brings bewilderment to the parents and relatives.

Moreover, the church trains the new convert to witness aggressively to their parents and relatives. The aggressive witness causes anger because the convert violates the values of hierarchy and smooth relationships, as well as accepted social roles and status. The parents and relatives listen to the new convert's testimony, patiently, until they reach a boiling point. Then they hit back, hard. As a result, the new convert takes refuge in the church community. Yet, the missing relationship is too great. Though the church community is strong, it cannot provide the support the convert needs. The church has thus gained one weak Christian while, through the convert's angry relatives, it has gained many strong enemies.

Thai culture is kind and generous to all religions, as can be seen from its history. Thailand has accepted primal religions, Hinduism, and Buddhism for more than two thousand years. The believers of these faiths lived in peace. King Rama V (1868-1919) issued a law out of love toward missionaries that they were free to preach the gospel. At the present time, the government gives money to missionaries to preach the gospel to the Thai (Mejudhon 1994: 1). It is a myth among Christians that Thais are against other religions. Usually, parents allow their children to learn about other faiths. Religion is good, from the Thai's viewpoint. The Thai learn about other faiths from primary school to high school.

The Royal Academy of Thailand records that the king is the protector of all religions (The Royal Academy 1995: 783). This evidence should rid Christians of the fear they have of the seekers' parents. In fact, Christians should get to know them because Thai culture is a relationship-based culture. A relationship provides a shock absorber and lessens anxiety for the parents when they know about the conversion of their children.

Suntaree Komin, a Thai scholar, conducted empirical research among the Thai. She found nine Thai value clusters: ego orientation, grateful relationship orientation, smooth interpersonal relationship orientation, flexibility and adjustment orientation, religio-psychical orientation, fun making, education and competence orientation, interdependence orientation, and achievement-task orientation (Komin 1993: 133). Christians violate the grateful relationship orientation, smooth interpersonal relationship orientation, flexibility and adjustment orientation, and the interdependence orientation when the new converts abruptly tell their parents of their conversion. The Thai like the proverb, "slowly but surely." They hate abrupt changes. Change is a slow process for them. They have sayings like, "slowly, slowly change" (*koy-pen-koy-pai*), and "I need time to prepare my heart and my mind" (*tong-tiam-toi-tiam-jai*). The Thai concept of time is cyclical (Feig 1989: 23-24).

When new converts witness aggressively to their parents and relatives, they violate their value of confrontation avoidance as well as their culture's value of hierarchy, which Feig considers as an important characteristic of the Thais (1989: 37, 76). While doing so, the new converts are usually under the spell of the "theology of redemption," according to which their parents and relatives are lost and will be in hell. Out of love, they are even more aggressive as their parents and relatives respond to their witness kindly and in quietness, or even with teasing remarks out of humor. As days pass by, new converts are more aggressive in witnessing. They overlook the ego-orientation value of their parents, who have strong self-esteem and strong self-identity as Thais. In order to keep their children meek and quiet, the parents fight back by scolding and criticizing. When the children talk back, their parents are enraged and ignore them, acting as if the children do not exist. Then the new converts withdraw into Christian communities and their other relational ties are broken.

As a result, these new converts lose their identity as Thais, which inhibits their spiritual growth. It seems to me that if converts were to remain bonded to their natural community—that is, to Thai culture—it would affect their identity as well as their bonding to Christian meaning. Because this does not happen, I believe that Christian churches in Thailand have many weak Christians.

As for the parents of the new converts, although they ignore their children completely, as Thai parents, they love them dearly. They long to bond with their own children and know what is going on in their lives so that they can help. This is an important duty of Thai parents, but they cannot do so as long as they feel that the church is stealing their children away. According to the parents, they invested their lives into their children, yet their children now belong to Christian churches, which have invested nothing in them. The result leaves an open wound for the Thai families because Christians violate Thai values and break the family's relational ties. The letter recorded below is from Nantachai Mejudhon's mother, written to him from Thailand when she learned of his conversion while he was living in the United States.

May 22, 1972

My Dearest Son,

> *Your last letter is the most important letter of my life. I read your letter at the office and in the bus and then at home in secret, afraid your younger brother would know about it. Usually, I allow him to read your letters as they inspire him. I have read your letter more than ten times now. I am glad that you have found peace and joy. Now that you are grown up and have a good education, you can think and make decisions on your own. I have tried*

to analyze your comment, *"I am still a good Buddhist in the way that I practice his teaching. I still respect and love Lord Buddha." I am trying to use this statement to comfort myself and put myself in the Buddhist middle way. Yet, I am confused and I ask myself, "Can he enter the monkshood again as he once did? Can my son still make merit as he once did? Does he have to give up all these rituals when he accepts Christianity?"*

Why do you write to me, "Please don't be sorry"? What about this religion could change the deep relational love between mother and son? I accept that I am too stupid to study and make experiments to find the truth like others. Even in the religion in which I worship and which I have respected from birth for more than sixty years I cannot find the truth yet. How could I find the truth in another religion? It is impossible.

I now accept this suffering because I have a lot of bad karma. I can no longer find peace and joy in my life. I have fought against all kinds of fate and shed my tears many times. I will try to quench my suffering, saying to myself, "It's my karma." The fate of karma predestines our life. Through suffering and pain, I will accept my karma and try my best to do good. I will try my best to do the mother's duty in this life, so that I don't have to suffer in another life. I think in my humble capacity. This world, this life is uncertain. That is the truth of truth.

Anyhow, I congratulate you, my son. Yet, I would like to plead and beg of you not to announce your new religion to any relatives. I plead with you not to be baptized like some others until you return and meet me, because I need your help in solving some problems. Please heed my requests in this matter. Good luck, my son. May you have peace and joy in our Lord Buddha's teaching. May you think about the grace of Buddha, Dharma, and Sangka, if you can.

From Mother,
Tipparat Mejudhon

P.S. I am frustrated and wonder how far this religion sets limitations and disciplines for other religions. Is it possible for this religion to get along with Buddhism in worship and rituals, or is absolute separation the only possibility?

The wounds caused by broken relationships can no longer be ignored. I believe the ritual of reconciliation in the Thai culture provides an answer for the dilemma mentioned above. This paper presents, in four parts, Thai culture's ritual of reconciliation as a discipling tool for new converts. The first part has been introductory. The second part is a theoretical framework for the ritual of reconciliation. The third part deals directly with critical contextualization proposing a way of creating a Christian ritual of reconciliation for bonding new Christian converts with their families. The last part is the conclusion.

Theoretical Framework

In order to understand this paper, we need to understand three important definitions: the definition of "reconciliation," the definition of "ritual," and the definition of "critical contextualization." I will present "reconciliation" as it is defined by Robert Schreiter. I will explain "ritual" (within the context of rites of passage) using A. H. Mathias Zahniser's thought as a framework. I will use the theoretical frameworks of Schreiter and Zahniser to analyze the Thai ritual of reconciliation. Finally, Paul G. Hiebert's theory of critical contextualization and Suntaree Komin's nine Thai value clusters will serve as a guideline for inventing a Thai Christian ritual of reconciliation. They are authorities in contextualization.

Robert Schreiter's Definition of Reconciliation

Robert Schreiter is an eminent Catholic scholar who has written many books about social reconciliation. He presents his idea about the definition of reconciliation as follows:

> There are at least three understandings of reconciliation that come close to the genuine meaning of reconciliation but distort and even falsify its true sense. These three are reconciliation as hasty peace, reconciliation instead of liberation, and reconciliation as a managed process (1997: 18).

Many people misunderstand "reconciliation" as hasty peace. They perform reconciliation to cover over problems. We need to understand the real meaning of "reconciliation." Robert Schreiter explains that reconciliation is a long process. Reconciliation does not require victims to quickly forget their pain and suppress their memory of a history of violence. Schreiter thinks that to trivialize and ignore the memory of victims is to trivialize and ignore human identity. To trivialize and ignore human identity is to trivialize and ignore human dignity. In this long process of reconciliation, Schreiter believes that only certain people have the moral authority to issue the call for reconciliation. Reconciliation demands special grace and kindness from victims. Oppressors cannot initiate it. Therefore, reconciliation is more likely to come from the victims in the situations, not from the wrongdoers. Reconciliation requires time for starting a new life for both victims and oppressors if reconciliation really takes place between them.

Moreover, Schreiter affirms that reconciliation goes hand in hand with liberation—without liberation, there will be no reconciliation. Schreiter states, "If the sources of conflict are not named, examined, and taken away, reconciliation will not come about. What we will have is a truce, not a peace" (1997: 23). He believes that true reconciliation must meet conflict and confront its cause. Schreiter points out that reconciliation is not a managed process. Reconciliation is spiritual. It is God who reconciles. It is God's grace welling up in one's life. Reconciliation is more of an attitude than an acquired skill or strategy.

Schreiter implicitly suggests that forms of reconciliation should be designed to fit various cultural contexts. He explains,

> By making reconciliation a skill it is accorded the highest (read: most scientific) form of rationality. But to reduce reconciliation to the technical-rational is to devalue it in other cultures (1997: 27).

Robert Schreiter's framework for the definition of "reconciliation" is summarized in a schematic representation on the facing page.

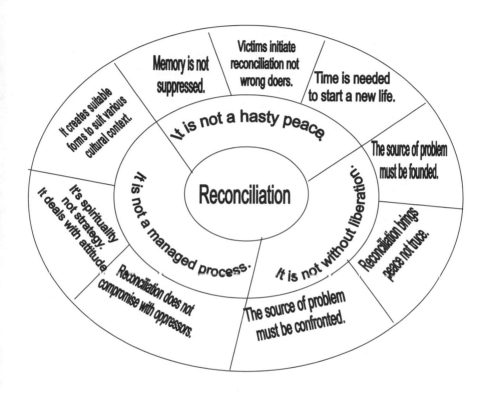

**Fig. 1: Schematic Representation of Schreiter's Definition
of Reconciliation**

A. H. Mathias Zahniser's Theory

A. H. Mathias Zahniser, the John Wesley Beeson Professor of Christian Missions, firmly believes that Christians can utilize symbols and ceremonies in making disciples across cultures, especially in times of crisis and transition. He points out four reasons for his belief:

> at times of crisis and transition people revert to traditional religious practices; (2) at times of crisis and transition people are ripe for bonding to meaning; (3) the discipling done at times of crisis and transition will help individuals, families, and their communities deal with daily, more ordinary needs in Christ; and (4) at times of crisis and transition outsiders need the loving service of the Christian community of faith (1997: 107).

In order to understand Zahniser's ideas, we should look closely at some definitions: the definitions of "ritual," "symbol," "rites of passage," and "liminality."

Scholars and anthropologists define "ritual" differently. Victor Turner, a renowned anthropologist, defines ritual as an aggregation of symbols (1968: 2). I think any ritual is rich with symbolic objects, symbolic actions, symbolic time and place. Victor Turner views rituals as performances. These rituals transform lives of ritual participants. Moreover, rituals reveal major classification, categories and contradictions of cultural process (Grimes 1995: 148).

As rituals are an aggregation of symbols, Turner also recognizes that symbols are the "molecules of ritual" (1969: 14). Of the many definitions of "symbol," I personally like that of Paul Tillich. He says, "Symbols point beyond themselves, in the power of that to which they point" (1997: 77). Tillich recognizes that symbols are powerful—that the forms of symbols contain powerful, important and deep meanings. These deep meanings justify the use of symbols. The national flags and national anthems of our countries are just such symbols, and they powerfully affect the hearts and minds of people.

Rites of passage are important rituals in all culture. Victor Turner explains rites of passage as follows:

Van Gennep himself defined *rites de passage* as 'rites which accompany every change of place, state, social position and age.' . . . Van Gennep has shown that all rites of passage or "transition" are marked by three phases: separation, margin (or limen, signifying "threshold" in Latin), and aggregation. The first phase (of separation) comprises symbolic behavior signifying the detachment of the individual or group either from an earlier fixed point in the social structure, from a set of cultural conditions ("a state"), or from both. During the intervening "liminal" period, the characteristics of the ritual subject (the "passenger") are ambiguous; he passes through a cultural realm that has few or none of the attributes of the past or coming state. In the third phase (reaggregation or reincorporation), the passage is consummated (1969: 94-95).

A. H. Mathias Zahniser puts the explanation about rites of passage of Gennep and Turner into the schematic diagram below (1997: 92).

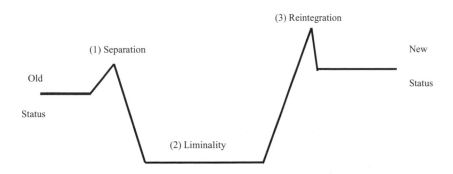

Fig. 2: Zahniser's Structure of a Rite of Passage

According to Zahniser,

> A rite of passage enables initiates to make a transition from
> one clearly defined position in society to another. These rites
> usually accompany the change from nonbeing to being in
> birth, from childhood to adulthood in puberty rites, from the
> single to the married state in marriage, and from life to the
> status of ancestor in the funeral (1997: 92).

In rites of passage, liminality or "threshold" is very important.
Initiates are in a gray area of life that causes them to deeply think
and feel. This experience encourages them to grow spiritually and
socially. Many Buddhist novices weep in the ritual process of monk
ordination and many Christians experience God's presence when
they are baptized. Zahniser also advocates anthropologist Kenneth
Tollefson's saying about the power of the rite-of-passage structure as
a "pedagogical opportunity for promoting personal development and
spiritual growth" (1990: 315). Tollefson believes that liminality
provides educational opportunity. The initiates experience the state
of marginality that helps them reflect on the past and the future. The
process of reflection encourages cognitive dissonance which
stimulates the initiates' reorientation of self-understanding and
perception of suitable social obligation and behavior. The state of
liminality is very important for the structure of the rites of passage.

On the facing page is a schematic presentation of my
theoretical framework concerning the ritual of reconciliation. Here, I
utilize Schreiter's theory about the definition of reconciliation, and
Zahniser's schematic presentation of rites of passage abstracted from
Arnold Van Gennep and Victor Turner.

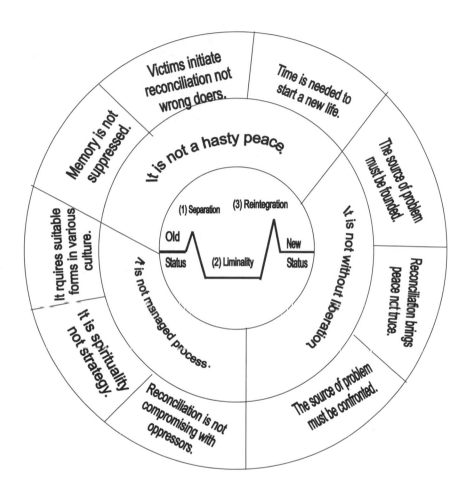

Fig. 3: The Schematic Presentation of the Ritual of Reconciliation

Critical Contextualization

I will now elucidate the concept of "critical contextualization." Paul Hiebert makes many suggestions in his book, *Anthropological Reflections on Missiological Issues* (1994). I will discuss their bearing on contextualization as follows: (1) exegesis of the culture; (2) exegesis of Scripture and the hermeneutical bridge; (3) critical contextualization's demand for a critical response; (4) new contextualized practices; and (5) checks against syncretism.

Hiebert explains exegesis of culture:

> The first step in critical contextualization is to study the local culture phenomenologically. Local church leaders and the missionary lead the congregation in uncritically gathering and analyzing the traditional beliefs and customs associated with some question at hand (1994: 88).

He also describes exegesis of Scripture and the hermeneutical bridge:

> The leader must also have a meta-cultural framework that enables him or her to translate the biblical message into the cognitive, affective, and evaluative dimensions of another culture. This step is crucial, for if the people do not clearly grasp the biblical message as originally intended, they will have distorted view of the gospel (1994: 89).

Hiebert explains that critical contextualization requires a critical response from local Christians in the light of their new biblical understanding. They should make decisions toward the new found truths; then Christian leaders will be able to help locals practice a new ritual that expresses the Christian meaning of the event. Hiebert suggests four criteria for checking against syncretism: that critical contextualization be biblically based; that believers be guided by the Holy Spirit; that the church acts as a hermeneutical community in contextualization; and that evangelical theologians from different cultures participate in discussion.

Using Paul Hiebert's theory of critical contextualization I will proceed to exegete the Thai ritual of reconciliation. Then I will present the exegesis of Scripture and the hermeneutical bridge of etic and emic Christians concerning the biblical meaning of "reconciliation." After this, I will briefly present a critical response to the ritual of reconciliation among Christian communities in Thailand. Following this, a Thai Christian ritual of reconciliation will be illustrated. My new contextualized practice will then be ready for checks against syncretism.

Exegesis of the Thai Ritual of Reconciliation

The Thai naturally participate in rituals of reconciliation through rites of passage, e.g., through monk ordination, funeral rites, conflict solving process, eloping, and a lot more. With the help of Schreiter and Zahniser's theory of the ritual of reconciliation, in order to find out its meaning and structure, I will analyze an example of the Thai ritual of reconciliation as it is recorded in a famous novel, *A Child of the Northeast*. Recorded below is an event concerning a couple in northeastern Thailand who committed fornication.

Early the next morning, when it was still dark as midnight, Koon awoke to hear a woman yelling at the top of her voice, right outside their house.

"Put down your ladder, Koon's papa!"

It was Auntie Kao, who was the wife of Uncle Yai and the mother of Kamgong. "Open your door," she yelled. "The water buffalo?" Koon's mother called out, opening the door and leaning out.

"Where is it now?" Koon's father asked.

"Still in Kamgong's bedroom," she said. "And her Papa is standing outside the door with his long knife."

His parents leaned out the doorway, and there was a hasty discussion. Koon soon understood that the water buffalo was Tid-Joon, son of Uncle Mek, and that he had been in Pi Kamgong's bedroom the whole night. Just before dawn, at the hour when the rooster was about to hop from his perch, Pi

Kamgong had called to her mother that Tid-Joon was in there, and had been with her the whole night.

At once, her father had jumped up and grabbed his long knife to stand guard in front of his daughter's door, so that Tid-Joon could not jump down from the house, leaving Kamgong up there, as daughters sometimes were left.

Koon's father sent Auntie Kao off to fetch Tid-Joon's mother and father. Then he dressed and went to tell Auntie Bua-si and Uncle Kem. They were more distant relatives, but in any important family matter, all of the family gathered—which was to say, almost the whole village.

"Mama, will Tid-Joon live with Pi Kamgong now?"

"Yes, son."

"Why don't they have a wedding, and invite people to eat lop and drink whiskey?"

"Because they are so poor. When two people marry this way, it is called chu sao. Kamgong's Papa says that he does not like Tid-Joon, and that Tid-Joon has no money. But that is not really true. The important thing is that Kamgong is the only child in the family who still lives at home and can help Uncle Yai and Auntie Kao. That's why Kamgong needs a little help herself . . ."

"So Tid-Joon went over there last night and sneaked into her bedroom and helped her?"

"Er . . ."

The sun still had not risen when they reached Uncle Yai's house, but Koon could see the dim shapes of many people clustered in the yard. Four of five of the oldest people in the village were up on the porch, chatting quietly with Koon's grandmother.

When they climbed into the house, Koon was very relieved to see that Uncle Yai was not standing in front of Pi Kamgong's door with a long knife, but sitting calmly enough on the kitchen floor and smoking a cigarette. And he was amazed to see that Tid-Joon's father had arrived already, and was sitting and smoking with Uncle Yai. He did not see Tid-Joon's mother.

And there was Pi Kamgong, the cause of all the trouble, sitting next to her mother, sitting hunched over and staring miserably at the floor.

"All right, everyone is here now," Koon's father said. "It is time for Tid-Joon to come out of the bedroom."

The door opened slowly and Tid-Joon crept forward. He crawled to his father's side on his hands and knees, and sat hunched over just like Kamgong, staring at the floor.

Koon was astonished. The swaggering young man he had seen at the well was not swaggering now!

"What do you all say to our mother speaking first?" Koon's father asked. No one replied. They all turned toward the old woman, and waited respectfully for her to speak. Koon's grandmother looked at Kamgong and Tid-Joon for a moment, then at the others. She said,

"A man and a woman become husband and wife in one of three ways. One, the man asks for her, and there is a wedding ceremony. Two, they run away together. Three, <u>chu</u> <u>sao</u> . . ."

"So what is to be done now?" Uncle Yai asked angrily.

Koon's grandmother raised her hand.

"If Tid-Joon asks forgiveness of our family, and of the spirits of our ancestors, that is enough."

She looked sternly at Uncle Yai and said, "Everybody in the village knows that Tid-Joon does not have a thing to offer but his apology, so that will have to be enough!"

"Our family accepts the whole blame," Uncle Mek said, "because Tid-Joon is our son, and he did wrong. But if the other family calls for some payment, I do not know what we will do, because we do not have anything, and that is the truth.

There is nothing of value in our whole place but three bahts and a chicken."

They talked until the sun began to rise, and it was then that Tid-Joon's mother appeared, carrying a tray on which she had placed one folded pakomah, some flowers, and the family's three baht. Tid-Joon sat up straight, for the first time, and Koon noticed the movement of the powerful muscles in his shoulders, arms and chest as he took the tray from his mother and crept on his knees toward the elders. He bent low before Uncle Yai, and before Auntie Kao; then he crawled toward Koon's mother and father, and bowed before them.

"And before our grandmother!" Uncle Yai said gruffly, and Tid-Joon quickly crawled to Koon's grandmother, and touched his head to the floor before her.

Koon's grandmother smiled down at him, and dabbed at her eyes with a square of red and black cloth.

"This Tid-Joon is a good boy," she said. "This boy has gone to the temple to be a monk in his time, and he will be a good husband and a father until he is an old man.

"Tid-Joon, listen to me. If you are a poor man, then you make merit with your good heart, and with the strength of your body."

Tid-Joon looked up, smiling gratefully at these sweet words from his bride's grandmother, and it was at the moment that Tid-Hod, the drunk, came struggling up the house ladder with the chicken under one arm, and stood steadily on the porch.

"Kamgong! What is this, letting that big water buffalo into the garden? Ha ha ha!"

"It is my karma, Tid-Hod," said Kamgong in a small shaky voice, not raising her head.

Tid-Hod sat down, leaned back on one elbow, and said that as soon as he had heard about this bad water buffalo, he had gone out and gotten a chicken for Tid-Joon to cook for his bride's ancestors. "After we make some lop from the chicken," he said, "and after the ancestors have had their share, we will all take a few bites ourselves."

Tid-Hod picked himself up and went off with Uncle Sang, Auntie Si-nin's husband, to kill the chicken and make the lop. It took them only a few minutes, and soon Koon's grandmother was lading chicken lop into a tiny bowl.

She put this bowl into a tray with some betel leaves, prettily folded and sprinkled with water, and the three baht from Tid-Joon's family. She carried the tray from the kitchen, and called Tid-Joon and Kamgong to follow her into Kamgong's bedroom, where she made them kneel down and ask forgiveness of Kamgong's ancestors, so that they could have a happy life together, and then she led them out to sit facing the people who by now filled the house, and also the porch.

"Tid-Hod brought a chicken for lop," she told them.

"Will there be enough rice for all these people?" one old woman asked.

"There will be enough," said Auntie Kao, Tid-Joon's mother. "Our neighbors have come, bringing four boxes."

Koon sat beside his father, sniffing the air hungrily. When six small bowls of chicken lop were set down between four boxes of rice, the people all reached forward politely, quickly rolling balls of rice and dipping them into the delicious food (Boontawee 1994: 84–90).

The events portrayed here illustrate a transition in the lives of Kamgong and Tid-Joon, from the status of single to the status of married, through fornication. They separated themselves to secretly enjoy their desire. The first state of separation was abruptly ended when Kamgong called at dawn to her mother acknowledging Tid-Joon's presence in her bedroom.

Then the liminality elucidates itself driving Kamgong and Tid-Joon into "threshold." They were not single, but they were not married either. They brought shame to both families and relatives. Kamgong's parents became victims. Tid-Joon polluted their virgin daughter without paying a dowry. Both Kamgong and Tid-Joon committed a cultural sin. They also committed a religious sin, breaking the third precept of Buddha. The spirits of Kamgong's ancestors were violated. The spirits could punish the whole clan of Kamgong and Tid-Joon. In liminality, Kamgong and Tid-Joon lost their old status. During, betwixt, and between these events, however, both of them probably learned about the difference between pollution and purity, as well as the importance of community. They probably reflected a lot about their past and future as they were confronted publicly by the victims of their sins.

Note that the victims initiated the process of reconciliation. It was a long process because the victims did not suppress their pain and anger. They pointed out the cause of the problem. The father wanted to liberate himself from shame, the loss of identity and the loss of dignity. Grandmother was the authority of the ritual of reconciliation. I believe that through God's image left in each victim, they could forgive Kamgong and Tid-Joon. Yet they also humiliated both oppressors. Thai culture demanded that both oppressors bow down to their victims' feet—the most humiliating of actions— signifying the submission of ego and oneself to the victim.

The ritual objects are humble and simple: a piece of cloth, a small amount of money, and flowers. A piece of cloth is a gift the Thai give to elderly people in sacred times such as festivals and ceremonies. Money represents a dowry. Tid-Joon's dowry, three baht, was all that his family had. Flowers represent friendship. Liminality ended when the victims forgave their oppressors and Grandma blessed them. Then Tid-Joon and Kamgong were reintegrated into a new status as a married couple. They reconciled to the victims and to the Buddhist precept of purity. They also apologized to Kamgong's ancestors' spirits. After that, celebration of the new status quickly followed.

This analysis reveals that the Thai ritual of reconciliation follows Schreiter's definition of reconciliation and the structure of rites of passage. The only superfluous action from the Christian perspective is the reconciliation to the ancestors' spirits. Apart from that, most of the ritual can be participated in by Thai Christians.

Some more information about the ritual can be helpful. This ritual of reconciliation is called the *Kama* and *Ahosikarma* Ritual. *Kama* and *Ahosikarma* are archaic words that come from Pali. *Kama* means "to ask for pardon; to humbly apologize." *Ahosikarma* means "forgiveness of the offence is granted" (Thai Royal Academy 1995: 128, 925).

Perhaps these concepts come from myths in primal religion, Hinduism, and/or Buddhism, being that these are the main strands of Thai syncretistic religion (Sataanandha and Boonyanate 1993: 6-12). Hinduism provides many myths about humans who offended gods and, thus, had to be reconciled to gods through sacrifices. Buddhism emphasizes reconciliation for broken human relationships. The Buddhist myth of Buddha's life tells about the great thief, Ongkulimand, who asked for pardon from Buddha, whom he wanted to kill. Buddha forgave him. Primal religionists in Thailand worship spirits both good and bad. When Thai people offend these spirits, they have to ask for forgiveness (*Kama*) and make an offering to suspend the offended spirits' chastisement.

Nowadays, the words "Kama" and "Ahosikarma" are frequently used in Thai language when relationships between persons are being challenged. The word "Ahosikarma" is shortened to "Hosi," being a vernacular expression. This demonstrates that the concept of reconciliation is still very important in Thai culture.

Exegesis of the Biblical Concept of Reconciliation

I will present here a meta-cultural exegesis of the biblical concept of reconciliation. I will employ the theological work of

Robert S. Schreiter, a C.P.P.S. American Theologian, William Barclay, a Scottish New Testament interpreter, Clearence B. Bass, an American Professor of Systematic Theology, and my own work, that of a Thai missiologist and theologian.

Schreiter also references a German theologian of New Testament, Cilliers Breytenbach:

> Cilliers Breytenbach has argued recently that the usages in the authentic Pauline passages in Romans 5 and 2 Corinthians 5 are not connected with the older biblical ideas of atonement, but reflect a more secular usage, namely, a making of peace after a time of war (1992: 42).

I think Breytenbach's idea elucidates human reconciliation in a way that can be easily understood by non-Christians.

Making reference to Latin American liberation theologian José Comblin, Schreiter notes:

> Combining the references in Romans and 2 Corinthians with the usages in Colossians and Ephesians, José Comblin has suggested that a theology of reconciliation can be discerned on three levels: a christological level, in which Christ is the mediator through whom God reconciles the world to God's self; an ecclesiological level, in which Christ reconciles Jew and Gentile; and a cosmic level, in which Christ reconciles all the powers in heaven and on earth (1992: 42).

Robert Schreiter condenses the exegesis of the New Testament texts regarding reconciliation into five points: (1) it is God who initiates and brings about reconciliation; (2) reconciliation is more a spirituality than a strategy; (3) reconciliation makes both victim and oppressor a new creation; (4) the new narrative that overcomes the narrative of the lie is the story of passion, death and resurrection of Jesus Christ; (5) reconciliation is a multidimensional reality.

I have clarified the first three points in the "Theoretical Framework" section of this paper, but have not touched on the fourth and fifth. Schreiter beautifully interprets the meaning of the passion, the death, and the resurrection of Jesus Christ. God illustrated his passion when he incarnated himself into the suffering, violence and death of humanity through his death on the cross. Human blood brings death; God's blood brings life. Jesus' resurrection heralds "new status" for all mankind, both victims and oppressors.

Schreiter also notes that reconciliation goes beyond problem solving. Reconciliation heals otherness and alienation, as stated in Romans 9-11; God reconciles Jews and Gentiles. Reconciliation includes all things in heaven and on earth (Eph. 1: 9-10; Col. 1: 19-20). Reconciliation, therefore, takes on a cosmic dimension. I think Schreiter has given us a cornerstone for the exegesis of the biblical concept of reconciliation.

William Barclay's exegesis confirms the first four points of Schreiter's conclusion. Barclay believes that God initiates reconciliation. It is completely by grace. The death of Christ changes our status with God. Christ's resurrection changes our state. Christ's justification puts us into a right relationship with God. Christ's sanctification affects our state. We can experience God's continuous saving grace (1975: 75-77). Barclay's exegesis seems to emphasize a specific dimension of reconciliation—that of God-man relationship.

Clearence Bass exegetes terminology regarding reconciliation. The exegesis is much more detailed than that of Barclay. However, the conclusion is the same in its lack of reference to social reconciliation, individual reconciliation, and cosmic reconciliation.

I exegete "reconciliation" differently. As a believer from Asia, I prefer to exegete the deep meaning of "reconciliation" from life stories. In this paper, I want to explore the reconciliation process recorded in the story of Joseph and his brothers in Genesis 37-47 and the story of Peter's reconciliation with Jesus in John 21. I see in these two incidents some structures similar to Schreiter's exegesis of "reconciliation."

(1) It is God who initiated the reconciliation. Probably, Joseph met God on the road to Egypt. He was a changed man while in Egypt; God was with him (Gen. 39: 3, 5, 21, 23). Jesus is God who incarnated himself into Jewish culture.

(2) Reconciliation is more a spirituality than a strategy. Joseph and Jesus encountered betrayal from someone whom they loved. Both of them experienced pain, violence, and injustice. However, they forgave. They took initiative in the reconciliation process. They confronted their oppressors. The causes of problems were clarified.

(3) Reconciliation makes both victims and oppressors a new creation. Joseph's brothers were changed. Joseph was changed. Peter became a pillar of the early church. Jesus, the Victim, became the Victor.

(4) The new narrative that overcomes the narrative of betrayal is the narrative of atonement. Suffering begets life and liberation. Death brings life.

(5) Reconciliation is a multidimensional reality. Individual reconciliation between Joseph and his brothers affects the clan and the nation. Peter's reconciliation affects the community, various nations, the world, and the cosmos as the gospel spreads out. Reconciliation is holistic. It affects the material world, the relational world, and the spiritual world.

(6) Reconciliation confirms that God's image remains in all cultures (Gen. 1: 27). People had reconciled through God's image before Christ came.

It seems to me that the exegesis of meta-cultural theologians provides strong ground for the claim that the Thai ritual of reconciliation is biblical.

A Critical Response

Through various seminars I have discussed the concepts involved in the Thai ritual of reconciliation with approximately one hundred missionaries to Thailand. Most agree that the Thai ritual of reconciliation is biblical and it can be contextualized. Thai Buddhists unanimously suggest that Christians use this ritual in discipling. Most Thai Christian leaders like the Thai ritual of reconciliation. Though few missionaries express concern about the use of symbolic objects, their use remains the only area of question. We are now ready to look at the contextualization of the ritual of reconciliation and its ability to bond new converts to their families.

New Contextualized Practice

On the basis of the frameworks and exegesis of Scripture, I believe that the concepts of reconciliation in the Thai *Kama* and *Ahosikarma* ritual can be stepping stones in Thai culture for the understanding of Christ as the Reconciler. I also believe that it can heal the broken relationship between new Buddhist converts (as well as old Buddhist converts) and their social networks. The contextualization of this ritual into a Christian *Kama* and *Ahosikarma* ritual must, therefore, be designed to help the new converts bond to their natural social networks and Christ, the Reconciler. This study will now lay out a Christian *Kama* and *Ahosikarma* ritual.

The Christian Ritual of Reconciliation, Kama and Ahosikarma

As a rite of passage, the Christian ritual of *Kama* and *Ahosikarma* is divided into three stages: (1) separation, (2) liminality, and (3) reincorporation.

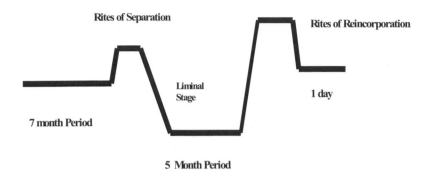

**Fig. 4:   The Rites of Passage Structure of the Christian Ritual
of Reconciliation**

According to the figure above, the rites of separation and the liminal stage take one year. Due to the Thais' value of grateful relationships and smooth interpersonal relationships, and their flexibility and adjustment orientation, the prolonged time provides a shock absorber, allowing the new converts to throw away their idols and to tell their parents about their conversion to Christianity. These are acts of separation from Buddhism. At the same time, the prolonged time provides a shock absorber for the parents when informed by their children of this important separation. During the liminal stage, the prolonged time allows the initiates to be bonded to the meaning of reconciliation to other persons, to God, to cultural communities, and to Christian communities, thus allowing them to be both Thais and Christians. This will result in a good sense of identity for the new converts. They will grow as Thais and Christians because they will have unbroken relational ties with their natural and cultural social networks, as well as with their Christian communities.

Due to the importance of this issue, I would like to concentrate on the bonding of the new converts to their relatives in each phase of the rite of passage in the *Kama* and *Ahosikarma* ritual. I will discuss this bonding within the context of the ritual of *Kama* and *Ahosikarma* as recorded in the event mentioned above. Moreover, I will use the nine value clusters of the Thai, their concepts of hierarchy, cyclical time and being, and their activity as a framework for the stages of separation, liminality, and reincorporation.

The Rites of Separation in the Christian Ritual of Reconciliation, Kama and Ahosikarma

    3. Putting away idols

    4. Informing the families of the conversion

    5. Negotiating

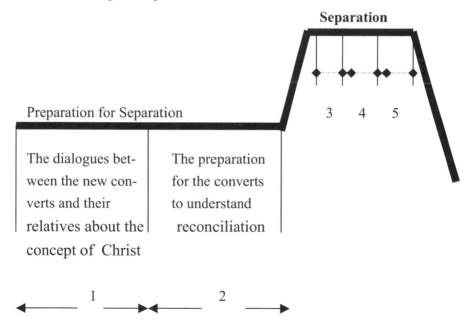

Fig. 5: The Rites of Separation

There are five steps in the rite of separation: (1) the religious dialogues between the new converts and their relatives about Christ and the church; (2) the preparation for the new converts to understand the concept of reconciliation; (3) putting away idols; (4) informing the families of the conversion; and (5) negotiating for confession and forgiveness. The religious dialogue between the new converts and their relatives is an important foundation for the Christian ritual of reconciliation, *Kama* and *Ahosikarma*.

Religious dialogue demands trust, respect, and love for parents on the part of the new converts. According to the apostle John, "There is no fear in love; but perfect love casts out fear, because fear involves punishment, and the one who fears is not perfected in love. We love because he first loved us" (John 4:18-20).

This kind of attitude will help the new converts to communicate their contact with Christianity to their parents from the beginning. This style of the communication will be effective only when it fits Thai cultural values. The parents will feel respected, trusted, and loved if the new converts ask for permission to go to the church and report what they learn from the church. The parents are willing to discuss religion with their children because the children's behavior indicates that they cherish the parents' identity, their concept of hierarchy, grateful relationship orientation, interpersonal relationship orientation, and interdependence orientations.

The new converts should also encourage Christians who are well aware of Thai culture to get to know their social networks. This will ease the fear and anxiety of Thai parents and help them to have a clearer view of Christians. They have various myths about Christians and churches. These myths should be corrected through the Christians' goodness.

The new converts must pay attention to their family's problems and needs. They must cooperate with their relatives to solve these problems, because collectivism is very important for the Thai. These behaviors will prevent new converts from alienating themselves from their relatives. They will also help bonding with relatives, and both sides will be prepared for the religious separation. The meekness and the vulnerability on the part of the new converts will prepare their social networks to negotiate in the liminal stage, as well as the rite of reincorporation.

The Liminal Stage of the Christian Ritual of Reconciliation, Kama and Ahosikarma

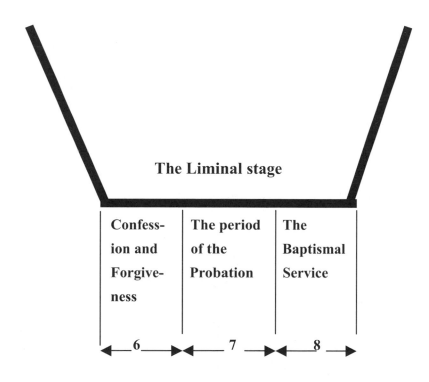

Fig. 6: The Liminal Stage

The liminal stage creates deeper bonding between the new converts and their social networks. The bonding is divided into three steps: (1) confession and forgiveness; (2) the period of the probation; and (3) the baptismal service.

The first step is the formal act of confession, in which the new converts who bring shame to their immediate families and relatives ask for forgiveness and bow down at the feet of their parents. The meekness in communication, the sacred indigenous objects, and the sacred ceremony speak to the hearts and minds of the Thai, allowing them to respond positively to the new converts.

This ritual of confession and forgiveness provides ways for the parents and relatives to vent their anguish, anger, frustration, disappointment, and concern before they can proceed further to truly grant forgiveness to the new converts. Their forgiveness is the action of reciprocity. When the new converts take the initiative to value the interdependent orientation in Thai culture by asking for forgiveness, they show respect for Thai culture and their parents' pain. As a result, the parents respect their decision to convert. A Thai poem states clearly the importance of interdependency in Thai culture:

> Tigers are tigers because of jungles;
>
> Jungles are jungles because of tigers.
>
> Soil is soil because of good grasses;
>
> Grasses are grasses because of good soil.
>
> (Praya Sri Sunthorn Woharn 1962)

Respecting interdependency creates bonds between new converts and their social networks. The bonding will go deeper in the periods of probation and baptismal service.

In the period of probation (Fig. 6, No. 7), the families receive back their authority over the new converts. They will set criteria together with the local churches for the new converts to prove their accountability in preparation for their baptism. Thai culture perceives and defines "activity" as *being* rather than *doing*. Therefore, the families will require the accountability of being from the new converts, and will be very happy that they can maintain their authority over them. If the new converts submit themselves to the family's authority, there will be deeper bonding because Thai culture requires the authority to be merciful to the submissive. As a famous Thai proverb suggests,

> The meek bow down with burden;
>
> They shall be blessed at the end (Ngamdee 1993: 36).

This bonding will prepare the parents and relatives for the baptismal service. This is one of the most difficult times for the convert and their families (Fig. 6, No. 8).

At this stage, liminality will soon end for the new converts, but suffering is at its peak for the new converts' parents and relatives. The bonding will go deepest if the new converts are sensitive to the pain of the parents because, from their viewpoint, the baptismal service signifies a complete separation from Buddhism and a full identification with Christianity. The children can comfort the parents in attitude and in action according to the Thai value of grateful relationship orientation. In Thai culture, gratitude is expressed through obedience, serving, and giving.

As the baptismal service approaches, the new converts should dialogue with their social networks about the concept of death and resurrection. In doing so, they should use stepping-stones such as familiar experiences in daily living and familiar concepts in Buddhism. Eliade suggests that the moon symbolizes death and resurrection (1987: 156-157). Professor Wit Wissawate lectured that in Buddhism, life is a continuous death and rebirth like electricity (1967). This will help social networks to understand the deep religious meaning of the ritual and they will be more appreciative because the Thai are religiously oriented. They should be led to understand the ritual not as a departure from Buddhism but as a fulfillment of Buddhist self-emptying. The baptismal service should symbolize the perfect bonding to the concept of self-emptying in Buddhism through Christ. The families should be invited officially to attend the ritual. Now the process of this Christian ritual of reconciliation takes us to the rites of reincorporation.

The Rites of Reincorporation of the Christian Ritual of Reconciliation, Kama and Ahosikarma

9. The parents' discourse

10. The symbolic serving

11. The feast

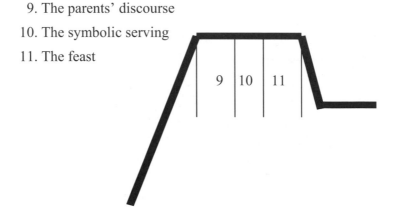

Fig. 7: The Rites of Reincorporation

The rites of reincorporation are divided into three steps: (1) the parents' discourse; (2) the symbolic serving; and (3) the feast. The bonding between the social networks and the new converts takes place in the first step. The parents are invited to give words of wisdom, which urge their children to fulfill their Christian duties to their families, communities, and the nation. The Thai like participating in formal ceremonies because of their value of hierarchy. If invited officially, they will usually agree to participate in religious ceremonies.

The feast provides another chance for bonding. The parents should be seated at the head of the table with their children, the other elderly relatives, and the church elders. The food being served should symbolize bonding and blessings. The rites of reincorporation end in joy and fellowship, but the bonding continues, as does the discipling of the new converts.

The bonding between the new converts and their social networks is not a sideline. It is their lifeline and it lasts as long as their life. If the bonding is life-long, the discipling of the new converts will last, and the church will have both strong Christians and good friends who are candidates for the kingdom. This indicates the effectiveness of the ritual.

The Effectiveness of the Christian Ritual of Reconciliation, Kama and Ahosikarma

The ritual is likely to be effective because it creates bonding between the new converts and their social networks throughout the process. As a result, the new converts are not cut off from their cultural roots. The problem of their crisis in self-identity is solved and discipling becomes possible.

The ritual trusts God as well as the parents and relatives of the new converts. Thais value ego orientation very highly, making respect and trust important ethical issues for them. Christians cherish the Thai self-identity, self-esteem, and self-respect.

This ritual accentuates six of the nine Thai value clusters: ego orientation, grateful relationship orientation, smooth interpersonal relationship orientation, flexibility and adjustment orientation, and interdependence orientation, as well as fun-pleasure orientation. The

Thai will respond to this much more than to the old model of aggressive evangelism.

This Christian ritual of reconciliation, *Kama* and *Ahosikarma*, fits the Thai's concept of time and hierarchy, allowing Christians to be viewed as humble, meek, gentle, and vulnerable, each of which is a religious model for Jesus' disciples. This is an effective way to win Thai hearts. As an anonymous ancient Thai poem says, "Be soft as a silk thread and tie a tiger down."

This ritual of reconciliation has been tested in at least three local churches. The results have been positive. People did not detect syncretism in the contextualization of the Christian ritual of reconciliation. I believe this ritual can be effectively used to heal memories of pain, violence, injustice, and oppression in war-torn countries like Laos, Cambodia, and Vietnam.

Conclusion

This study presents what is perhaps the core problem for Christianity in Thailand. When Thais become Christian, the relational bonds between new converts and their natural social networks are broken. As a result, the new converts lose their identity as Thais and become weak Christians. The parents and relatives thus turn against the church and become strong enemies of Christian conversion. This study has determined the cause of this problem to be the violation of Thai cultural values. It has pointed out that Thai culture uses the ritual *Kama* and *Ahosikarma* to heal such broken relationships. This Thai ritual can be contextualized to become a Christian ritual of reconciliation and resolve the problem mentioned above. The study has demonstrated that the ritual is a rite of passage and has given the ritual's respect for Thai values as evidence for its potential effectiveness. The study thus concludes that the Christian ritual of reconciliation, *Kama* and *Ahosikarma*, can be a means to solve the problem of the church gaining one weak Christian, yet many strong enemies, with each new convert. It will provide an effective means for helping new converts to be reconciled to their culture and to understand "reconciliation" itself.

CHAPTER 10

Abortion and *Mizuko* Rites in Japan:
How Buddhism Responds to Needy Women

Mark Dominey

Introduction

Abortion is, for most Buddhists and Christians alike, both the taking of a life and a sin. However, in the secular industrialized world, abortion has become an easy legal option and far too commonplace. In the United States, opinion is sharply divided by groups antagonistic to one another, with the Pro-Life position maintained mostly by Christians. In postwar Japan, on the other hand, there has never been such antagonistic division and anti-abortion groups are negligible.

Japan actually legalized abortion in 1948 and most people simultaneously see it as a regrettable taking of innocent life, but a necessary evil that cannot be helped. From the period of 1955 to 1964 there were actually more reported abortions than live births. In the early 1980s a high of 28% of pregnancies ended in abortion (in 2000 the figure was 22.3%), a few percentage points behind the rate in the United States. Today, millions of Japanese women have had abortions and for the past six years, the number has been growing among teenagers at an alarming rate.[1]

Buddhist sects in Japan have been mostly silent concerning the moral aspects of this problem, but the Christian churches in Japan have remained even more silent. There is no palpable Christian anti-abortion movement, much less a noticeable effort to even raise Christian consciousness on the matter. Nor are there Christian support groups available to help the millions of Japanese women who are actively seeking spiritual answers to their sad experience. Indeed, millions of women, including those in the churches, still await a truthful and sincere response that will help them find peace with God over their hidden past.

However, since the mid-1970s, there has been a noticeable development within Japanese Buddhism, which is attracting large numbers of women (and some men) who seek some sense of resolution over their abortion experience. New religious rituals for aborted children called *mizuko kuyô*, have appeared in a large number of temples, which serve as funerary and pacification rites for the spirits of aborted fetuses. Because this phenomenon appeared suddenly and became widespread, it soon caught the attention of many scholars of Japanese religions (Brooks 1981; Smith 1988; Werblowsky 1991). It has been thoroughly studied in the West by LaFleur (1992) and Hardacre (1997).

This chapter will outline the phenomenon and offer some brief suggestions for missionaries and Japanese Christians to consider. In light of the widespread abortion problem, the needs of Japanese women themselves, and the idolatrous response of temples to those needs, perhaps most important will be the question of whether Christian churches in Japan should develop some kind of memorial or rite for aborted fetuses, provide active help for the grieving women, or even see this as an opportunity for evangelism.

The Scope of the Abortion in Japan

There are over 64 million women in Japan but no one knows precisely how many have had abortions.[2] Certainly those that have experienced an abortion number in the tens of millions. Since 1948 there have been at minimum 35 million (recorded) abortions in Japan, a number that would add at minimum another 28% to the current population. The true number is much higher, because there has long been a problem with chronic intentional under-reporting by doctors, who keep the procedure off the books in order to avoid taxes. In fact, Norgren states that both Japanese and American researchers believe that the actual abortion rate in the 1980s and 1990s was 1.5 to three times the official rate (2001: 5). Werblowsky references Japanese medical and social science colleagues as saying that the true number is closer to ten times the reported figure (1991: 312). From the mid-1950s to the mid-1960s, over half of all pregnancies are officially thought to have ended in abortion. Recent government statistics put the number at over 340,000 cases per year (Kitamura 2002: 16-17).

One thing that seems clear is that the number of unwanted pregnancies (and consequently abortions) would have been less if the Japanese government had only legalized oral contraceptives before 1999. Amazingly, it took almost 40 years for the pill to be approved in Japan, and only after public outcry at the swift approval process for Viagra—which took less than a year! According to the Alan Guttmacher Institute, Japan is "curious" in its attitudes toward the pill (Kihara et al. 2001), no doubt the result of years of anti-pill official propaganda that has left the public misinformed and relying on the efficacy of condoms. Kitamura records condom failure as the reason for 52% of unwanted pregnancies in Japan (2002: 23). As many researchers (Norgren, Hardacre, Kihara, Kitamura) have already noted, one has to consider the possibility that the official opposition to the pill from medical associations and even the Ministry of Health and Welfare might have actually been due to the unstated reason that abortions are more lucrative than dispensing pills and even births.

Although the lowest recorded official number of abortions was in 1991, since then there has been a rapid increase due to a huge increase in teen pregnancy. The Japan Ministry of Health and Welfare issued a report (Aug. 8, 2002) remarking that abortions among teenage girls had reached a record high for the sixth straight year (46,571 for girls age 19 and under), almost twice the number as in 1995 (26,117). Moreover, the segments of women receiving the greatest number of abortions were the 20–24 and 25–29 years old age groups (82,540 and 72,621, respectively), indicating that unwanted pregnancies are, by a far margin, now the result of sex outside of marriage.

Unfortunately, there is now a measured rise in abortions performed in Japan that has not been seen for 50 years. Overall, the increase in sexual activity among young people in the 1990s as well as less availability of reliable contraception has resulted in more unwanted pregnancies and more abortions among teens in particular. Many of these women deal with their abortions by turning to *mizuko* rites.

Japan's *Mizuko Kuyô* Phenomenon

The Japanese term *mizuko* literally means "water baby" and suggests the unborn fetus in its amniotic sack. *Mizuko* always means a child who has died, either by miscarriage or induced abortion. The term *kuyô* refers to "rites" (lit. "offer sustenance") where offerings are made, often with the notion of merit transfer, commonly seen in Japanese ancestor worship. The rituals now termed *mizuko kuyô* can be best thought of as ancestor worship for ones departed descendants, even if strictly speaking they are not parental ancestors, but children who precede their own mothers in death. Nowadays, the *mizuko* are more likely to be the result of abortion than miscarriages. Often such deaths are unknown to or not recognized by their father, though technically belonging to the pantheon of his family lineage. The responsibility to do something about these departed children thus falls on the mothers, who do so silently.

The bodhisattva Jizô (Sk. Ksitigarbha) is central to *mizuko* practices and the cult of Jizô in Japanese Buddhism is important in understanding people's thinking about what has happened to their child and what is required for the departed soul to find peace and enlightenment. Jizô has since ancient times been seen as having a special role in protecting children in Japan. There is a great deal of popular lore, mostly indigenous, about Jizô in this capacity. Stone idols of Jizô appear in almost every neighborhood and many, if not most, temples. It is very common to see these statues with a bib (usually red) tied around their necks, and they often take on an infant-like appearance, due to having the shaved head of a priest. Often the Jizô statues are small and child-like. Jizô also frequently appears as a priest holding a staff and a jewel. Needless to say, all Japanese children from a young age learn of Jizô as a merciful and kind protector "buddha" to be prayed to and revered for helping protect children from accidents, etc.

Jizô was imported to Japan by Koreans in 577. In 5th century China Jizô (Ch. Dìzàng) was known as one who could intercede with the Kings of Hell. In the Muromachi era (1338-1573) Jizô began to be seen as a guarantor of long life, safe childbirth, and safety for children. During the Edo period the association with children expanded with popular lore such as miracle tales and hymns. The notion of *Sai-no-kawara* arose, which is a liminal "riverbed of judgment" akin to limbo, where the souls of dead children were thought to congregate and pile up stones to make stupas as a devotional act on their parents' behalf while being chased by demons (*oni*). As protectorate of children, the notion that Jizô would have a special role in caring for the souls of *mizuko* is easily understandable, even though there is no historical evidence that Ksitigarbha ever had this role outside of Japan, even in China. Nevertheless, as a bodhisattva Jizô shows compassion on all people in the same way as Kannon (Avelokitesvara or Kuan Yin) or Amida (Amitabha), who have mercifully stopped short of their own enlightenment in order to help humanity as Buddhist saviors.

Temples performing *mizuko* rituals typically sell small Jizô figurines (idols) that represent an aborted fetus. It can be quite overwhelming to see the number of such statues lined up at larger temples. For example, temples such as Shiunzan near Chichibu in Saitama or Hasedera in Kamakura have many thousands. Brooks reported ten to twenty thousand *mizuko tôba* at a temple in Kyoto (1981: 122). Mothers come to find their own statue and make offerings, such as children's clothing (knitted caps are popular, as well as infant shoes or coats in winter), milk, candy, or toys (pinwheels are very common); high school girls often offer keychains. Purchasing a Jizô statuette is just part of the *mizuko kuyô* rites; money is paid to the priest at various times to perform Buddhist prayers on behalf of the dead spirit.

Of course, one major reason for this type of religious behavior is that it parallels ancestor worship in form. What is notable is that these rights are for the unborn, who have not even been named. As Smith writes, "in the case of mizuko there is obviously a fundamental inversion of the typical and expected sequence in the ancestor-descendent continuity. A child here dies before its parents" (1988: 9). It is because the *mizuko* deaths differ from one's seniors that there is some confusion about what is to be done. Although *mizuko* rites are becoming more common, they are not "ordinary."

It needs to be stated that most women who have abortions are probably not involved in *mizuko* rites. In both 1983 and 1984, researches estimated that about 18% of the women reported to have had abortions in those years had performed *mizuko kuyô*. Hardacre estimates that the effective market makes up only 15 to 20 percent of women who have had abortions. She concludes: "This is a minority practice, rejected by most abortion recipients and most religious institutions" (1997: 99). However, if *one in five* Japanese women who have had an abortion are willing to pay money and go through rituals to overcome their hurts and fears, then this still represents a sizeable number of people interested in spiritual answers to a problem that includes unresolved guilt, grief, fear of spirit attack, and as I will show below, even a recognition that a sin has been committed for which some sort of atonement is needed.

One difference in *mizuko* rites is the need to express apology, an understandable sentiment that is arguably exacerbated in the Japanese cultural context. According to a translation of a brochure from Shiunzan,

> The principal things that have to be done for its sake are the making of a full apology and the making of amends to such a child... If the parents merely carry out ordinary memorial rites but fail to make a full apology to their child, their *mizuko* will never be able to accept their act (LaFleur 1999: 194; 1992: 221).

According to the temple brochure, the next thing to do is to set up an image of Jizô in both the home and at a temple grounds. Shiunzan reasons,

> Such a Jizô can do double service. On one hand it can represent the soul of the *mizuko* for parents doing rites of apology to it. Simultaneously, however, the Jizô is the one to whom can be made an appeal in prayer to guide the fetus through the realm of departed souls (ibid).

The Jizô image also does a double duty as a memorial tablet for the infant. Parents are urged to offer water and rice to it daily, praying for the well-being of the *mizuko* and chanting sutras to it, as well as making monetary offerings "to buddha" because "you never had to pay anything for the upbringing and education of a *mizuko*" (ibid: 195). Here we can ironically see the debt one might feel towards one's own parents inverted as unfulfilled duty towards one's children. But perhaps more serious for Buddhists would be the problem of incurred karmic debt.

Buddhist Teaching about Abortion

What does Japanese Buddhism teach regarding the death of infants and abortion? Simply put, killing in any form is a serious sin and abortion is viewed as the taking of a life. Moreover, there is no debate among Japanese Buddhists that life begins at conception and that fetuses are fully human. However, ultimately, since Buddhism is nontheistic, there is no God who will stand in judgment over abortion. Only negative karma is a concern, not eternal damnation. Lay people may be taught the Five Precepts for "right" actions which include not taking any life and avoiding sexual misconduct, but for ethical decision-making, avoiding more suffering seems to be primary. Historically, abortion was seen as immoral. Stevens writes,

> Since birth control could be interpreted as an attempt to interfere with the workings of karma, there was a tendency within Buddhism to discourage artificial contraception... Abortion, however, was an abomination... the Buddhist position against abortion was clearcut and has only been questioned in modern times (1990: 139).

While sects today may be reluctant to take a firm position against *mizuko* because there is no explicit canonical warrant, those promoting *mizuko* rites may be criticized for their silence since their livelihood depends on it.

In postmodern Japan, reincarnation (as a human, much less as a beast or in hell) is for all practical purposes no longer believed a likely outcome by the vast majority of secular Buddhists. This is not so much a loss of faith as the logical development of the extreme Mahayana doctrine syncretized with ancestor worship, which has progressively moved from individuals taking responsibility for their own enlightenment through ascetic practices to what I want to call "lazy Buddhism," whereby one does almost nothing but rely on others (*tariki*), namely saviors like Amida or Kannon—and the rituals performed by descendents—to guarantee enlightenment. Indeed, Japanese Buddhism as a whole is arguably the most simplified and highly developed of the various Mahayana schools in Asia, and most people nowadays assume that they will enter the Pure Land after death on the basis of both the merit transfer rituals and the unlimited benevolence of bodhisattvas. Proper funeral rites and the accompanying memorials including the purchase of a proper posthumous name (*kaimyô*) are the key in this merit transfer, a matter that is left to the family. In sum, Japanese Buddhism teaches a kind of universalism for all will become buddhas through proper ritual.

In contrast, during the Edo period, babies were not normally given funerals because people generally hoped they would be reborn in the human world. Graves were not built nor memorial services performed. Hardacre writes:

> When Buddhist rites were performed, they usually took the form of "feeding the hungry ghosts," or rites of prayer and intercession (*kitô*), rather than rites of merit transfer on which adult funerals and memorial rites are based (1997: 54).

Brooks believes that "it is debatable whether or not *mizuko kuyô* is authentically Buddhist" (1981: 120). True, but most Japanese probably perceive that it is. However, in the case of rituals that have developed for the pacification of *mizuko* spirits, we see an interesting conflict of ideas about Buddhist afterlife and departure from normal rites. First, most temples do not intern the remains of fetuses (though by law they are required to be cremated from the fourth month of gestation). There are exceptions. Sôjiji temple in Tokyo keeps the bones of *over half a million* babies (Brooks 1981: 121). But the statues of Jizô replace the graves per se, or the home altar for many women. Second, in contrast to the death of traditional ancestors, many mothers pray for their aborted children to quickly be reborn, usually into their family as a sibling, if the reason for the abortion was an untimely pregnancy or before marriage.[3] This affirms reincarnation. Yet the possibility of rebirth is also juxtaposed by the possibility of becoming a Buddha and many mothers desire that the child's spirit will, by ritual, become enabled to watch over them as a guardian spirit, a sentiment expressed on votive prayer plaques (*ema*) found at many temple compounds.[4] Especially for those who do not want more children, this is the common conclusion. In short, the popularization of abortion has not been matched by a coherent response from Buddhist dogmatists and people have been left confused over what really happens to their dead child and how they should deal with the matter.

Still, there is measurable confusion about where their *mizuko* have gone. Over 45% say that their *mizuko* are "always in my heart," about 40% see them as having souls which have gone to "the other world," 25% see them as having "returned" to their "ancestors," and 20% each believe that they are either in heaven or reborn (Hardacre 1997: 97). The multiple responses that people gave indicate that they are unsure. Even some priests do not agree. Some have pointed out that creating a *mizuko* creates bad karma, but others have suggested that it is the *mizuko* who carries the bad karma and suffers. Although confusion remains about the specifics, as Brooks notes, "some credit should be given to Japanese Buddhists for accommodating Buddhism to the particular needs of the Japanese people" (1981: 139). In general, it seems that nowadays many women choose to think of their aborted children as having become godlike rather than returning in rebirth as humans.

The Concept of Spirit Retribution in *Mizuko* Rites

In spite of official Buddhist dogma, one important element in understanding *mizuko kuyô* is the notion of spirit retribution (*tatari*). According to many temples that are promoting *mizuko* rites, the spirits of aborted infants are not in peace, but suffering in a dark and confused state, vengeful over their mother's rejection of them, and prone to attack the living. Many see the spirits as confused souls that need to be placated and sent on by ritual to their own path to buddhahood, but it should not be forgotten that abortions are deaths that results from violence to the fetus. Nevertheless, if proper measures are not taken to assist the suffering soul, it may spiritually attack the family that aborted it. Common among the types of symptoms that suggest *tatari* would be nightmares, feeling as if something is suffocating you in your sleep (*kanashibari*), bedwetting, and even a child's poor performance in school. Although such problems may have other explanations, for women who have experienced abortions and have not resolved their grief and guilt, especially those who maintain a belief in the worldview that includes spirit retribution, the conclusion that a vengeful child spirit is involved seems reasonable. In fact, a large number of Japanese women these days assume that *mizuko* spirits will become vengeful and cause troubles if they are not placated through the proper temple *kuyô* rites.

The notion that innocent children somehow transform into attacking spirits is not unlike existing concepts of "hungry ghosts" (*gaki*) or those who died without family to perform rites (*muenbotoke*), which are also angry and attack due to neglect, and which, unlike *mizuko*, have a longer doctrinal history in Mahayana outside of Japan. Both Hardacre and LaFleur have given plenty of evidence to show that the *mizuko* phenomenon is created and maintained by temples, many of which would appear to be unscrupulous in their desire to manipulate women through fear and maintain a new and lucrative source of income. Although the *mizuko* cult can be found in temples of all six major sects, the largest sect in Japan (Jôdo or Pure Land sect) has officially spoken out against the practices, particularly the notion of *tatari*.[5] Many priests in all sects are concerned about the sensationalism that some temples have resorted to in order to promote the new rites. Japan's mass media and the tabloid press have also had a large role in shaping and promoting the *mizuko* phenomena. Articles with testimonies of attacks by vengeful fetuses have become a virtual genre and appear alongside temple advertisements in women's magazines, so that the practice has become highly commercialized. As the concept of spirit retribution became popular through the mass media and the teachings of new religions, Hardacre notes that "Older women who had had abortions decades earlier found their unresolved feelings stirred again by the spiritualists, and many sought ritual atonement." Consequently, a number of these women began visiting their neighborhood temples seeking a ritual, whether or not one had ever been offered. Some temples have felt it convenient to oblige, whether out of compassion for the dead souls, a desire to meet the felt needs of the women, or simply to make more money.

Temples and the Business of *Mizuko* Rites

Because many temples have fostered a fear of spirit retribution, and due to the sheer numbers of women who have experienced abortions in Japan, there is undeniably a significant "market" among women desiring spiritual answers to dealing with their abortions. Consequently, a relatively new Buddhist response has developed as a "cottage industry" alongside its already massive money-making funerary business. Simply stated, *mizuko kuyô* exists because there is a demand for it. Women are motivated to approach temples for rites of spirit pacification both by guilt or grief and by fear.

However, many temples that offer *mizuko kuyô* do not explicitly teach *tatari* but offer the rituals because of the demand,

and many do so reluctantly. One temple near my home seems fairly typical of those temples that offer *mizuko* rites more out of the demand than a desire to create one. It really offers a smorgasbord of rituals, something for everybody, though it is particularly devoted to the Fudô Myôô cult, as well as Jizô, and it advertises its regular *mizuko kuyô* services on its homepage (URLs for temples cited are listed in the Bibliography under the temple's name, in this case Enjôin 2003). It unabashedly declares its loyalty to syncretism with news on its participation in the local Shinto festival (*Yôno no mikoshi*) and the seven Chinese Taoist gods of good luck (*shichifukujin*). *Mizuko* rites are just one service out of the many that it offers the festival-loving Japanese community.

Shingon and Tendai sects are the most esoteric and magical, so it is not surprising that *tatari* is promoted in such places. One Shingon website (Tatsueji 2003) offers *goma* and other esoteric rites performed by a priestess (!) and not surprisingly is devoted to the Fudô and Dainichi Nyôrai cults, along with Jizô. Both *kaimyô* and *tôba* (thin sticks of wood usually inscribed with the ancestor's name and Buddhist phrases) are apparently sold as part of the rituals. Basic rites can be requested for a one-time fee of ¥30,000. Needless to say, the online application could not be easier for women to access nationwide (the website is also available by cell phone and elaborate directions to the temple are posted for those coming from various regions by car, bullet train, and even international flights). Indeed, one can argue that temples in Japan are entering the 21st century much faster than churches. By contrast, at the time of writing there appears to be only one Evangelical organization with a website in Japanese denouncing abortion from a pro-life perspective (Pro-Life Japan – Machida 2003), but offering only a couple of paragraphs of text ("Fetuses are human... we are opposed to abortion... repent and believe in Jesus..."), though plenty of gruesome photos.

Of all the sects in Japan, only Jôdo Shinshû has issued a clear policy on *mizuko kuyô*, absolutely prohibiting it. Nevertheless,

Hardacre found Jôdo Shin temples that *did* offer it anyway, albeit without the telltale statuettes. Jôdo Shin's opposition stems mostly from its strong belief that salvation is assured through Amida, but it has spoken out against the concept of *tatari.* Moreover, priests have stated that "purchasing a ritual will not wipe out sin. Instead, only sincere repentance can save the *mizuko*" (Hardacre 1997: 194).

Hardacre studied 157 temples and found that 44% were offering *mizuko* rites, with another 16% not having any policy for or against. Only 46% of the temples in her survey did not perform them (1997: 208-209). In order of involvement, Shingon temples were the most likely to offer rites (81%), which is not surprising considering their strongly shamanistic bent. A majority of Nichiren temples also offered ceremonies (72%). Next in involvement are Jôdo (47%) and Tendai temples (42%), followed by Zen (36% with Sôtô sects much more involved than Rinzai). Most surprising was her finding that 13% of the Jôdo Shin temples she surveyed offered *mizuko kuyô* even though the sects headquarters had strongly opposed them.

Ceremonies include the offering of candles, flowers, and incense, the priest's prayers, and the audience participating by offering more incense and reciting the Heart Sutra or the *Sai-no-kawara wasan.*

> Through the prayer and devotion of their parents here at this ritual, they will be set at rest and receive the protection of all the Buddhas. Prayers will be granted and sickness and misfortune avoided through the great mercy and protection of the Buddhas (Hardacre 1997: 179).

Some temples hold *mizuko* festivals on special days and women can be seen attending in groups or pairs.

For interning the *mizuko,* some temples require a meritorious Buddhist name (*kaimyô*) to be purchased and some do not; these can be quite expensive, though they are generally cheaper than those sold for the adult dead. During the spring and autumn equinoxes, and at the around the Bon festival, it is common to set up *tôba* and many temples make them for *mizuko* instead of setting up the small Jizô images. Some temples also sell *ihai* (stone tablets for the *kaimyô*) to be put in a family altar. Consequently, women who approach temples for help will often have purchased an idol to be interned or to take home. If the statue is interned on the temple grounds, then usually she will appear from time to time to make personal offerings before it and to pay for the rites performed by a priest.

Clearly, the amount of money that temples make in this *mizuko* industry is large. One temple in Shiga Prefecture, which advertises on the web (Zenkôji 2003), seems typical in offering several options and price packages ("offerings") for the ceremonies ranging from ¥3,000 to ¥30,000.[6] Even at a modest price, some temples are making a killing. Jolivet (citing another work) claims that Shôjuin "baby" temple (*akachan dera*) in Tokyo alone interns some 550,000 cremated fetuses (1997: 137).[7] However, Shiunzan Jizôji temple charges from ¥150,000 to ¥230,000 per statue, not including annual internment fees (ibid: 139). This is a huge *mizuko* temple with thousands of statues. Although it is located in a remote area about an hour outside of Tokyo (Chichibu in Saitama), it attracts people from the surrounding area seeking anonymity. Surely Hardacre is right to declare the fetus as being "marketed" by the religious industry in Japan.

Another temple in Suita city (Emmanji) has posted an elaborate website offering information in a question and answer format, mostly warning of terrible spirit retribution from *mizuko* and the hope of salvation through *mizuko kuyô*. Prices range from ¥5,000 to ¥50,000 and application can be made online. A variety of amulets for sale are also pictured including a cute one with the image (probably unlicensed by Sanrio Corporation) of Hello Kitty. A major ceremony is held annually around the Bon festival for *families* with "games and puppet shows for the kids" and "free bags of snacks for everyone!" Thus, we find the *destruction* of an unborn child is ritualistically and ironically transformed into a *celebration* for families. This shows the real power that rituals have and the importance of the role that religion can play in Japan.

As outlined above, fear of spirit retribution drives some women to the *mizuko* rites. Most are at least in part involved in the practice in an attempt to resolve their guilt, grieve their loss, remember the dead, and move on with life. Awashimadô Shûtokuji temple claims that "When you pray with the desire to perform the rites for the *mizuko* from the bottom of your heart, all will be saved" (temple website, my translation). It is an attractive appeal.

But people are also driven by their own sense of guilt over having taken a life. Hardacre sees the desire for closure still strong in older women. "At the end of their reproductive lives, many were drawn to the possibility of appropriate ritual, whether or not they feared spirit attacks." Moreover, "Unresolved feelings about abortion are widely reported, especially by women in their fifties and older; the majority of women born between 1920 and 1940 have had abortions" (Hardacre 1997: 78, 158). A 1992 Japanese survey of the personal meaning people found in the rites showed that a majority (73%) saw it as a way of "Atoning for a sin" (*tsumi no tsuginai*). The second most common result was "Easing my feelings."[8] Indeed, some 85% of people surveyed who were involved in *mizuko kuyô* felt a sense of sin (*tsumi*) toward their child and over 70% of them fear that they will suffer a spiritual attack if they do not perform some kind of rites (ibid., 96). Some people end up involved in repeated rites because of pressure from the temples.

How Might Evangelicals Respond?

Evangelicals almost all agree that abortion is an offense to God. A fetus is consistently referred to as a living human child made by God for his purposes (Ps. 139:13-16; Jer. 1:4-5; Luke 1:11-17, 41-44; cf. Gal. 1:15; etc). Consequently, infants in the womb are not to be killed (Ex. 21:22-25; 23:7; Jer. 20:17) and believers have a moral responsibility to work for both justice in society and protection of the innocent. Remaining silent is not an appropriate Christian response to the problem of abortion.

If Japanese Buddhism can be called a "funeral religion" deriving the bulk of its money from the sale of rituals that it offers as a monopoly, then sales of *mizuko* rites and related paraphernalia are a significant portion of the income which props up the whole superstructure of temples. There are serious ethical questions that remain unchallenged by Christians in Japan. Many of the larger *mizuko* temples in Japan display thousands of statuettes and sometimes tens of thousands of *tôba*—an amount that represents millions of dollars in income per temple. For example, Shiunzan temple already had over 6000 idols at the time of Brooks' study (1981: 141) costing at least 70,000 yen each, some five million dollars in today's currency. Werblowsky reported that Hasedera temple had sold at least 50,000 statues and he personally saw 20,000 *mizuko ihai* interned in one other temple (1991: 298, 309). The continuous rituals demand further payments and the real amount of money temples are making can only be imagined. It is a topic demanding further investigation.

Although Christians should not seek to profit from abortion, a better response could be made. While the opportunity exists to reach out to women who are looking for spiritual answers to their ordeal, the church seems to be afraid to raise the issue. Why? Perhaps a fear of syncretism or an inability to contextualize the gospel through the church within Japanese culture are some reasons that the problem of aborted children has not yet been adequately addressed by the Japanese church and legitimate alternatives to *mizuko kuyô* have not been presented. However, by overlooking this trend in society, the church is likely making a mistake and missing an opportunity for ministry and growth.

I believe there are at least seven reasons why ignoring the reality of *mizuko kuyô* is a mistake: (1) Ignoring it will not make it go away; (2) it creates a climate of denial in the church; (3) it does not honor the dead children; (4) it deprives people of the truth and the help they need; (5) it overlooks serious sin within society, but also that cripples even believers; (6) it can leave people feeling that they have no alternative but to go to temples to find relief; and (7) it does not offer an alternative to temple grave sights for memorializing the fetuses. Obviously, churches should not be erecting idols, but at the very least they can offer counseling.

One area that has long been ignored is what a new believer is supposed to do about a *mizuko* idol already installed at a temple. In my experience, this matter is never even brought up, though much discussion about what to do with a family altar may take place. It is as if a "don't ask, don't tell" policy is in place. Some may feel that if there are no remains, then merely abandoning the Jizô statue is enough. I recommend that women at least be asked if they have one somewhere and be offered help in what to do. Merely abandoning the Buddhist memorial site is probably not enough, for it functions as a grave, and women are wont to remember the child, as evidenced by the offerings of toys, candy, milk, clothing, etc. Westerners in particular, may be tempted to feel that some form of functional substitute is not necessary, but the evidence of temple rites suggests otherwise.

Abortion is a serious problem in many countries, but Japan is unique in the Buddhist world for its response to this social problem through ritualization. If nothing else, *mizuko kuyô* can be seen as emblematic of the very real spiritual and felt needs that exist in Japan. Missiologists should seriously consider a significant response to this palpable social problem and Christians everywhere should reach out to the hurting in a tangible way with compassion, the message of the gospel, and above all else, with love.

In order to reach out to the Japanese, a wide variety of missionary efforts have been made, with teaching of English probably being one of the most popular methods used by Western missionaries. However, in considering the felt needs of the target community, it is highly desirable that spiritual interests be given the greater attention and that relationships be built with people who are seeking spiritual answers to spiritual problems.

This chapter has identified Japanese women who have experienced abortion (of which there are tens of millions) as a significant group, which although somewhat hidden in society, is nevertheless displaying a strong tendency to seek spiritual answers to their grief, shame, guilt, and fears. Their spiritual interest is made obvious by the *mizuko kuyô* phenomenon. The lack of an appropriate response, much less an organized strategic outreach by churches to minister to their needs and confusion, is lamentable. Perhaps one reason for a lack of response is that whereas most pastors are men, those who carry the pain of abortion are women.[9] Pastors may be insensitive to the needs of even their congregations (most of whom typically are women). Abortion also carries a good deal of stigma in Japan making it difficult to discuss.

Still, women who have had abortions may be more open spiritually and possibly will be more likely to listen to and respond to the gospel, especially as it speaks to the issues of forgiveness and the fate of their lost children. Those who have had an abortion are usually aware that they have committed a sin and need help in finding forgiveness. The gospel speaks directly to the issues and there is no better solution to the guilt, fear, and pain that these women experience. The church must first help its own members—who likely have the same incidence of abortion as the general population—to find peace with God over the matter. Creating a healthier climate where it can be discussed would be a great first step.

I personally was ignorant of the hidden problem of abortion grief in my own church in Japan. One seeker came to me distraught over a recently broken relationship and seeking spiritual advice. I understood her tears to be merely a sign of sadness over the ending of her relationship with her boyfriend. After becoming a Christian, however, she still suffered from depression, cried easily, complained about sleep problems, and for two years in a row—around the same date—collapsed on a train in what even doctors feared was epilepsy. Brain scans found no physical problem.

However, later I learned of her abortion and discovered that she was actually suffering from Post Abortion Syndrome (PAS), a form of Post-Traumatic Stress Disorder (PTSD), the symptoms of which are outlined in Massé and Phillips (1998: 16-20) and Burke and Reardon (2002: 272-276). Now I realize that her collapsing on the train coincided with the anniversary of her baby's demise and her overwhelming grief in psychosomatic display. Besides the unexplained crying, sleep problems, and suicide attempt, I missed other classic signs, such as the desire to enter an occupation to help small children (she was in training to become a daycare worker). According to the Elliot Institute *Survey of Psychological Reactions Reported after Abortion* (Appendix C in Burke and Reardon 2002: 287-300) in which 260 women who had contact with selected post-abortion recovery ministries in the U.S. were questioned (using a Likert scale) on their post-abortion experiences, women who had experienced abortion were significantly more likely to report hysterical outbreaks, feelings of guilt, unforgiveness, fear of punishment by God, fear of harm coming upon their other children, worsening of negative feelings on the anniversary date of the abortion, nightmares, flashbacks to the abortion, and so on.

Although the Elliot Institute did not survey the general population, its results give us an idea of the range of problems many women feel after abortion. Not surprisingly, the overwhelming majority of respondents admitted experiencing guilt (92.6%), sorrow (91.8%), shame (91.0%), self-condemnation (90.9%), depression (88.2%), remorse (82.6%), sense of loss (86.2%), unforgiveness of self (85.7%), grief (84.7%), regret (84.8%), a general sense of emptiness (83.4%), anxiety (81.4), and self-hatred (76.8%). Almost all (94.0%) regretted having an abortion and the majority (70.2%) feared punishment from God. Half (51.5%) felt their negative feelings became worse on the anniversary of the abortion. However, most (60.1%) for some reason felt unable to grieve. When asked, "Do you feel fully reconciled with your abortion experience today?" over half answered "No," and many reported outbursts such as uncontrollable weeping (69.8%). Although these grim statistics are limited to the sample of respondents who presumably were in contact with post-abortion ministries because of lingering unresolved grief, one can easily see a pattern of needs for pastoral response. Most disturbing, over half (55.8%) reported suicidal feelings, with 28.2% indicating that they had already attempted suicide. Many still felt preoccupied with thoughts of death (42.8%).

Furthermore, for many, their relationship with the unborn child appears not to have ended. Some 36.5% strongly agreed that they were "preoccupied with thoughts of the child I could have had." Over half reported some kind of "flashbacks to the abortion" (63.4%), and nearly half (46.4%) experienced nightmares or insomnia (44.8%). One surprising find in the Elliot Institute survey was that 17.7% of the respondents claimed to have had a "waking or sleeping visitation from the aborted child." Of these, 23.9% described the mood as "vengeful," though 74.1% described the mood as "forgiving." Interstingly, nearly half also indicated a "fear of harm to my other children" (25.2% agreed and 23.4% strongly agreed). Nearly half (48.8%) also indicated that they sometimes talked to their child after the abortion. Apparently such experiences are not limited to Buddhist contexts and a cross-cultural comparison could be made.

Counseling proved effective in the case of the grieving Japanese woman I encountered. Once the problem was addressed properly, this grieving Christian became able to forgive herself and her boyfriend, for both his abandonment and pressure to have the abortion, and she found answers to questions that she could not put into words during our first encounters, *namely the question of where her baby's soul had gone.*

A Theological Problem

Where do the souls of aborted fetuses go? This is a tremendously important question and is beyond the scope of this brief study. Many Evangelical theologians (MacArthur 2003; Hayford 1990; Lightner 1977) hold that those who are unable to decide either for or against Christ—who because of their infancy are unable to exercise faith—may be saved, though the Bible seems silent on this issue. Lightner, for example, presents a compelling case for the salvation of aborted and miscarried infants. Considering Jesus' words in passages such as Matthew 18:14 and John 3:18 and 36, Lightner concludes: "Those who can't believe can't disbelieve either, and therefore we may be sure they will spend eternity in Heaven, not Hell." (See also 2 Sam. 12:22-23; cf. 2 Sam. 18:33).

At any rate, this theological problem is different from the classic problem of the fate of those who have not heard because infants have no known ability to respond to general revelation. If one believes that the souls of these children are not judged for their sin nature, then there is reason to believe that heaven will be populated by many millions who have not even been born. Many Japanese reject Christianity when confronted with the awful fact that their ancestors are in hell; in the case of infants lost to abortion, there is the option of presenting them as in heaven with Christ, not hurting, and hoping that their mothers will believe and join them. What is clear, however, is that believers seeking to enter into grief counseling of abortion victims need to have a coherent and well thought-out biblical response to the burning question, "Where is my child now?"

Christian Rites for Fetuses in Japan?

Could there be a role for an indigenous Japanese Christian memorial for aborted fetuses? It is significant that while in the West cemeteries are not usually built to memorialize aborted fetuses, memorial sites and accompanying rituals do exist in Japan, in Buddhist form. This is a problem that the both missiologists and the Japanese church should consider more deeply. An appropriate ritual, which recognizes the value of the life taken, gives opportunity to express grief, memorializes the dead, and helps women who want to turn from their sins to the hope that is in the gospel, could very well be a helpful component in Japanese church life. One need not approach the matter from the perspective of finding a functional substitute; the need to recognize the value of a departed soul in a dignified Japanese manner is reason enough to consider this issue.

Norgren (2001) has detailed the politics and development of reproductive policy in Japan. Sadly, Evangelicals have not even appeared on the radar screen in this debate. Although overturning laws on abortion in Japan may seem extremely unlikely, making its position public should be a goal of the church as it is a form of salt and light in the dark world.

Creating abortion recovery support groups would seem to be a good idea for Japan. Literally millions of women have been through a similar experience, though few if any churches in Japan are offering an appropriate forum such as a support group for them to find fellowship or comfort.

Conclusion

In conclusion, it appears that *mizuko kuyô* arose in order to "answer" a "problem" that developed when abortions became commonplace in the post-war era. Although this activity takes a decidedly Buddhist form, whether due to its promotion by temples or the worldview expectations of Japanese women, or both, there remains an underlying desire on the part of women to care for, memorialize, and seek peace with their aborted children, as well as to atone for sin and experience forgiveness. Whereas the Buddhist establishment has chosen to meet these felt needs, the Christian church has barely begun to grapple with the problem and could offer a much better response, which is biblical, practical, helpful, and could lead to the conversion of Japanese to Christianity. I propose the following action steps as a start:

1) *Lead believers to pray about this significant moral issue and that God would intervene to save lives—physically and spiritually.*

2) *Help believers become better informed on the issue of abortion. Many who have not personally experienced it have not given it much thought.*

3) *Be prepared to counsel those who come forth with lingering grief and guilt. Offer women a supportive environment with adequate confidentiality. Equip Christian women—especially those who understand the experience firsthand—to work as peer counselors.*

4) *Organize post-abortion recovery groups for women with the purpose of helping them find peace with God through the gospel. This could prove to be an effective evangelistic outreach.*

5) *Mobilize Christians into action, if possible, to raise the awareness of society at large about the evil that is in taking the life of the unborn.*

6) *Respond to Buddhism's false teaching of spirit retribution. Expose mizuko kuyô as idolatry.*

7) *Consider appropriate and indigenous Christian rituals to memorialize children lost through abortion and*

miscarriage. Allow for the internment of aborted children or their memory at church grave sites.

8) *Publish books, or at least create a website, which will offer the public more information.*

9) *Promote adoption, which is virtually unheard of in Japan. Work toward alternatives to unwanted pregnancies and see the establishment of crisis pregnancy centers.*

10) *Expose the Buddhism's unethical side reflected in the money-making funeral industry that exploits those who are vulnerable.*

Notes

[1] According to a white paper issued by the Health, Labor and Welfare Ministry, in 2001 there was the highest ever recorded number of abortions by Japanese teenage girls (46,500) and the total for the whole population stood at 341,588 (*Daily Yomiuri* 8/9/2003).

[2] According to the Ministry of Public Affairs, Posts and Telecommunications in 2000 there were 64,987,000 females of which 56,011,000 were over age 15 (*Asahi Shimbun* 2001: 56).

[3] During the Edo period the word *mabiki* ("spacing") was used as a euphemism for infanticide. The normal meaning of the word refers to keeping rice plants spaced apart. One Japanese writer in an essay on Jizô

notes the ironic contradictions between the goal of Buddhism, which is to be born in the Pure Land, and the wishes of the parents of *mizuko*, which is often that the child reincarnate and return to them in a later birth. Terauchi writes, "According to Buddhist teaching, when people die they become buddhas... From the parents' perspective it's unfortunate if one gets them to change all the way into buddhas... They want them to be born again one more time so they can enjoy the pleasures of life. The Jizô cult speaks to the wishes of that kind of parent" (Terauchi 2000: 96, my translation). Nevertheless, he adds that Jizô himself is put into a worse conundrum than either the parent or the aborted child: "After finally saving the misfortunate *mizuko,* Jizô goes and has it reborn, returning it to the mother's body. But then the mother complains 'Two is already more than enough...!'" (Terauchi: 98-99, my translation).

[4] Below are transcriptions of a couple of randomly chosen *ema* (handwritten plaques offered as prayers) to the spirits of aborted children that I found hanging at Hasedera Temple in Kamakura:

To you who couldn't be born:
Nine years have now gone by. Mommy and Daddy are living separately from one another. I met someone with whom I've been thinking it would be good to have your little brother or sister. Will you let [or forgive] me? I was finally able to get a person with whom I can face the future and walk together hand in hand. Please watch over us somehow. From now on I think I want to live for others. Somehow, somehow, please watch over your Mama who has become able to move forward.

Takako

To my 3 kids:
I am really sorry. I hope that you can definitely be born [again] sometime, but please stay by my side. Please pray that Mommy will be able to get hold of true happiness. And that both I and all the important people in my life will be happy.

Kaoru

For more on this ritual and the types of prayers women offer, see Werblowsky (1991).

[5] The six main sects of Buddhism in Japan along with their share in the total number of temples are as follows: Jôdo Shin (29%), Zen (36%), Shingon (17%), Jôdo (11%), Nichiren (9%), Tendai (6%). Of course, not everyone in the other sects besides Shin believes in *tatari* attacks from *mizuko*. One Buddhist writer questions why fathers are not the targets of spirit retribution and casts doubt on the whole premise: "If the fetus is going to attack the mother after aborting it, then it has to attack the father too. Put another way, men don't believe in things like spirit retribution. Because they don't believe in it, they aren't intimidated by it. I wish women had just that much wisdom…" (Unrin 2000:103, translation mine).

[6] They also do memorial services for dead pets, which though beyond the scope of this study, raises the question of whether there are legitimate limits to Christian contextualization and functional substitution of rituals.

[7] Japanese law actually requires cremation of fetuses after the fourth month and some people have a need for interning the remains.

[8] The survey was by Takahashi Saburuo, "Mizuko kuyô ni kansuru tôkei chôsa shiryô" (unpublished survey, Kyôto Daigaku Kyôyôbu Shakaigaku Kyôshitsu, 1992: 10).

[9] I do not mean to suggest that men who are involved in abortions in some way do not also suffer. There is a growing movement in the West recognizing the need for men also to receive counseling for post-abortion syndrome. See *www.safehavenministries.com* or *www.lovematters.com/men* for example.

CHAPTER 11

Holistic Mission:
A Thai Church's Ministry to the Whole Person

James W. Gustafson

[This chapter is a slightly revised form of the article entitled, "The Integration of Development and Evangelism," which was published in *Missiology*, 26.2 (April, 1998): 131-142.]

In June 1983, participants from a broad spectrum of evangelical churches, missions, and aid agencies met at Wheaton College, Illinois, to discuss the issue, "The Church in Response to Human Need." The consensus of those meetings as found in the resulting "Wheaton '83 Statement" was that "we do not emphasize Evangelism as a separate theme, because we see it as an integral part of our total Christian response to human need" (Samuel and Sugden 1987: 254-265). The declaration and the main body of the Wheaton '83 Statement highlight a struggle on the part of evangelicals to move from a separatistic understanding of the relationship of evangelism and social action to a more holistic or integrated understanding of the relationship between the two.

The beginning of an evangelical consensus is documented as early as 1974 when the Lausanne Covenant proclaimed,

> Although reconciliation with man is not reconciliation with God, nor is social action evangelism, nor is political liberation salvation, nevertheless we affirm that evangelism and socio-political involvement are both part of Christian duty (Lausanne Committee 1974: para. 4).

Although this early statement advocated that both evangelism and social action are part of Christian duty, thus implying that the results of evangelism should impact society, the nature of that relationship was not spelled out (Samuel and Sugden 1987: 175).

Almost a decade later, the consensus of the "Consultation on the Relationship Between Evangelism and Social Responsibility" held in Grand Rapids, Michigan, in 1982, was that social action is an adjunct to the task of evangelism. Development was seen as a "consequence of evangelism," a "bridge to evangelism," and a "partner to evangelism" (Lausanne Committee 1982: para. a).

Commenting on the growing consensus in the evangelical community on the relationship of evangelism to development, Tite Tienou in his paper given at the Wheaton Consultation in 1983 noted,

> Social transformation is part of the message of and a natural outgrowth of evangelism...(but) it will likely not take place through a dead evangelism: evangelism will likely not result in social Transformation unless the church and Christian community witness by their lifestyles that they have been transformed. If we really mean business let us deflate our empty words and inflate our actions (Samuel and Sugden 1987: 179).

Today, some 20 years after the above statements were made, we are still discussing the relationship between development and evangelism. It seems that consultation statements and an overall consensus of opinion do not necessarily bring about policy changes or action within the larger evangelical community! The question that springs to mind is *why*? If, in fact, after over two decades of discussion and dialogue on the subject, we have really arrived at a consensus, why then is holistic ministry not being more widely practiced by the evangelical community around the world?

I believe the answer is to be found in a number of obstacles that impede the progress of the implementation of the holistic mission of the church around the world today.

Obstacles to the Practice of Holistic Ministry in the Church

1. A Continuing Separation of Evangelism and Development: A Narrow Understanding of Evangelism

In spite of the rhetoric of the Wheaton '83 Statement, the fact is that the evangelical community at large remains, to this day, committed in largely to a "separatistic" concept of the relationship of development to evangelism. Development and evangelism are still regarded by the majority in evangelicalism as two distinct, if necessary, "duties" of the church. The use of such terms in the above statements on the relationship of evangelism and development as "linking," "bridging," "consequence of," and "partner to" betray a continuing bifurcation of the relationship of these two important entities. They are considered to be different parts of the same being. They are seen as "different" concepts and only related to each other as independent parts of a broader church mission.

This mindset is enhanced by, or perhaps enhances, the structural distinction of two separate organizational components of the broader church movement, the mission agencies, and the aid and development agencies. At the very least, these two entities of the Christian movement are different departments in the same denomination; at the most, they are entirely independent organizations, the one seen as focused on "spiritual" ministry and the other on "socio-economic" work. They are often linked by the "add-on-an-evangelist" syndrome where development projects are given spiritual credibility by the addition of an evangelist who is related to a separate department or organization.

I believe that this continuing tendency to separate development and evangelism is the result of a "truncated" concept of evangelism. This concept sees evangelism as "spreading the good news that Jesus Christ died for our sins and was raised from the dead according to the Scriptures" (Lausanne Committee 1974: para. 4). The "verbal" expression of the good news is seen as evangelism. It is proclamation oriented and dedicated to the verbal presentation of the gospel of Jesus Christ to all humanity. The myth perpetuated by this understanding of evangelism is that "hearing" the gospel is the equivalent to "being reached" by the gospel.

I would be the last to deny that this is what evangelism is about. It is, however, not the whole picture. The gospel of Jesus Christ is not just a *word*; it is a *living word.* The gospel is *life,* which includes the making of prepositional statements about its nature but at its *best* is the *incarnation* of the Word of God into the cultures and lives of humankind around the world. It is "doing the gospel" which is mandated by Scripture. Jesus himself is our model. As we read in John 1:14, he "became flesh" (all that it meant to be human) and "dwelt among us" (lived with us as one of us) and was "full of grace and truth" (the gospel). As a result, "we beheld his glory" (we saw the truth by his grace). Jesus was the first evangelist and his method of incarnation remains what evangelism is about to this day.

Evangelism is about enabling the gospel of the grace of God in Jesus Christ to be born into our lives, our cultures, our societies, our organizations, and our traditions. It is about enabling that gospel of grace to live in and permeate us and our context in such a way that it "transforms" us and our environment to become what we and our environment are meant to be in Christ. Evangelism *is* transformation,

transformation *is* development, and development *is* evangelism in a very real sense.

There is a need to replace the narrow concepts of evangelism held by many today with a more biblical understanding of the holistic nature of evangelism. Until we do this, we will remain bound in the confines of our separatistic thinking, robbing evangelism of its natural process in all of life and development of its power.

2. A Secular Definition of Development: A Constrictive Interpretation of Development

Since development is persistently separated from evangelism in the minds of many Christians, it is easy to see how for them development becomes a concept defined not by the teaching of God's Word, but by the secular mind that coined the term. As long as development is perceived of as separate from evangelism, in whatever way, it will continually fail to be defined in a way consistent with the Word of God. As long as development is defined in a secular manner, there is no possibility of integrating it with the biblical concept of evangelism.

The influence of the secular mindset is strong. It is based on normative value premises about what is or is not desirable that are often in conflict with the teaching of the Word of God. It is geared toward indicators of success that often have little to do with development as understood from a biblical perspective. An example of this can be seen in the economist's approach to secular development that has economic growth as its ultimate goal. Even at the micro level of grassroots development projects, this mindset persists. As its goal is to increase income, its focus is individualistic and often pits individual entrepreneurs against each other in competition. The better-off poor minority is its target since they are more likely to succeed, given the economic definition of success, than are the poorest majority. It is an up-and-out mode of development based on Adam Smith's famous notion that "if each individual consumer, producer and supplier of resources pursues self-interest, he or she will, as if by an 'invisible hand,' be promoting the overall interests of society" (Todaro 1989: 5).

More important for us than the fact that Adam Smith's principle is not working in Third World settings today is the fact that the whole economic development mindset, with its focus on individualism and self-attainment, is in total contrast to the Word of God. The focus of God's Word is on the good of the group or the "body." It teaches self-denial and service to others as the way life should be lived. Its central theme is to love God above all else and to love others as we love ourselves. A development mindset that is based on individualistic self-attainment is contrary to the basic thrust of God's Word and as such needs to be rejected as a definition of what development is about for the church.

The secular development mindset both repels and appeals. On the one hand, it puts the term "development" into a conflictive position with evangelism and accuses it of being less than spiritual. As a result, development programs connected to the church are often accused of bringing spiritual death or of squelching the growth of the church. On the other hand, the secular mindset often dictates the norms for both policy and procedure, for both programs and standards for evaluating those programs within Christian development organizations.

What is badly needed is a critical evaluation of the secular development mindset that will determine which aspects of the mindset are consistent with and which are opposed to the Word of God. As Christians, our definition of development must stem from principles and values from God's Word and not from the theories of secular development. Biblical theology ought to dictate our development principles and values. The Word of God must be the norm from which all of our development theory is drawn. If the church does not re-interpret the meaning of development in the light of Scripture, there is no way that development can be integrated with evangelism. However, if development is interpreted by the Word of God, both development and evangelism will be found to merge and mesh until they are firmly integrated.

3. A Crisis of Faith: Theological Infidelity

Tite Tienou's statement that social transformation (development) will not occur through "dead evangelism" is an important point (Samuel and Sugden 1987: 179). He defines "dead evangelism" as that done by the Christian community that is not being transformed and is not living out that process of transformation in their lifestyle. The immediate question that springs to mind is, how can there be dead evangelism within the church of Jesus Christ given the nature of the gospel and its power to transform? From my experience of almost three decades in holistic ministry in Thailand, I am convinced that the answer to that question is that there is a crisis of faith in the church today that is sapping it of the transforming power of God.

According to the Word of God in Romans 1:16-17, the gospel is "the power of God for salvation." The power of the gospel lies in the fact that it reveals God's righteousness, which is given freely to all people. The only requirement is that they in faith accept God's righteousness and as a result, experience his transforming power. In short, the gospel is completely and solely a word about what *God* has done for human beings by his *grace*.

Moffatt has noted that "the Bible is a religion of grace or it is nothing at all...no grace, no gospel" (1932: 15). God's purpose is to bring humankind to salvation by the power of his grace and not by the efforts or personal goodness of any human being (Eph. 2:8-9). In the gospel it is only what God has done and will do that counts. The problem is that every fiber of human nature causes us to think that we can earn God's favor and indeed, that we *must*, if we are to be accepted by God.

I am deeply concerned about what I feel is a departure from the gospel of grace in the church around the world today. The focus of a large segment of the church is on *law* and not *grace*. Even if the rhetoric is *grace*, the practice is *law*. The emphasis of much Christian teaching is on being good enough to please God. Law and obedience to the law are held up as the indicators of a person's salvation, this in spite of the Word of God in Romans 3:20, which tells us that there in no way a person can be saved by obedience to the law. In fact, the basic function of the law, according to God's Word, is to drive humankind to despair of their own ability to save themselves and to cast themselves in total dependence on the grace of God in Jesus Christ. It is *only* by the power of God's grace that we are saved and transformed into all that God desires us to be.

I feel that the church is often "duped" by the "religious" value system of the society it is in, which teaches that humans must work at being morally good in order to please God and find salvation. The overriding concern becomes morality, and the method and message become *law*. The basic problem with this way of thinking is that it is not the teaching of the gospel. The gospel of God teaches that human beings are not and cannot be good enough to please God by obedience to the law. There no one good except God himself (Luke 18:19). This goodness (righteousness) of God is free to all who believe and accept it (Eph. 2:8-9). This goodness of God is the power of God (Rom. 1:16-17) that will utterly transform those who experience it to become what God intends them to be (Rom. 12:2).

This is development in the true sense of the word. It is also evangelism of the best kind. As the church truly understands and believes the gospel of God's grace and not only accepts it personally but lives out the gospel in every aspect of its organizational life and work, the power of God's grace will enable the ongoing transformation of both the church and its society. By God's grace evangelism and development are bonded to each other. Both are empowered by the grace of God, and both are the expressions of God's grace as it is lived out in the church and its society.

4. A Cultural Insensitivity: Cultural Imperialism

Perhaps one of the greatest obstacles to the church's being the source of social transformation within its own society is the fact that the church today in most settings is culturally a foreigner in its own culture. Especially in Third World countries, this is true. The church has often been established with the motto "the West is best" in mind. As a result, "formal correspondence" becomes the model on which most churches in the Third World are based, and Western Christianity is the model to which they conform. Local culture is seen as "sinful" and not measuring up to God's standard. Little thought is given to the fact that Western culture itself does not measure up to God's standard. The forms and expressions of the church in the West are seen as the real Christian expression of the gospel and are copied religiously. Anything departing from this norm is seen as syncretistic and heretical.

In fact, this very Western, formal correspondence Christianity is the most syncretistic of all. Although the form of the church remains that of the West, more often than not, the content (values) remain that of the local culture. The problem that this creates is twofold. On the one hand, the form of Western Christianity is foreign to most cultures of the world (as well as being extremely foreign to its own diversified culture today). It does not have entry into these cultures and is not easily understood by them. On the other hand, if the Western form of Christianity is always an outsider and is rarely understood in non-Western cultures, then what it houses (its content—belief or values—which is the power of the gospel of God's grace in Jesus Christ will never have a chance to impact the hearts and minds of those non-Western cultures. If this, in fact, is the case, as it certainly is from my study and experience, then it is no wonder that the church is generally unable to impact its culture and society with the power of the gospel. Evangelism and development are dead because Western Christianity blocks the effective communication of the gospel of God's grace, which alone is the dynamo that can empower the church's movement into its society.

The overall problem is a lack of cultural sensitivity on the part of the church today. Cultural sensitivity provides the means for enabling the power of the gospel to address clearly the context of any culture and thereby bring about the necessary transformation of society. There are two basic aspects to cultural sensitivity. First, cultural sensitivity enables us to use local forms and expressions to communicate clearly and effectively the gospel of God's grace and its implications in a way that can be understood easily and simply by people in culture. This is what Jesus did when he "became flesh" and "dwelt among us." Second, cultural sensitivity enables us to pierce to the core of local culture and detect those aspects of the value system that need to be confronted and transformed by the grace of God. As these are detected and the gospel is clearly and simply communicated and lived out in culturally appropriate ways, it will confront the local value system by the power of God resulting in a process of transformation (a change in values and lifestyle).

A Case in Point: Holistic Ministry in Northeast Thailand

For over 30 years, I have worked with my wife and a growing number of Northeastern Thai colleagues, to do holistic ministry in Northeast Thailand. The name for this ministry in Thai is *patina tung krop* or "integrated holistic development." It is *development* in the sense that it seeks to transform people from where they are to what they are meant to be in Christ. It is *holistic* in the sense that it deals with the whole person and all areas of his or her life. It is *integrated* in that all aspects of the ministry are tied together and could not exist or function independently of each other.

This integrated holistic development was begun with the establishment of the Center for Church Planting and Church Growth in Northeast Thailand (CCPCG) in 1977. Its original purpose was to plant "contextualized dynamic equivalence" churches in Northeast Thailand, the poverty belt of the country. Since its beginnings in 1977, the Center and its ministry have grown. It has given birth to over 40 "mother" churches and over 200 "daughter" churches. In 1983, it started the Issaan Development Foundation (IDF) to deal with the social, economic and physical needs of the people of Northeast Thailand. In 1993, the CCPCG changed its name to The Institute for Sustainable Development (ISD). With the name change came a more holistic focus for the organization. The ISD today does research and curriculum development training in all areas of holistic ministry related to the churches for which it is responsible.

In late 2002, the IDF underwent a series of changes, one of which was the independent formation of the Isan Aquatics Farm (IAF) development organization that has assumed the socio-economic development roles of the IDF. The ISD and the IAF are today working together to facilitate the growth and expansion of contextualized churches in Northeast Thailand.

Both the ISD and the IAF are owned and operated by Northeastern Thai who are committed to the same integrated holistic ministry. They work together to enable the local churches in the area to "do the gospel" in their own communities. The ISD focuses on research and training in all areas of the ministry. This includes those areas related to the churches' faith and practice: church planting, faith (theology) and culture, and musicology (using local instruments, song and dance, as well as the life of the church in society. The IAF is concerned with enabling the local church to impact the socio-economic areas of its context.

Core Principles

At the heart of the holistic ministry of the ISD and IAF are a number of core principles, which are important for the practice of integrated holistic ministry.

1. Authority

Thomas J. Peters and Robert H. Waterman, Jr. (1982) in their important book on management, *In Search of Excellence,* have quoted Thomas Watson, Jr., president of IBM, concerning the importance of beliefs or values in the success of any organization. He writes,

> I firmly believe that any organization in order to survive and achieve success must have a sound set of beliefs on which it premises all its policies and actions. Next I believe that the most important single factor in corporate success is faithful adherence to those beliefs. And, finally, I believe that if an organization is to meet the challenge of a changing world, it must be prepared to change everything about itself except those beliefs, as it moves through corporate life (Peters and Waterman 1982: 280).

What Watson has said about the management of business organizations applies also to the church. Central to the activities of the holistic ministry of the ISD and the IAF has been the authority of the Word of God. At the heart of Scripture is the gospel of God's grace and power. This gospel of God's grace, with all of its implications, is the core belief on which all policies and practices of the IDF and IAF are based.

2. Integration

Every aspect of the ministry is tied together (integrated) by the grace of God. The belief of the IAF and ISD is that God's grace is relevant to every aspect of both personal and organizational life.

There are no spiritual and secular distinctions in the holistic ministry of these two organizations. All of life is spiritual and all of life is impacted by God's grace.

3. Focused Flexibility

All aspects of the work of holistic ministry are focused and flexible at the same time. They are focused on God's Word and his fantastic grace. They are flexible in seeking to allow his grace to be seen and understood by the Northeastern Thai communities in which they work. It is only as God's grace is understood and responded to that the work of transformation can begin in the lives and environment of Northeasterners.

4. Contextualization

Knowing that people can communicate clearly with each other only to the extent that they share a common culture, and that effective communication is what is "heard," not necessarily what is "said," the IAF and ISD have worked from the beginning to enable Jesus Christ (the Living Word) to be born into Northeast Thai culture. The worship and life of the church (musicology, language, ceremonies, etc) as well as the structure, management system, and the development programs are part of the holistic ministry that seeks to enable the gospel of God's grace to be born into and to be lived out in Northeastern Thai culture.

5. Power Encounter

As the gospel of God's grace is incarnated into Northeastern Thai culture, it is naturally understood and focuses on the local cultural value and belief system of the Northeastern Thai society. The result is "power encounter" at the level of values and belief systems that result in decisions, which in turn begins the process of transformation. It is within the holistic or socio-economic development programs of the IDF and the IAF that this process occurs most effectively.

6. Local Church Focus

The local church and its community are the focus of the holistic ministry of the IDF and the IAF. The ultimate goal of holistic ministry is to enable the local church to become the "local development organization" in its own context. As this process takes place, the local church begins to impact its community with the transforming power of God's grace. This is "doing the gospel" at its best, with a group of believers living out the values and beliefs of the gospel in their own communities. A development study done by Esman and Uphoff (1984) of 150 local development organizations has confirmed that the establishment of intermediate local development organizations such as the IAF and ISD is crucial for the facilitation of local development organizations such as local churches at the village level (Esman and Uphoff 1984).

7. Process/Broker Approach

The IAF and ISD maintain a "process/broker" relationship to the local churches who act as the local development organizations in their communities. Studying the approaches of 41 local development organizations, David Gow found that those organizations with the greatest success in helping the poor help themselves were those that followed a process/broker approach (1979: 89-90). The "process" part of the approach is highlighted by a "down and in" movement on the part of the local development organization—the starting point of good holistic ministry is with the poor themselves. As the local development organization begins to work in a participatory manner with the local poor, an understanding of the context of those being helped is achieved and the grace of God is able to "empower" the poor in an effective and transforming way. The "broker" function of the local development organization is that of linking the local context to extra-local resources. Through the brokering process, the local poor are linked to markets, knowledge, supplies, funds and other appropriate sources for ongoing development.

Some Conclusions

Given both the concepts and the practice of integrated holistic development or ministry that have been briefly outlined in the first part of this paper, what implications does this have for us as we seek to do holistic ministry in a needy world? The following are a few brief conclusions that I feel are important as the church seeks to do holistic ministry today.

1. There is a danger in being co-opted by the secular mindset.

There is a real danger in secular donor organizations setting up the basic principles for development programs that do not coincide with either the tenets of God's Word or the development needs at the grassroots level. The basic question is, based on the principles of God's Word, which should take priority, funding sources or local development organizations priorities?

There is also a danger of funding sources dictating the standards on which success will be evaluated. The danger of being driven by quantitative economic indicators of success is all too clear for anyone who has worked in development at the grassroots level. At the very least, it forces local development organizations to concentrate exclusively on those poor who can help achieve the quantitative goals (that is, the entrepreneurial poor). At the most, it usurps the gospel's emphases on qualitative indicators of development (e.g., values and beliefs). What is needed today is the establishment of indicators of success that are drawn from the basic principles of the Word of God and show progress in the direction of holistic transformation.

2. We need to see our role as holistic and not single faceted.

It is easy and perhaps natural (given the separation of development and evangelism today) for Christian aid and development organizations to assume that the church that they are seeking to help is mature and capable of receiving the socio-economic programs that the aid organizations bring without disruption. This assumption, however, is *not* true in the majority of cases. In the implementation of any socio-economic development program there must be a concurrent emphasis on the spiritual dimension of development. Values of local church members must be challenged progressively by the transforming power of God's grace. Only as local church members are "being transformed" by the power of the gospel can they in turn become "transformers" of their own communities. It is not enough to add on an evangelist to the local development programs. What is needed is "holistic development," which addresses the social/cultural/spiritual dimension of development as well as the economic dimension. Whole people are in need of "holistic transformation," which is the ultimate goal of holistic ministry. For a comprehensive bibliography of holistic development resources see Appendix 1.

3. There is a need to allow the grace of God to permeate our Christian organizations to the extent that it becomes the key in determining their policies and actions.

As Bishop Lesslie Newbigin has noted,

> It is a sign of our spiritual weakness that we lust for tight organizations where everything is governed by a set of inflexible rules. The multiplication of rules is a sure sign of spiritual decay (1954: 106).

We need to combat the *law-oriented* organizational mindset of most Christian organizations with a *grace-oriented* mindset. As the grace of God becomes the basis for our organizational operations, the results will be twofold: (1) the power of God will infuse our organizations; and (2) the dichotomy of "spiritual" and "socio-economic" will disappear and in its place will be holistic ministry.

4. We need to avoid the search for simplistic answers to the needs of the poor.

I am convinced that we are easily enamored by the sensationalism of *global* thinking and planning. Westerners, especially, have a tendency to want to generalize answers to the world's problems. It would be magic to be able to develop a global answer to the problems of poverty around the world. In reality, however, given the fact of cultural diversity alone around the world, this is not a possibility. What is needed is *"area specific"* focuses that result in a variety of holistic ministry programs, each aimed at the needs of specific situations and their contexts.

I am also convinced that we need to resist the *"resource development syndrome"* that seeks to simplify and sensationalize the local setting in order to stimulate funding. If development programs that relate to real grassroots situations do not stimulate the Christian community at large to contribute to their success, then the education of the larger Christian community in the realities of holistic ministry should be the approach taken, not capitulation to the skewed values of a Christian community seeking sensationalism.

5. We need to focus on enabling the local church to do holistic development.

Too often, Christian development organizations do the work of development themselves and do not seek to equip the local church for the task. Enabling local churches to be the resource base for ongoing community development will have a more far-reaching effect than the development organizations doing the work on their own. It is a fact that the best possible initiators of grassroots development or holistic ministry are local people. The local church is the obvious source of any Christian holistic ministry at the grassroots level. It is the enablement of local churches to be local development organizations in their own communities that is of crucial importance today. As local churches are enabled and equipped to reach into their own contexts with the power of God's grace, the holistic mission of the church will be realized, and the church around the world will be both transformed and become transformer of society by the power of God's grace in Jesus Christ.

Appendix 1: Bibliography on Holistic Development

(Compiled by Dr. David Lim, this bibliography is an important tool for doing a study of holistic development from a variety of perspectives.)

Adeney, Miriam. *God's Foreign Policy*. Grand Rapids: Eerdmans, 1984.

Alinsky, Saul. *Reveille for Radicals*. New York: Random, 1969.

Andres, Tomas. *Community Development: A Manual*. Quezon City: New Day Publishers, 1988.

Andrews, Dave. *Can You Hear the Heartbeat?* Manila: OMF Literature, 1989.

Bakke, Ray. *A Theology As Big As the City*. Downers Grove: IVP, 1997.

_____. *The Urban Christian*. MARC Europe, 1987.

Bobo, Kimberly. *Lives Matter: A Handbook for Christian Organizing*. Kansas City: Sheed & Ward, 1986.

Boff, Leonardo. *The Church: Charism and Power*. Maryknoll: Orbis, 1985.

_____. *Ecclesiogenesis*. London: Collins; Maryknoll: Orbis, 1986.

Bonk, Jonathan. *Missions and Money: Affluence as a Western Missionary Problem*. Maryknoll: Orbis, 1991.

Bosch, David. *Transforming Mission: Paradigm Shifts in Theology of Mission*. Maryknoll: Orbis, 1991.

Bradshaw, Bruce. *Bridging the Gap.* Monrovia: MARC, 1994.

Cheyne, John R. *Incarnational Agents: A Guide to Developmental Ministry.* Monrovia: MARC, 1996.

Christian, Jayakumar. *God of the Empty-Handed: Poverty, Power and the Kingdom of God.* Monrovia: MARC, 1999.

Conn, Harvey (ed.). *Planting and Growing Urban Churches.* Grand Rapids: Baker, 1997.

Cook, Guillermo. *The Expectation of the Poor: Latin American Basic Ecclesial Communities in Protestant Perspective.* Maryknoll: Orbis, 1985.

Cox, Harvey. *The Secular City.* New York: Macmillan, 1965.

Craig, Jenny. *Servants Among the Poor.* Manila: OMF Literature, 1997.

De Santa Ana, Julio (ed.). *Good News to the Poor: The Challenge of the Poor in the History of the Church.* Maryknoll: Orbis, 1978.

_____. *Separation Without Hope? Essays on the Relation Between the Church and the Poor During the Industrial Revolution and the Western Colonial Expansion.* Maryknoll: Orbis, 1977.

_____. *Towards a Church of the Poor.* Geneva: W.C.C., 1979; Maryknoll: Orbis, 1981.

Frieden, Bernard, and L. B. Sagalyn. *Downtown, Inc.: How America Rebuilds Cities.* Cambridge, MA: MIT Press, 1989.

Greenway, Roger. *Discipling the City, 2nd Ed.* Grand Rapids: Baker, 1992; Manila: OMF Literature, 1998.

Grigg, Viv. *Companion to the Poor.* Monrovia: MARC, 1984.

_____. *The Cry of the Poor.* Monrovia: MARC, 1992.

Goudzwaard, Bob, and Harry de Lange. *Beyond Poverty and Affluence: Toward an Economy of Care.* Grand Rapids: Eerdmans, 1995.

Guder, Darrell. *The Incarnation and the Church's Witness.* Monrovia: MARC, 1999.

Haugen, Gary. *Good News About Injustice: A Witness of Courage in a Hurting World.* Downers Grove: IVP, 1999.

Hendricks, H. *Social Justice in the Bible.* Maryknoll: Orbis, 1985.

Jang, Mark, and Joann Slead, eds. *Complex Humanitarian Emergencies: Lessons from Practitioners.* Monrovia: World Vision, 2000.

Lagarejos, A. *The Church of the Poor: A New Perspective on the Church, the State and the Poor.* Pasig City: Educational Resources Development Center, 1999.

Lim, David. "The Unique Christ for Peace and Justice," in Bruce Nicholls (ed.), *The Unique Christ in Our Pluralist World.* Grand Rapids: Baker, 1994. Pp. 214-230.

_____. *Transforming Communities.* Manila: OMF Literature, 1992.

Linthicum, Robert. *City of God, City of Satan.* Monrovia: MARC, 1991.

_____. *Empowering the Poor.* Monrovia: MARC, 1991.

McAlpine, Tom. *By Word, Work and Wonder.* Monrovia: MARC, 1995.

Maggay, Melba. *Transforming Society.* Quezon City: I.S.A.C.C., 1996.

Maglaya, Felipe. *Organizing People for Power: A Manual for Organizers.* Manila: Asia Committee for People's Organizations, 1982.

Mangalwadi, Vishal. *Truth and Social Reform.* Delhi: Nivelit, 1989.

Miller, Donald. *Discipling Nations.* Seattle: YWAM, 1999.

Montgomery, Jim. *I'm Gonna Let It Shine.* Pasadena: William Carey Library, 2001.

Myers, Bryant. *Walking with the Poor.* Maryknoll: Orbis, 1999.

_____. *Working with the Poor.* Monrovia: World Vision, 1999.

Ogden, Greg. *The New Reformation.* Grand Rapids: Zondervan, 1990.

Perkins, John. *With Justice For All.* Ventura: Regal, 1982.

Pierce, Gregory. *Activism that Makes Sense: Congregations and Community Organization.* New York: Paulist, 1984.

Ringma, Charles. *Catch the Wind.* Manila: OMF Literature, 1992.

Samuel, V., and C. Sugden. *Mission as Transformation.* Oxford: Regnum, 1999.

Schumacher, E. F. *Small is Beautiful.* London: Abacus, 1974.

Simpson, D., and C. Stockwell. *Congregations and Community Organizing.* Chicago: Inst. for the Church in Urban Industrial Society, 1987.

Simson, Wolfgang. *Houses that Change the World.* Carlisle: OM Publishing, 2001.

Snyder, Howard. *Liberating the Church.* Downers Grove: IVP, 1983.

Suderman, Robert. *Calloused Hands, Courageous Souls: Holistic Spirituality of Development and Mission.* Monrovia: MARC, 1999.

Tiersma, J., and C. Van Engen, eds. *God So Loves the City.* Monrovia: MARC, 1994.

Tillapaugh, Frank. *Unloashing the Church* Ventura: Regal, 1992.

Tonna, Benjamin. *Gospel for the Cities.* Maryknoll: Orbis, 1982.

Wolterstorff, Nicholas. *Until Justice and Peace Embrace.* Grand Rapids: Eerdmans, 1983.

World Council of Churches. *Christian Faith and the World Economy Today.* Geneva: W.C.C., 1992.

Yamamori, T., B. Myers, and D. Conner, eds. *Serving with the Poor in Asia.* Monrovia: MARC, 1995.

_____, _____, and K. Luscombe, eds. *Serving with the Urban Poor.* Monrovia: MARC, 1998.

REFERENCES

Chapter 1: Counting the Buddhist World Fairly

Anderson, Gerald H., ed. *International Bulletin of Missionary Research.* 23.1. New Haven: Overseas Ministries Study Center, 1999.

Barrett, David B, and Todd M. Johnson. "Annual Statistical Table on Global Mission: 1999." In *International Bulletin of Missionary Research.* 23 (1999): 24-25.

Beaver, R. Pierce et al, eds. *Eerdmans' Handbook to the World's Religions.* Grand Rapids: Eerdmans Publishing Company, 1982.

Dhammananda, K. Sri. "Do You Know?" Keynote speech given at the opening ceremony of the 14th YBAM Bienniel Convention. <http://www.geocities.com /~buddhistnews/page207.html> December 31, 1998.

Hopfe, Lewis M. *Religions of the World.* 4th ed. New York: Macmillan Publishing Company, 1987.

Johnstone, Patrick. *Operation World.* Grand Rapids: Zondervan Publishing House, 1993.

Lausanne Committee for World Evangelization. "The Thailand Report — Christian Witness to Buddhists. 15." Wheaton: Lausanne Committee for World Evangelization, 1980.

Tambiah, S. J. *Buddhism and the Spirit Cults in Northeast Thailand.* Cambridge: Cambridge University Press, 1970.

Tweed, Thomas A. "Nightstand Buddhists and other Creatures: Sympathizers, Adherents, and the Study of Religion." In *American Buddhism: Methods and Findings in Recent Scholarship.* Eds. Duncan Ryuken Williams and Christopher S. Queen. Surrey: Curzon Press, 1999.

Winter, Ralph D., and David A. Fraser. "World Mission Survey." In *Perspectives on the World Christian Movement: A Reader.* 3rd ed. Pasadena: William Carey Library, 1999.

Chapter 2: The Power of the Kingdom for Encountering Buddhist Worldviews

Bright, John. *The Kingdom of God.* Nashville: Abingdon, 1953.

Carson. D. A. *Exegetical Fallacies.* Grand Rapids: Baker Book House, 1984.

Cheu, Hock-Tong. *Buddhism in Chinese Culture.* Subang Jaya: Pelanduk Publications, 2000.

Clark, David K. *Dialogical Apologetics: A Person-Centered Approach to Christian Defense.* Grand Rapids: Baker Book House, 1993.

Covell, Ralph. "Jesus Christ and World Religions." *The Good News of the Kingdom: Mission Theology for the Third Millennium.* Eds. Charles Van Engen, Dean S. Gilliland, and Paul Pierson. 162-171. Maryknoll: Orbis Books, 1993.

Coward, Harold. *Scripture in the World Religions.* Oxford: Oneworld, 2000.

Dumbrell, William J. *Covenant and Creation: An Old Testament Covenantal Theology.* Exeter: Paternoster Press, 1984.

France, R. T. "The Church and the Kingdom of God: Some Hermeneutical Issues." *Biblical Interpretation and the Church.* Ed. Donald A. Carson. 41-42. New York: Thomas Nelson, 1984.

_____. *Divine Government: God's Kingship in the Gospel of Mark.* London: SPCK, 1990.

Gethin, Rupert. *The Foundations of Buddhism.* Oxford: Oxford University Press, 1998.

Griffiths, Paul J. *An Apology for Apologetics: A Study in the Logic of Interreligious Dialogue.* Maryknoll: Orbis Books, 1991.

_____. *Christianity through Non-Christian Eyes.* Maryknoll: Orbis Books, 1994.

Groome, Thomas. *Christian Religious Education: Sharing our Story and Vision.* San Francisco: Harper and Row, 1980.

_____. "The Critical Principle in Christian Education and the Task of Prophecy." *Religious Education.* 72 (3) (1977): 262-66.

_____. *Sharing Faith: A Comprehensive Approach to Religious Education and Pastoral Ministry.* San Francisco: Harper and Row, 1991.

Gross, Rita M., and Terry C. Muck, eds. *Buddhists Talk about Jesus and Christians Talk about the Buddha.* New York: Continuum, 2000.

Hiebert, Paul G. "Evangelism, Church, and Kingdom." *The Good News of the Kingdom: Mission Theology for the Third Millennium.* Eds. Charles Van Engen, Dean S. Gilliland, and Paul Pierson. 153-161. Maryknoll: Orbis Books, 1993.

_____. *Anthropological Reflections on Missiological Issues.* Grand Rapids: Baker Book House, 1994.

Jones, E. Stanley. *Along the Indian Road.* New York: Abingdon Press, 1939.

_____. *Christ at the Round Table.* New York: Abingdon Press, 1928.

_____. *The Christ of the Indian Road.* New York: Abingdon-Cokesbury Press, 1925.

_____. *The Unshakable Kingdom and the Unchanging Person.* Nashville: Abingdon, 1972.

Kraemer, Hendrik. *The Christian Message in a Non-Christian World.* New York and London: International Missionary Council, 1947.

Ladd, George E. *A Theology of the New Testament.* Grand Rapids: Eerdmans Publishing Company, 1993.

Newbiggin, Leslie. "The Gospel among the Religions." In *Faith Meets Faith.* Eds. Gerald H. Anderson and Thomas F. Stransky. 3-19. Grand Rapids: Eerdmans Publishing Company, 1981.

_____. *The Open Secret: Sketches for a Missionary Theology.* Grand Rapids: Eerdmans Publishing Company, 1978.

_____. *Trinitarian Faith and Today's Mission.* Richmond: John Knox Press, 1964.

Pannenberg, Wolfhart. *Theology and the Kingdom of God.* Philadephia: Westminster Press, 1969.

Peters, George W. *A Biblical Theology of Missions.* Chicago: Moody Press, 1972.

Schreiter, Robert J. *Constructing Local Theologies.* Maryknoll: Orbis Books, 1985.

Smallbones, Jackie. "Thomas Groome's Shared Christian Praxis." *Christian Education Journal.* 7 (1) (1986): 57-67.

Stott, John. *Christian Mission in the Modern World.* Downers Grove: InterVarsity Press, 1975.

Swidler, Leonard, ed. *Toward a Universal Theology of Religion.* Maryknoll: Orbis Books, 1987.

Thomas, Chacko C. "The Work and Thought of Eli Stanley Jones with Special Reference to India." Ph.D. dissertation. University of Iowa, 1955.

Verkuyl, Johannes. "The Kingdom of God: Test of Validity for Theology of Religions." In *The Good News of the Kingdom: Mission Theology for the Third Millennium.* Eds. Charles Van Engen, Dean S. Gilliland, and Paul Pierson. 71-81. Maryknoll: Orbis Books, 1993.

Williams, Paul. *Mahayana Buddhism: The Doctrinal Foundations.* London: Routledge, 1989.

_____. *The Unexpected Way: On Converting from Buddhism to Catholicism.* Edinburgh: T & T Clark, 2002.

Wright, Christopher. "The Christian and Other Religions: The Biblical Evidence." *Themelios.* 9 (2) (1984): 4-14.

Yong, Amos. "Discerning the Spirit(s) in the World of Religions: Toward a Pneumatological Theology of Religions." In *No Other Gods Before Me? Evangelicals and the Challenge of Religions.* Ed. John G. Stackhouse. 37-61. Grand Rapids: Baker Academic, 2001.

Chapter 3: Practical Applications of the Good News into Doctrinal Black Holes in Buddhism

Bavinck, J. D. *An Introduction to the Science of Missions.* Philadelphia: Presbyterian and Reformed, 1961.

Cotterrell, Peter. *The Eleventh Commandment.* Leicester: InterVarsity Press, 1981.

Davis, J. R. *The Path to Enlightenment.* London: Hodder & Stoughton. 1997.

Davis, J. R. *Poles Apart?* Bangalore: The Theological Book Trust, 1996.

Humphries, Christmas. *Buddhism.* London: Penguin Books, 1951.

King, Winston. *Buddhism and Christianity.* London: Allen & Unwin, 1963.

McGavran, Donald A. "The Bridges of God." In *Perspectives on the World Christian Movement: A Reader.* Eds. Ralph D. Winter and Steven C. Hawthorne. 3rd ed. Pasadena: William Carey Library, 1999.

Peiris, Lakshman. "Reaching Buddhists." In *Composite Position Paper of Pre-COWE Group Study.* Unpublished occasional paper. Manila, n.d.

Petchsongkram, Wan. *Talk in the Shade of the Bo Tree.* Trans. and ed. Frances Hudgins. Bangkok: Thai Gospel Press, 1975.

Richardson, Don. "Finding the Eye-Opener." In *Perspectives on the World Christian Movement.* Ed. Ralph D. Winter. Rev. ed. Pasadena: William Carey Library, 1992.

Chapter 4: The Value and Limits of Dialogue

Abe, Masao. "Kenosis and Emptiness." In *Buddhist Emptiness and Christian Trinity: Essays and Explorations.* Eds. Roger J. Corliss and Paul F. Knitter. 5-25. Mahweh, NJ: Paulist. 1990.

Arndt, William F., and F. Wilbur Gingrich. *A Greek-English Lexicon of the New Testament and Other Early Christian Literature.* A translation and adaptation of Walter Bauer's *Griechisch-Deutsches Wörterbuch zu den Schriften des Neuen Testaments und der übrigen urchristlichen Literature.* 2nd ed. Chicago: University of Chicago, 1979.

Blosser, Philip. "Review of Russell H. Bowers, Jr.'s Someone or Nothing? Nishitani's *Religion and Nothingness* as a Foundation for Christian-Buddhist Dialogue." In *Japanese Journal of Religious Studies.* 23 (Spring 1996): 209-11.

Bowers, Jr., Russell H. "Defending God Before Buddhist Emptiness." In *Bibliotheca Sacra.* 154 (October-December 1997): 396-409.

_____. "Someone or Nothing? Nishitani's *Religion and Nothingness* as a Foundation for Christian-Buddhist Dialogue." In *Asian Thought and Culture.* Vol. 27. Gen. ed. Charles Wei-Hsun Fu. New York: Peter Lang, 1995.

Carson, D. A. *The Gagging of God: Christianity Confronts Pluralism.* Grand Rapids: Zondervan, 1996.

Carter, Ben M. "Evangelical Buddhism. 54th Annual Meeting of the Evangelical Theological Society." Toronto. Nov. 20-22, 2002.

Cobb, Jr., John B. *Beyond Dialogue: Toward a Mutual Transformation of Christianity and Buddhism.* Philadelphia: Fortress, 1982.

Cobb, Jr., John B., and Christopher Ives, eds. *The Emptying God: A Buddhist-Jewish-Christian Conversation.* Faith Meets Faith Series. Gen. ed. Paul F. Knitter. Maryknoll: Orbis, 1990.

Davies, Eryl. "1993." In *Foundations* 24 (1990): 16-21.

Davis, John R. *Poles Apart: Contextualizing the Gospel in Asia.* Bangalore: Theological Book Trust, 1998.

Dumoulin, Heinrich. *Christianity Meets Buddhism.* LaSalle, IL: Open Court, 1974.

Gross, Rita M., and Terry C. Muck. *Buddhists Talk About Jesus— Christians Talk About the Buddha.* New York: Continuum, 2000.

King, Winston. "Buddhist-Christian Dialogue: Past, Present and Future: Masao Abe and John Cobb Interviewed by Bruce Long." In *Buddhist-Christian Studies* 1 (1981): 12-29.

Griffiths, Paul, and Delmas Lewis. "On Grading Religions, Seeking Truth, and Being Nice to People—A Reply to Professor Hick." In *Religious Studies* 19 (1983): 75-80.

Hesselgrave, David J. *Communicating Christ Cross-Culturally: An Introduction to Missionary Communication.* 2nd ed. Grand Rapids: Zondervan, 1991.

Huff, Peter A. "The Challenge of Fundamentalism for Interreligious Dialogue." In *Cross Currents* 50, 1/2 (Spring/Summer 2000): 94-102.

Ingram, Paul O. *The Modern Buddhist-Christian Dialogue: Two Universalistic Religions in Transformation.* Studies in Comparative Religion. Vol 2. Lewiston, NY: Edwin Mellen, 1988.

Louw, Johannes P., and Eugene A. Nida. *Greek-English Lexicon of the New Testament Based on Semantic Domains.* 2nd ed. New York: United Bible Societies, 1989.

McGrath, Alister E. "The Christian Church's Response to Pluralism." In *Journal of the Evangelical Theological Society* 35 (December 1992): 487-501.

_____. *A Passion for Truth: The Intellectual Coherence of Evangelicalism.* Downers Grove: InterVarsity Press, 1996.

Neill, Stephen. *Christian Faith and Other Faiths.* Downers Grove: InterVarsity Press, 1984.

Netland, Harold A. *Dissonant Voices: Religious Pluralism and the Question of Truth.* Grand Rapids: Eerdmans, 1991.

Neusner, Jacob. "Can People Who Believe in Different Religions Talk Together?" In *Journal of Ecumenical Studies* 28 (1991): 88-100.

Ng, Daniel. "A Survey of Christian Models in Religious Dialogue." In *Regent Chinese Journal* 1 (1993): 8-16.

Nishitani, Keiji. *Nishida Kitarō.* Trans. Yamamoto Seisaku and James W. Heisig. Nanzan Studies in Religion and Culture. Gen. ed. James W. Heisig. Berkeley: University of California, 1991.

Schreiter, Robert J. "Interreligious Dialogue: A Hundred Years On." In *New Theology Review.* 6 (1993): 6-17.

Sharpe, Eric J. "The Goals of Inter-Religious Dialogue." In *Truth and Dialogue in World Religions: Conflicting Truth-Claims.* Conference on the Philosophy of Religion, University of Birmingham, 1970. Ed. John Hick. Philadelphia: Westminster, 1974.

Slater, Robert Lawson. "The Coming Great Dialogue." In *Christianity: Some Non-Christian Appraisals.* Ed. David W. McKain. New York: McGraw-Hill, 1964.

Suzuki, D. T. "Lectures on Zen Buddhism." In *Zen Buddhism and Psychoanalysis.* Eds. Erich Fromm, D. T. Suzuki, and Richard DeMartino. New York: Harper, 1960.

Tennent, Timothy C. *Christianity at the Religious Roundtable: Evangelicalism in Conversation with Hinduism, Buddhism, and Islam.* Grand Rapids: Baker Book House, 2002.

Tracy, David. *Dialogue with the Other: The Inter-Religious Dialogue.* Louvain Theological & Pastoral Monographs. Louvain: Peeters, 1990.

Waldenfels, Hans. *Absolute Nothingness: Foundations for a Buddhist-Christian Dialogue.* Trans. J. W. Heisig. New York: Paulist, 1980.

_____. "Buddhism and Christianity in Dialogue: Notes on the Intellectual Presuppositions." In *Communio: International Catholic Review* 15 (1988): 411-22.

Watty, William W. "Evangelization as Dialogue: A Caribbean Perspective." In *International Review of Mission* 83 (1994): 429-36.

Wentz, Richard E. "The Prospective Eye of Interreligious Dialogue." In *Japanese Journal of Religious Studies* 14 (March 1987): 3-17.

Wiebe, Donald. *Religion and Truth: Towards an Alternative Paradigm for the Study of Religion.* Religion and Reason, vol. 23: Method and Theory in the Study and Interpretation of Religion. Gen. ed. Jacques Waardenburg. New York: Mouton, 1981.

Chapter 5: The Transfer of Merit in Folk Buddhism

Beyer, Stephen. *The Buddhist Experience.* Belmont, CA: Wadsworth Publishing, 1974.

Burnett, David. *The Spirit of Buddhism.* East Sussex: Monarch Publications, 1996.

Coleman, James William. *The New Buddhism: The Western Transformation of an Ancient Tradition.* New York: Oxford University Press, 2001.

Davis, John. *The Path to Enlightenment: Introducing Buddhism.* Suffolk: Hodder & Stoughton, 1996.

_____. *Poles Apart?* Bangalore: The Theological Book Trust, 1996.

De Silva, Lynn. *Buddhism Beliefs and Practices in Sri Lanka.* Battaramulla, Sri Lanka: SIOLL School of Technology, 1974.

Dhammananda, K. Sri. *What Buddhists Believe.* Kuala Lumpur: Buddhist Missionary Society, 2002.

Harvey, Peter. *An Introduction to Buddhism.* Cambridge: Cambridge University Press, 1990.

Holmberg, David H. *Order in Paradise: Myth, Ritual, and Exchange among Nepal's Tamang.* New York: Cornell University Press, 1989.

Lausanne Committee for World Evangelization. *Christian Witness to Buddhists.* Wheaton: LCWE, 1980.

Niles, D. T. *Buddhism and the Claims of Christ.* Richmond, VA: John Knox Press, 1967.

Po-Yee, Iris Wong, and Kevin Sinclair. *Culture Shock China.* Portland: Graphic Arts Center Publishing Co, 1990.

Schumann, Hans Wolfgang. *Buddhism.* Wheaton: The Theosophical Publishing House, 1973.

Smith, Alex G. *Buddhism Through Christian Eyes.* Littleton: OMF International, 1999.

_____. *Siamese Gold: A History of Church Growth in Thailand, An Interpretive Analysis 1816-1982.* Bangkok: Kanok Bannasan, 1992.

_____. *Strategy to Multiply Rural Churches: A Central Thailand Case Study.* Bangkok: OMF Publishers, 1977.

_____. "Missiological Implications of Key Contrasts between Buddhism and Christianity." In *Sharing Jesus in the Buddhist World.* Eds. David Lim and Steve Spaulding. Pasadena: William Carey Library, 2003.

Spencer, Cornelia. *The Land and People of China.* Philadelphia: J. B. Lippincott, 1972.

Spiro, Melford E. *Buddhism and Society.* San Francisco: Harper and Row Publishers, 1970.

Stott, John. *Romans: God's Good News for the World.* Downers Grove: InterVarsity Press, 1994.

Tambiah, S. *Buddhism and the Spirit Cults in Northeast Thailand.* Cambridge: Cambridge University Press, 1970.

Tsering, Marku. *Sharing Christ in the Tibetan World.* Upper Darby, PA: Interserve USA, 1998.

Weerasingha, Tissa. *The Cross and the Bo Tree.* Taichung, Taiwan: ATA, 1989.

Wells, Kenneth. *Thai Buddhism, Its Rites and Activities*. Bangkok: The Police Printing Press, 1960.

Chapter 6: The Serpent Power and the New Adam

Bannerjee, Akshaya Kumar. *Philosophy of Goraknath with Goraksha Vacana-Sanghraha*. Gorakhpur, 1961.

Bhagwandas, Mohanlal. *Comparative and Critical Study of Mantrasast*. Ahmedabad, 1944.

Bharati, Agehananda. *The Tantric Tradition*. Bombay, 1976.

Briggs, George Weston. *Goraknath and the Kanaphata Yogis*. Calcutta, 1938.

Kloetzli, Randolph. *Buddhist Cosmology*. Delhi, 1961.

Eliade, Mircea. *Yoga: Immortality and freedom*. Princeton, 1969.

Olesen, Bjarne Wernicke. *Devi og Saktismen*. Manuscript. Aarhus, 2002.

Chapter 7: An Exploration of the Book of Ecclesiastes in the Light of Buddha's Four Noble Truths

Bodhi, Bhikkhu. *The Buddha and His Dhamma*. Kandy: Buddhist Publication Society, 1999.

Bruce, F. F. *The Books of Acts: The New International Commentary on the New Testament*. Grand Rapids: Eerdmans Publishing Company, 1954.

Camus, Albert. *Qohelet and His Contradictions*. Sheffield: Almond Press, 1989.

Crenshaw, J. L. *Ecclesiastes: Old Testament Library*. Philadelphia: Westminster Press, 1987.

Dahood, M. J. "Canaanite-Phoenician Influence in Qoheleth." In *Biblica*. Vol. 33 (1952).

Davidson, Robert. *Ecclesiastes and Song of Solomon*. Edinburgh: Saint Andrew Press, 1986.

De Silva, Lily. *Nibbana as Living Experience*. Kandy, Sri Lanka: Buddhist Publication Society, 1996.

De Silva, Lynn A. *Emergent Theology in the Buddhist Context*. Colombo: Ecumenical Institute for Study and Dialogue, 1979.

_____. "Good News of Salvation to the Buddhists." In *International Review of Missions*, LVII (Oct. 1968).

_____. *Why Believe in God,* Colombo: Christian Study Centre, 1970.

_____. *Why Can't I Save Myself: The Christian Answer in Relation to Buddhist Thought*. Colombo: Christian Study Centre, 1967.

Dunn, J. D. G. *The Acts of the Apostles: Epworth Commentaries*. Peterborough: Epworth Press, 1996.

Eaton, Michael A. *Ecclesiastes: Tyndale Old Testament Commentaries*. Leicester: InterVarsity Press, 1983.

Elwood, Douglas J. *Asian Christian Theology: Emerging Themes,* Philadelphia: Westminster, 1980.

Erickson, Millard J. *Christian Theology*. Grand Rapids: Baker Book House, 1988.

Fernando, A. *Acts: The NIV Application Commentary*. Grand Rapids: Zondervan Publishing House, 1999.

Fox, Michael V. "The Meaning of *hebel* for Qohelet." In *Journal of Biblical Literature*, 105 (1986): 409-427.

Gordis, Robert *Koheleth, The Man and His World: A Study of Ecclesiastes*. New York: Schocken Books, 1968.

Guruge, A. W., ed. *Return to Righteousness: A Collection of Speeches, Essays and Letters of Anagarika Dharmapala*. Colombo: Ministry of Education and Cultural Affairs, 1965.

Harrison, Everett F. *Romans: The Expositor's Bible Commentary, Vol. 10*. Grand Rapids: Zondervan Publishing House, 1976.

Harvey, Peter. *An Introduction to Buddhism*. Cambridge: Cambridge University Press, 1992.

Hengstenberg E. W. *A Commentary on Ecclesiastes*. Evansville: Sovereign Grace, 1960.

Hughes, Selwyn. *Ecclesiastes: The Search for Meaning*. Surrey: CWR, 1993.

Kalupahana, David J. *Buddhist Philosophy: A Historical Analysis.*
Honolulu: University of Hawaii Press, 1976.

Kersten, Holger. *Jesus Lived in India.* Dorset: Element Books, 1995.

Kerston Holger, with E.R. Gruber. *The Original Jesus: The Buddhist
Sources of Christianity.* Dorset: Element Books, 1995.

Kidner, Derek. *The Message of Ecclesiastes.* Leicester: InterVarsity Press,
1976.

Larkin, W. J. *Acts: The IVP New Testament Commentary.* Downers Grove:
InterVarsity Press, 1995.

Longman III, Tremper. *Ecclesiastes: The New International Commentary
on the Old Testament.* Grand Rapids: Eerdmans Publishing Company,
1998.

Marshall, I. H. *Acts: Tyndale New Testament Commentaries.* Grand Rapids:
Eerdmans Publishing Company, 1980.

Matthews, Bruce. *Craving and Salvation: A Study in Buddhist Soteriology.*
Waterloo, ON: Wilfrid Laurier University Press, 1983.

Murphy, Roland, and E. Huwiler. *Proverbs, Ecclesiastes, Song of Songs:
New International Biblical Commentary.* Peabody: Hendrickson
Publishers, 1999.

Murphy, Roland E. *Ecclesiastes: Word Biblical Commentary, Vol. 23.*
Waco: Word Books, 1992.

Olyott, Stuart. *A Life Worth Living and a Lord Worth Loving: Ecclesiastes
and Song of Solomon.* Hertfordshire: Evangelical Press, 1986.

Richards, L. O. *Expository Dictionary of Bible Words.* Basingstoke:
Marshall Pickering, 1988.

Scott, R. B. Y. *Proverbs and Ecclesiastes: Anchor Bible Commentary.*
Garden City: Doubleday, 1965.

Seow, C. L. *Ecclesiastes: Anchor Bible Commentary.* Garden City:
Doubleday, 1997.

Seybold, Kiel K. "Hebhel." In *Theological Dictionary of the Old
Testament.* Eds. G.J. Botterweck and H. Ringgren. Grand Rapids:
Eerdmans Publishing Company, 1978.

Stott, John R. W. *The Contemporary Christian*. Leicester: InterVarsity Press, 1992.

_____. *The Message of Romans*. Leicester: InterVarsity Press, 1994.

Thera, Piyadassi. *The Buddha's Ancient Path*. Kandy, Sri Lanka: Buddhist Publication Society, 1996.

Van Leeuwen, R. C. "Vanity." In *The International Standard Bible Encyclopaedia, Vol. 4*. Ed. G.W. Bromiley. Grand Rapids: Eerdmans Publishing Company, 1993.

Wiersbe, Warren W. *Be Satisfied*. Wheaton: Victor Books, 1990.

Wijebandara, Chandima. *Early Buddhism: Its Religious and Intellectual Milieu*. Kelaniya, Sri Lanka: The Postgraduate Institute of Pali and Buddhist Studies, 1993.

Wright, C. *Thinking Clearly About the Uniqueness of Jesus*. Crowborough: Monarch Publications, 1997.

Wright, J. Stafford. *Ecclesiastes: The Expositor's Bible Commentary*. Grand Rapids: Zondervan Publishing House, 1991.

Chapter 8: A Contextualized Presentation of the Gospel in Thai Society

Van Leeuwen, R. C. "Vanity." In *The International Standard Bible Encyclopaedia. Vol. 4*. Ed. G. W. Bromiley. Grand Rapids: Eerdmans Publishing Company, 1993.

Carey, Keith. "Reaching Buddhists through Old Testament Wisdom Literature." In *International Journal of Frontier Missions* 2 (October 1985): 335-341.

Cooke, Joseph. "The Gospel for Thai Ears." Typewritten. 1978.

Cooke, Mary. "A Thai's Attitude toward Religion." Unpublished notes. Bangkok: Overseas Missionary Fellowship, n.d.

Davis, John. *Poles Apart: Contextualizing the Gospel in Asia*. Bangalore: Theological Book Trust, 1998.

Dinkins, Larry. "Eight Bridges to Witnessing." *Lingo* 22 (June 1988): 19-21.

_____. "Response to Bangkok Post Article on Why Missionaries Have Failed." *Lingo* 22 (June 1988): 14-18.

Engel, James. *Contemporary Christian Communications: Its Theory and Practice.* New York: Thomas Nelson Publishers, 1979.

Filbeck, David. *Social Context and Proclamation: A Socio-Cognitive Study in Proclaiming the Gospel Cross-Culturally.* Pasadena: William Carey Library, 1985.

Guthrie, Donald. *New Testament Theology.* Downers Grove: InterVarsity Press, 1981.

Gusawadi, Brasert. "Witi Atibaay Tang Hang Kwam Rod Doy Chai Ruub Wongglom Sung Maaythung Gaay Jai Lae Winnyaan." (A Method of Explaining the Way of Salvation Using a Circle with the Meaning of Body, Mind and Spirit.) Unpublished paper. Bangkok: Overseas Missionary Fellowship, n.d.

Hesselgrave, David, and Edward Rommen. *Contextualization: Meanings, Methods and Models.* Pasadena: William Carey Library, 1989.

Hughes, Philip. "The Use of Actual Beliefs in Contextualizing Theology." In *East Asia Journal of Theology* 2 (February 1984), 251-258.

Johnstone, Patrick, and Jason Mandryk. *Operation World: When We Pray God Works.* 3rd ed. Cumbria, UK: Paternoster Lifestyle, 2001.

Kirsch, A. Thomas. "Notes on Thai Religion." In *Clues to Thai Culture,* 146-163. Ed. Central Thai Language Committee. Bangkok: Overseas Missionary Fellowship, 1981.

_____. "The Thai Buddhist Quest for Merit." In *Clues to Thai Culture,* 120-136. Ed. Central Thai Language Committee. Bangkok: Overseas Missionary Fellowship, May 1981.

Komin, Suntaree. *Psychology of the Thai People: Values and Behavior Patterns.* Bangkok: National Institute of Development Administration, 1990.

Koyama, Kosuke. *Waterbuffalo Theology.* Maryknoll: Orbis Books, 1974.

Kraft, Charles. *Christianity in Culture: A Study in Dynamic Biblical Theologizing in Cross-Cultural Perspective.* Maryknoll: Orbis Books, 1979.

Kung, Hans, Joseph van Ess, Heinrich von Stietencron, and Heinz Bechert. *Christianity and the World Religions: Paths to Dialogue with Islam, Hinduism, and Buddhism*, trans. Peter Heinegg,. New York: Doubleday, 1985.

Ladd, George Eldon. *A Theology of the New Testament*. Grand Rapids: Eerdmans Publishing Company, 1974.

Lien-Hwa, Chow. "Towards Evangelical Theology in Buddhist Culture." In *The Bible and Theology in Asian Contexts*. Eds. Bong Rin Ro and Ruth Eshenaur. Taiwan: Tai Shin Color Printing, 1984.

Mejudhon, Nantachai. "Meekness: A New Approach to Christian Witness to the Thai People." D. Miss. dissertation. Asbury Theological Seminary, 1997.

Mothanaprakoon, Ezra. "A Critique of Buddhist Soteriology from a Biblical Perspective." Unpublished paper. Manila: Far East Advanced School of Theology, 1987.

_____. "Thai Buddhism." Unpublished paper. Singapore: Bible Institute of Singapore, 1981.

Petchsongkram, Wan. *Talks in the Shade of the Bo Tree*. Trans. and ed. Frances Hudgins. Bangkok: Thai Gospel Press, 1975.

_____. "Teaching New Christians." Unpublished paper. Bangkok: Overseas Missionary Fellowship, n.d.

Phra Sasanasobhana. Phraputtajao *Song Soon Arai*. (What Did the Buddha Teach?) Trans. Phra Khantipalo and Phra Nagaseno. Bangkok: The War Veterans Organization of Thailand, 1967.

Shin, Hong-Shik. *Principles of Church Planting as Illustrated in Thai Theravada Buddhist Context*. Bangkok: Kanok Bannasan (OMF Publishers), 1989.

Smith, Alex. *Buddhism through Christian Eyes*. Littleton: OMF International, 2001.

_____. *Siamese Gold—A History of Church Growth in Thailand: An Interpretive Analysis 1816-1982*. Bangkok: Kanok Bannasan (OMF Publishers), 1981.

_____. *Strategy to Multiply Rural Churches: A Central Thailand Case Study*. Bangkok: Kanok Bannasan (OMF Publishers), 1977.

_____. "The Way to Freedom—The Way to a New Life." Unpublished paper. Bangkok: Overseas Missionary Fellowship, n.d.

Weerasingha, Tissa. "A Critique of Theology from Buddhist Cultures." In *The Bible and Theology in Asian Contexts*. Ed. Bong Rin Ro and Ruth Eshnaur. Taiwan: Tai Shin Color Printing, 1984.

Wisley, Tom. "Dynamic Biblical Christianity in the Buddhist/Marxist Context: Northeast Thailand." Ph.D. Dissertation. Fuller Theological Seminary, 1984.

Chapter 9: The Ritual of Reconciliation in Thai Culture

Barclay, William. *The Letter to the Romans*. Philadelphia: Westminster Press, 1975.

Boontawee, Kampoon. *A Child of the Northeast*. Bangkok: Duangkamol, 1994.

Eliade, Mircea. *The Sacred and the Profane: The Nature of Religion*. San Diego: Harcourt Brace and Company, 1987.

Feig, John Paul. *A Common Core: Thais and Americans*. Intercultural Press, 1989.

Grimes, Roland L. *Beginning in Ritual Studies*. Rev. ed. Studies in Comparative Religion. Ed. Frederick M. Denny. Columbia: University of South Carolina Press, 1995.

Hiebert, G. Paul. *Anthropological Reflections on Missiological Issues*. Michigan: Baker Books, 1994.

Komin, Suntaree. *Psychology of the Thai People: Values and Behavioral Patterns*. Bangkok: NIDA, 1993.

Mejudhon, Nantachai. "Meekness: A New Approach to Christian Witness to the Thai." D. Miss. Dissertation. Asbury Theological Seminary, 1994.

Ngamdee, Yinglak. *Supasit Kampangpey Lae Samnuan Thai* (Proverbs, Saying and Thai Expressions.) Bangkok: Agsarapipat, 1993.

Praya Sri Sunthorn Wohan, Noi. *Archanyang Kun Kamklong Lokaniti* (The Poetry of the Laws of Life.) Bangkok: Kurusapa Publishing House, n.d.

Sataanandha, Suwanna and Nuangnoy Boonyanate. *Rongroy Kwamkit Kwamchur Thai* (The Belief System of the Thai.) Bangkok: Chulalanogkorn University Publishing House, 1993.

Schreiter, Robert J. *Reconciliation: Mission and Ministry in a Changing Social Order.* New York: Maryknoll, 1996.

Tenney, Merill C., ed. *Pictorial Bible Dictionary.* Grand Rapids: Zondervan Publishing House, 1962.

Thai Royal Academy. *Pojananukrom* (Dictionary.) Bangkok: Agsorncharoentasana, 1994.

New American Standard Bible. La Habra, CA: The Lockman Foundation, n.d.

Tollefson, Kenneth. "Maintaining Quality Control in Christian Missions." In *Missiology* 18/3, 1990.

Turner, Victor. *The Drums of Affliction: A Study of Religious Processes among the Ndembu of Zambia.* Oxford: Clarendon for the International African Institute, 1968.

_____. *The Ritual Process: Structure and Anti-Structure.* New York: Aldine De Gruyster, 1969.

Wissawate, Wit. "The Series of Lecture on Buddhist Philosophy." Bangkok: Chulalongkorn University, 1967.

Zahniser, A. H. Mathias. *Symbol and Ceremony: Making Disciples Across Cultures.* Monrovia: MARC, 1997.

Chapter 10: Abortion and Mizuko Rites in Japan

Asahi Shimbun Japan Almanac 2002. Tokyo: Asahi Shimbun, 2001.

Brooks, Anne P. "Mizuko Kuyô and Japanese Buddhism." In *Japanese Journal of Religious Studies* 8 (1981): 119-147.

Burke, Theresa, and David C. Reardon. *Forbidden Grief: The Unspoken Pain of Abortion.* Springfield: Acorn Books, 2002.

Catholic World News (Dec. 26, 2000) at <www.cwnews.com>.

Daily Yomiuri (Aug. 9, 2002): "Rise in Teen Abortion Prompts Govt Sex Study."

Hanazono Yukio. "Problem of Slow Increase Should Be Solved." In *Church Information Service News*. Bilingual. Dec. 2002, no. 56.

Hardacre, Helen. *Marketing the Menacing Fetus in Japan*. Berkeley: University of California Press, 1997.

Hayford, Jack. *I'll Hold You in Heaven*. Ventura: Regal Books, 1990.

Johnston, William Robert. "Historical Abortion Statistics, Japan." Updated Apr. 15, 2002 at <www.johnstonsarchive.net/policy/ abortion/ab-japan.html>.

Jolivet, Muriel. *Japan: The Childless Society? The Crisis of Motherhood*. London: Routledge, 1997. Originally published in French as *Un pays en mal d'enfants*. Paris: Éditions La Découverte, 1993.

Kihara, Masako Ono, Jane S. Kramer, Deborah Bain, Masahiro Kihara, and Jeff Mandel. "Knowledge of and Attitudes toward the Pill: Results of a national survey in Japan." In *Alan Guttmacher Institute Family Planning Perspectives*. Vol. 33, no. 3, May/June 2001). <http://www.agi-usa.org/pubs/journals/ 3312301.html>.

Kitamura Kuniô. *Piru*. (The Pill.) Tokyo: Shûeisha Shinsho, 2002.

Lightner, Robert P. *Heaven for Those Who Can't Believe*. Schaumburg, IL: Regular Baptist Press, 1977.

LaFleur, William R. "Buddhism and Abortion: 'The Way to Memorialize One's Mizuko'." In *Religions of Japan in Practice*. Ed. George J. Tanabe, Jr. Princeton: Princeton University Press, 1999.

_____. *Liquid Life: Abortion and Buddhism in Japan*. Princeton: Princeton University Press, 1992.

_____. "Contestation and Consensus: The Morality of Abortion in Japan." *Philosophy East and West*. Vol. 40, no. 4 (October 1990).

MacArthur, John. *Safe in the Arms of God: Truth from Heaven about the Death of a Child*. Nashville: Thomas A. Nelson, 2003.

Martin, Elaine, and Richard W. Anderson. "Rethinking the Practice of Mizuko Kuyo in Contemporary Japan: Interviews with practitioners at a Buddhist temple in Tokyo." In *Japanese Journal of Religious Studies* 24/1-2 (1997), 121-143. The full text is available at <http://bama.ua.edu/~emartin/ publications/ mkarticl.htm>.

Massé, Sydna, and Joan Phillips. *Her Choice to Heal: Finding Spiritual and Emotional Peace after Abortion.* Colorado Springs: Chariot Victor Publishing, 1998.

Norgren, Tiana. *Abortion before Birth Control: The Politics of Reproduction in Postwar Japan.* Princeton: Princeton University Press, 2001.

Population Council. News Release, Dec. 26, 2000, reporting data listed in *Studies in Family Planning.* Vol. 31, no. 4 (Dec. 2000).

Pro-Life Japan—Machida (Chiisana inochi wo mamoru kai). <http://homepage3.nifty.com/look-at-jesus/pljm/index.htm>.

Reisser, Paul, M.D., and Teri Reisser. *Help for the Post-Abortion Woman.* Grand Rapids: Zondervan, 1989.

Selby, Terry L., with Mark Brockman. *The Mourning After: Help for the Postabortion Syndrome.* Grand Rapids: Baker Book House, 1990.

Smith, Bardwell. "Buddhism and Abortion in Contemporary Japan: Mizuko Kuyô and the Confrontation with Death." In *Japanese Journal of Religious Studies* 15 (1988): 3-24. Also *in Buddhism, Sexuality, and Gender.* Ed. José Ignacio Cabezón. Albany: State University of New York Press, 1992.

Stevens, John. *Lust for Enlightenment: Buddhism and Sex.* Boston: Shambhala, 1990.

Terauchi Daikichi. "Gendai no Mizuko Jizô." (Contemporary Mizuko Rites.) In *Jizô-sama Nyûmon.* (An Introduction to Jizô.) Ed. anon. Tôkyô: Taihô Rinkaku, 2000.

Unrin Zuihô. "Mizuko Kuyô ni Omou Koto" (Thoughts on Mizuko Rites.) In *Jizô-sama Nyûmon.* (An Introduction to Jizô.) Ed. anon. Tôkyô: Taihô Rinkaku, 2000.

Werblowsky, Zwi. "Mizuko Kuyô: Notulae on the Most Important 'New Religion' of Japan." In *Japanese Journal of Religions Studies* 18 (1991): 295-344.

Temple Websites Cited:

Awashimadô Shûtokuji (Feb. 18, 2003) <http://park.zero.ad.jp/~zbc46685/mizuko.htm>.

Enjôin (Feb. 18, 2003) <http://www.evam.ne.jp/enjyoin/>.

Tatsueji (Feb. 18, 2003) <http://www1.ocn.ne.jp/~tatsueji/>.

Zenkôji (Feb. 18, 2003) <http://www.mediawars.ne.jp/~zenkouji/kuyou.htm>.

A number of reference materials and an especially good bibliography (all in Japanese) on the subject of *mizuko kuyô* can be found at Japanese website <http://*www.ne.jp/asahi/time/saman*> posted by the Mizuko Kuyô Culture and Society Research Group (*Mizuko Kuyô no Bunkai to Shakai Kenkyûkai*).

Chapter 11: Holistic Mission

Esman, Milton J., and Norman T. Uphoff. *Local Organizations: Intermediaries in rural development*. Ithaca: Cornell University Press,1984.

Gow, David D. *Local Organizations and Rural Development: A Comparative Reappraisal*, Washington, DC: Development Alternatives, 1979.

Lausanne Committee for World Evangelization. "Lausanne Covenant." In *Let the Earth Hear His Voice*. Ed. J. D. Douglas. Minneapolis: World Wide Publications, 1975.

Moffatt, James. *Grace in the New Testament*. New York: Ray Long and Richard R. Smith, 1932.

Newbigin, Lesslie. *The Household of God*. New York: Friendship Press, 1954.

Peters, Thomas J., and Robert H. Waterman, Jr. *In Search of Excellence*. New York: Warner Books, 1982.

Samuel, Vinay, and Christopher Sugden, eds. *The Church in Response to Human Need*. Oxford: Regnum Books; Grand Rapids: Eerdmans, 1987.

Todaro, Michael P. *Economic Development in the Third World*. New York: Longman, 1988.